PRAISE FOR *RETAIL HELL*

"[Freeman is] a retail-centric Perez Hilton."

—*Publishers Weekly*

"[*Retail Hell*] was delivered this morning and . . . I've been laughing 'til I'm burple in the face!"

—Michael Tonello, bestselling author of *Bringing Home the Birkin*

". . . An amusing window into the world of hyper-consumption . . . full of outrageous—and humorous—tales of shoppers behaving badly, all in pursuit of an 'It' bag."

—*LA Times* fashion critic Booth Moore

"Gucci hawker-turned-author Freeman Hall shares hilarious tales of his twenty-year servitude as a sales guy, from crazy customers to the cloyingly cheerful store culture."

—*Washington Post Express*

"An entertaining look at the view from his side of the handbag counter. . . . Meet the Piggy Shoppers, the Discount Rats, and the Bloodsuckers—all of them customers who shop at fine stores, terrorize the sales staff, and now are exposed . . . ."

—*Reuters*

"*Retail Hell* . . . omits few offenses that writer Freeman Hall faced on the sales floor. Readers . . . will get a glimpse of the crassness of shoppers and salespeople, depending on the situation."

—*Women's Wear Daily*

Retail Hell

HOW I SOLD MY SOUL TO THE STORE

Confessions of a Tortured Sales Associate

FREEMAN HALL

Avon, Massachusetts

Published by
Adams Media, a division of F+W Media, Inc.
57 Littlefield Street, Avon, MA 02322. U.S.A.
www.adamsmedia.com

Paperback ISBN 10: 1-4405-0577-2
Paperback ISBN 13: 978-1-4405-0577-5
Paperback eISBN 10: 1-4405-0876-3
Paperback eISBN 13: 978-1-4405-0876-9

Hardcover ISBN 10: 1-60550-102-6
Hardcover ISBN 13: 978-1-60550-102-4
Hardcover eISBN 10: 1-4405-0433-4
Hardcover eISBN 13: 978-1-4405-0433-4

Printed in the United States of America.

10   9   8   7   6   5   4   3   2   1

Library of Congress Cataloging-in-Publication Data
is available from the publisher.

This book is available at quantity discounts for bulk purchases.
For information, please call 1-800-289-0963.

For my mom, Janie Burchett, who encouraged me to follow my dreams and taught me that where there's a will, there's a way.

Author's Note

The situations and characters in this book are based on my twenty-plus years of retail experience. However, the names of stores and people have been changed, timelines are out of sync, and the situations have been cleverly disguised, ripped inside out, and run over several times. For the purposes of the book, my Retail Hell takes place at a department store I'll call The Big Fancy. As satisfying as it would have been to name names, my ass would be sued up one side of the escalator and down the other. And that would be painful on my ass.

Contents

Act 2: Sinners, Serpents, and the Craziest Crazy-Lady Customers 97

Act 3: Misfire and Brimstone at The Big Fancy 193

Free Gift with Purchase! BONUS SECTION

INTRODUCTION:
FREEMAN'S INFERNO

Move over, Dante.

A Wednesday afternoon at The Big Fancy. Someone out sick. Someone at lunch. Someone in a training class. And my manager in a meeting with the store manager. Probably playing footsie. I'm flying solo at the handbag counter.

As usual, because I'm by myself, the gates of Retail Hell open up: An indecisive woman wants me to retrieve every evening bag we have inside of a glass case, forcing me down on my knees at least sixty-five times. Another woman fires off a barrage of mind-numbing questions about a Juicy Couture bag. The phone rings nonstop: "Why aren't the markdowns done?" "Can you check on a handbag?" "Is Tiffany there? No? Then can you help me?" A well-known customer who returns a lot of merch rolls up to the counter carrying two shopping bags loaded with handbags. She wants to have some returned, some exchanged, and others checked to see whether they went on sale so she can get price adjustments. Her receipts look like a pile of wilted lettuce leaves and don't match the price tickets, which are not attached to any of the bags. While she's trying to straighten out her mess, another customer gets pushy and begs me to ring up a wallet because apparently *she's* the only person on lunch break and in a hurry. I make the annoying Returner wait and ring up the wallet, only to get a code on the register not approving the sale. I call Credit and am immediately bounced to hold. A woman wearing a dirty Mickey Mouse sweatshirt appears at the counter with a $3,000 Marc Jacobs handbag stuffed into a plastic grocery bag. She wants to return it and get her cash back. I can already tell she's a Nasty-Ass Thief. Another phone line begins to ring. I debate answering it, but risk losing my connection with Credit . . . which would mean I'd have to start all over. The Returner asks me if I can call someone else to help her. The Juicy Couture Questioner seconds her motion. And like the cherry on top of a shit sundae, a new customer forces her way up to the counter and shouts in my face:

"Excuse me, do you work here?"

I look like an octopus at the Aquarium of Insanity. How can she even ask me that?

A dumb-ass question deserves a dumb-ass answer:

"No, I sure don't."

I turn my back on her and continue to wait for Credit while praying to God to please keep me from freaking out and picking up the fucking register and hurling it at all of them.

I wasn't born a Retail Slave. I didn't pop out from my mother's womb with a feverish desire to sell things people don't want or need. I don't have the bouncy game-show-host personality that would make it easy for me to go up to strangers and say, "Hi! How are you today? How can I help you? Would you like to see our new Coach bags for spring? Let me tell you what's on sale! Can I answer any other idiotic questions you might have? Please! Treat me like shit and ruin my day!"

No, I wasn't born a Retail Slave, but I was born into a family *full* of them. My uncommon first name, Freeman, was bestowed upon me in honor of my grandfather, who was named Freeman in honor of his father Freeman. Yep, that's three Freemans in the family. But the name wasn't the only thing gifted to me by my elders. I also inherited their retail genes.

My great-grandfather Freeman owned a furniture and appliance store in Reno, Nevada, where I'm from. He was known as a tenacious salesman who could sell a refrigerator to an Eskimo. My grandfather Freeman, on the other hand, spent most of his life at the store on the other side of sales: in the service department. His willingness to fix problems could turn a ferocious customer into a purring pussycat.

How could I dodge that retail bullet?

My mom, a divorced, single mother of two, spent most of her life in retail, hawking everything from jewelry to drapery to tractors. She could charm anyone into maxing out their AmEx for an antique bauble, saying, "You need to buy this! It's going to be a collector's item someday. $3,999 is a real bargain."

I, however, showed no signs of a soul headed for a life in retail. As a kid, I hated cleaning and folding, didn't like talking to strangers, loathed math, couldn't do ten things at once, wasn't aggressive, despised cheerleading, and did not like being told what to do. Not exactly a blueprint for a life in retail.

I had a different plan. I wanted to be just like Steven and Stephen—Spielberg and King. In fifth grade, my English teacher was surprised by my disturbing and detailed book report on *The Exorcist*. But rather than sending me to the school counselor, she recommended I read *'Salem's Lot*. I thought it would be a lame snooze, but it scared the shit out of me. Stephen King had sunk his teeth into me and that was it. I was his forever. At about the same time, Spielberg put out *Close Encounters of the Third Kind* and became my hero. And even though I cherished *Jaws*, the book, my love for the director was cemented once I saw the movie. For days I slept curled up at night, rather than stretched out. My legs were not about to become fish sticks.

At a young age, my heart was set on emulating my idols and crafting a million-dollar screenplay . . . so what in Retail Hell happened to me?

I'll tell you what happened. In a word: clothes.

We all have our addictions. Belgian chocolate. QVC porcelain dolls. Crack cocaine. Mine just happens to involve shirts and pants. Designer shirts and pants. And trendy shoes that look hot with them.

No big surprise there. Young gay guy lured to the dark side by fashion. It's not headline news. But as I neared adulthood, my love for cool clothes got the best of me when I won the underage lottery by scoring a fake ID.

In college, during the early 80s, I fed my film obsession by working at a majestic old movie house downtown, selling tickets to classics like *E.T.* and *Flashdance*. The assistant manager was a cool guy who was several years older. He also happened to be the owner of a driver's license displaying a picture that looked exactly like me. After begging and offering everything in my bank account (a whopping $50), he agreed to get a new license and sell me the "lost" one.

This was a huge social coup for me. Most of my friends were over twenty-one, and I hated not being able to hang with them at clubs and casinos. Thanks to my older, blond-haired, blue-eyed twin, that was about to change.

Fake ID in hand, I rushed to my favorite department store (one of only two in Reno). If I was going to dance and drink the night away at the only gay club in town, I had to do it looking like I'd just stepped out of the pages of GQ. I was a broke college kid, but I desperately wanted a pair of Calvin Klein jeans. Everyone wanted his name on their ass, and I was no different. But sadly, the only thing I could afford on my meager movie-house paycheck were Calvin's undies—and that was only if I bought them at Marshalls! After trying on a bunch of sale-rack rejects, I found a funky brand-name shirt that would have to do. As the cute Preppy Sales Guy rang up the shirt, I asked him if the Calvin jeans ever went on sale.

"Not often," he replied, "But if you want to get a discount on them, you should work here. Employees get 20% off."

I did a double take. What? Was he shitting me? Twenty percent off? Department store salespeople get discounts? On Calvin Klein jeans? I could not believe my ears. I felt dizzy.

"Even on the Calvins?" I asked.

"Yes, even on the Calvins. It's on everything," he replied, "I got a pair for only fifteen bucks."

I almost passed out.

"You know what else?" he said, "They also automatically give you a credit card when you start, even if you've never had credit before. All employees get an eight-hundred-dollar limit."

Break out the smelling salts. A CREDIT CARD!!? I didn't have one, but I had wanted one for a long time. Badly.

Was that all I had to do? Work at the department store for discounts and credit cards?

I suddenly saw myself with a closet full of Calvin Klein everything. Put me on the cover of GQ!

"You know what else?" Preppy Sales Guy said, leaning in, "Major studs shop here."

His gaydar was on target. I gave him a sheepish smile and said, "Wow. I hadn't thought about that before."

After that, I only had one question: "Where's the personnel department?"

A week later I landed a gig with the department store and was in Retail Shangri-La, with Visa card in hand, surrounded by fabulous designer clothes and potential dates. It was not long before I had my very own CK jeans, and I proclaimed, "The only thing coming between me and my Calvins is a cute boy." Along with my dream jeans, I racked up pieces from Perry Ellis, Ralph Lauren, and Lacoste; a Swatch watch; Wayfarer shades; and the ever-popular Sperry Topsiders. My fashion planets had aligned. The world was at my feet. And I looked damn good!

Working in men's sportswear was my first retail job (aside from selling lemonade and movie tickets), and it wasn't particularly hellish. In fact, sometimes it was quite retailicious: flirting with cute male customers, taking long breaks, gossiping about coworkers, having vodka collins lunches, creating hip displays, opening boxes of clothes I wanted to buy. In the stockroom I had an entire rolling rack acting as my own personal hold shelf. It was loaded with merch I planned on buying as soon as it all dropped to 75% off and funds became available in my checking account.

Of course, there were hellacious moments, like a customer reaching into the middle of a table of sweaters and yanking from the bottom, knocking them all over like dominos after I'd just spent an hour folding. Or a customer yelling at me because he wanted a Polo shirt on sale the day after a sale ended. Or the scary old man coming on to me in the fitting rooms, asking if the Speedo looked good on him. *Ewww.*

Good times, bad times—through it all, my retail genes were raging. Although there was no pressure from the store to make sales because we weren't on commission, I had a way of talking men into buying loads of clothes. I had mastered the art of sales-associating in Men's Sportswearland. Because of my stellar retail skills, my manager deemed me her assistant—with no pay raise. My pay raise consisted of all the extra hours I'd be working. *Umm, say that again? Extra hours?*

And just like that, my honeymoon with Calvin Klein was over.

Every day was a twelve-hour day with mountains of paperwork. I directed merchandise floor moves, set up all the sales, handled tedious transfers, counted merch until my head hurt, stayed late, and came in early. The store began to feel like an unforgiving, chaotic, and demanding dungeon, with customers yelling and complaining, markdowns always needing to be done, phones ringing, registers breaking, and my manager freaking out every five minutes.

I became a slave to retail. My love for writing and watching films took a back seat to the store. The pay sucked and my credit card was maxed, but it didn't matter at the time because I still lived at home, and most of my hard-earned money was spent on partying and new outfits for partying. As days slipped into years, my life became an endless, monotonous cycle of reporting to the store, hanging clothes, moving clothes, picking up clothes, ringing clothes up, and shopping for clothes. I was barely putting pen to paper. My movie muse was dead. The store had me by the balls.

That is, until I went to see *Fatal Attraction*.

Remember it? Glenn Close plays the jilted lover of Michael Douglas, and she stalks the shit out of him, going so far as to boil his kid's pet rabbit and then pretend to drown in a bathtub. For me *Fatal Attraction* was pure cinematic genius. Audience participation at its best. There's nothing like hundreds of people freaking out and wetting their pants in front of a theater screen. I wanted to write something just like it. My imagination reeled. And just like that, I went back to movie-watching binges, reading scripts, and writing out my ideas.

The Retail Slave I'd become was suddenly wide awake.

Time to revive my Million-Dollar Screenplay dream.

I decided to abandon the slimy retail riverbank and float downstream to a place I was sure had sandy white beaches, picturesque blue skies, lazy palm trees, and half-naked men serving bottomless margaritas. The day I left Reno it was pouring rain and cold, but my head was filled with California sunshine and visions of becoming a Hollywood hotshot—a rich and famous screenwriter with a private office on the Universal lot next to Steven.

But there's a fine line between heaven and hell, and little did I know I was about to sell my soul to another store.

A really Big Fancy store.

ACT 1

The Big Fancy Underworld

The devil made me do it.

Hell in a Handbag

Leo DiCaprio opens the envelope and says, "And the Oscar for Best Original Screenplay goes to . . . Freeman Hall—Love in a Fitting Room." Applause thunders across the Kodak Theatre. As I reach center stage and the Oscar is handed to me, Leo gives me a friendly guy-to-guy hug. The dude is total actor candy. My speech kicks ass. I thank director Ron Howard for not getting angry when I slipped my script into his shopping bag. I also give a shout-out to God, my mom, my sister, my acupuncturist, my fifth-grade teacher, my beta fish, Sid Vicious . . .

"EXCUSE ME!"

What?

Who is that?

Excuse me, but I'm not finished with my acceptance speech. Be quiet.

"EXCUSE ME!"

There it is again. Sounds like a woman. Whatever. Some jealous screenwriter in the audience. As I take my Oscar backstage, I am so glad I didn't cry. Tom Hanks pats me on the back. Meryl Streep winks at me. I feel a little lightheaded. Oprah's people stop me. I promise my first interview to her, of course. Jennifer Aniston bumps into me. She's smoking hot! Hugh Jackman bumps into me. He's smoking hot! Jerry Bruckheimer approaches me and says he wants me to write . . .

"EXCUSE ME! You *do* work here, don't you?"

Crap.

I really wanted to hear what Jerry had to say.

Suddenly it's all gone. The stage. The audience. Leo. All of it. Gone.

Another Academy Award dream lost. Oprah wouldn't want to interview me any more than she would an Olive Garden dishwasher. My Oscar night fantasy evaporates into the unnatural yellow glow of track lights bouncing off mirrored columns while Celine Dion goes on and on about her heart going on and on. The Kodak Theatre's slick stage is replaced by worn carpet the color of moldy oatmeal and a maze of glass fixtures and shelves holding overpriced designer handbags. My fingers are not clasped around Oscar's gold body, but instead around the leather straps of a Coach signature satchel. I am in the middle of the handbag department of The Big Fancy, where I work as a sales associate.

I may as well be a million miles from Hollywood, even though the Kodak Theatre is actually mere miles away. No award ceremonies or after-parties in my immediate future . . . only a tangle of handbags to be tidied for tomorrow.

It's five minutes to closing. I get out of my head and reposition my eyes toward the counter. The late-night interruption of my Tinsel Town dream had come from a short, plump thing with bacon-colored hair so greasy it looks like she just came out of the shower. Her clothes are disheveled and she sports orange safety-goggle-looking glasses in need of cleaning. A beat-up Big Fancy shopping bag sits on the counter in front of her.

Return time.

When I arrive at the counter, the greasy little hobbit immediately turns all bitchy. "What's wrong with you?" she asks, peering at me over the top of her orange glasses. "I was asking for your help several times and you just stood there like you were in a trance."

"I was. The Oscar trance."

And if you hadn't bothered me, I'd still be there, at the Governor's Ball showing off my statuette, drinking champagne out of Leo's shoe.

The Greasy Hobbit is not interested in my trance.

"I need to return," she says. "There's also a wallet inside."

I open the bag and immediately recognize the white plush Ferragamo dustcover. A large $2,000 calfskin tote bag and $500 wallet sat inside. Greasy shoves a receipt in my face.

Of course, my eyes immediately go to the salesperson number: 441064.

Fuck me with a handbag. It's my employee number and I don't even remember selling it to her. The last thing I need is a huge return. The day had been slow with sales and busy with problems. Her return is going to be the nail in my coffin.

To make matters worse, the outside of the $2,000 Ferragamo tote isn't exactly in "I never used it" condition. Its days of immaculateness are long past—scratches, dents, and scuff marks are scattered across its body. WTF? Had she loaned it to Edward Scissorhands?

"This bag has been used," I announce, repeating a line I say often at The Big Fancy.

Greasy peers at me through the orange glasses, attempting to turn me into stone with her goblin eyes, "I'm telling you I didn't use it, the scratches must have been there before."

"And *I'm telling you* there is no way you would have paid $2,000 for a bag with scratches."

"Well, I did," she says, "I just decided not to keep it. I never used it. I don't know what I was thinking spending that kind of money."

I bite my tongue. Greasy didn't buy this Ferragamo bag. No lie detector needed here—I remember who purchased the Ferragamo a few months ago. The buyer had been a tall blond woman who had sucked the life out of me. A total Therapy-Digger. During our lengthy time together, I had showed her every handbag in the joint while she spared no details of her train-wreck life: She was overworked at her job, hated her coworkers, had an elderly mother in rehab and a teenage daughter who wasn't speaking to her, and—the topper—she had just discovered her husband was having an affair. Apparently she found some photos of him in a pair of pink lace panties. It wasn't clear if the other woman was a woman or a man dressed as a woman.

Oh yeah. Good times.

The writer in me had wanted to take notes, but the Retail Slave in me had just wanted her to be gone. The whole session gave me a headache. I had played the good little sales associate, offered exceptional service, played her shrink, and then told her she needed to buy the bag to get back at her panty-loving husband. Proclaiming the Ferragamo the bag of her dreams, that's what she did. And now some *other* woman was here returning it all beat to shit? Like a thousand times before, I am about to become the casualty of another Therapy-Digger, but decide to go down fighting.

Not so fast, Greasy Little Hobbit, it's late and my feet hurt.

"But you didn't buy this bag."

"Yes, I did!"

"Umm. No you didn't."

"Are you calling me a liar? I told you it's my bag."

"Well I'm the original salesperson and you're not the woman I sold it to."

Busted! Greasy Hobbit sighs and rolls her eyes behind her smudgy glasses. Then she sort of snarls her lip at me.

"Whatever," she says, "It's my sister's. She gave it to me and I don't appreciate being interrogated. I want to return it."

"I'm not allowed to take back used handbags."

"What are you talking about? I never used it!"

I point to several mauled areas of the Ferragamo.

"That's ridiculous. I return things all the time and I've never had a problem!" she says, ignoring my observation, "I have my receipt! I know the policy at this store. You have to return it. I never used that bag."

We'll see about that, Frodo.

I quickly open the Ferragamo and pull out the paper stuffing. Sure enough, I find makeup stains smeared across the bottom. I show them to her.

"I don't know what you're talking about. I don't see anything," says Greasy.

"You don't see those brown stains?"

"It's from the paper."

While checking out the lining, I feel a lump in the zipper pocket. I unzip it and pull out two tampons, a paper clip, and a penny.

"I think you left these behind," I say, handing them to her.

This happens all the time when women return bags they've used. Tampons, lipstick, coins, Tic Tacs, and condoms are the top things found.

Greasy sighs loudly as if I were the problem, rather than all the personal garbage she's left in the bag. "I was just trying my things in it. I really don't see what the problem is here. It's none of your business what I keep in my handbag."

It is when my commission's at stake! I'm not your Designer Handbag Rental Service! My name is not Bag Borrow or Steal.com!

After finding those incriminating items, I keep going. I unzip every freakin' pocket. And there are a lot of them on this Ferragamo tote. The last one I check, the one with a long zipper compartment on the outside, holds the smoking gun. I reach in and immediately feel something made of a soft, silky-like fabric. It's a bra! Greasy left her bra in a $2,000 Ferragamo! I yank it out—almost as dramatic as a magician making a rabbit appear. *"Voilà!"* I so want to say, *"Madam, you are a filthy liar!"*

But instead I say, "You also left your bra."

Or maybe it belongs to your "sister's" husband?

I hold it up like evidence in a murder trial. But then I get a closer look. The bra is old and ratty, all shredded and discolored. And to my horror, all over the cups are tiny white flakes that begin to flutter around, dusting the counter like a light snowfall. Are these flakes dandruff? Or dead skin?

I drop the bra to the counter while yelping, "OH MY GOD!"

This is one of those moments in which you don't know whether to run away screaming or to call a Hazmat team. I'm overcome with visions of contracting piggy flu or lice or some other nasty disease. I need an antibacterial bath, STAT.

Greasy snatches the bra and dismisses its grossness. "You're overreacting. That's just my workout bra. There's nothing wrong with it."

"It proves you were using the bag, which is why I can't return it. Especially now that your flaky bra was inside it."

"EXCUSE ME? What did you just say? How insulting and rude. I have never been treated this way at a Big Fancy Store. There is nothing wrong with my bra."

"Ma'am," I say, as cool as a Gucci bag, "It's all over the counter."

"Those are just dust particles from the bag," Greasy snaps.

"Bags that have never been used don't have dust particles. They also don't have tampons, dirty bras, and makeup stains inside."

Greasy's face turns so red, I begin to think she is going to rise up off the aisle and release enough hellfire to turn my ass into ashes.

"THIS IS NOT THE BIG FANCY WAY! I WANT TO SEE YOUR MANAGER!" she screams, flailing her arms around as if she's an air-traffic controller at Hobbiton International Airport.

I remain calm. "We're closing, and my manager is off right now."

"THEN I DEMAND YOU GET THE STORE MANAGER!"

"The store manager isn't here now either."

"WELL SOMEONE MUST BE RUNNING THIS STORE! I AM A PAYING CUSTOMER HERE! I DON'T HAVE TO PUT UP WITH YOUR RUDE BEHAVIOR!"

And so it comes to this. Like countless other times when customers threw fits after we denied them the right to return their old, used, disgusting handbags. I pick up the phone and page the night manager. Since neither my manager nor the store manager is around, The Big Fancy assigns the duty of temporary leadership to another department manager. When Sierra, the children's shoe manager, answers, I know I'm screwed. Besides having a spine like a stick of chewing gum, she is a total Big Fancy Rah-Rah Bitch. I leave Greasy to smolder while I continue the closing duties of straightening hundreds of handbags. As soon as Sierra shows up, Greasy erupts like a volcano, spewing about my poor customer service skills and how awful I am. After Greasy's ten-minute tirade winds down, the night manager approaches me and says, "I'm going to go ahead and authorize the return as a customer service issue. She's pretty upset about the way you handled it and I think it's the best direction for us to take."

I want to strangle Sierra with the DKNY in my hand. "You've got to be fucking kidding me. Did you see the bag?" I counter, "It's beat to shit and her DIRTY BRA was inside it! We can't even resell it, and now I'm in the hole."

"I realize you're upset, but please don't use that language with me. I'm here to take care of the customer. If she goes to Suzy tomorrow or calls Corporate, they'll take it back anyway. Just save yourself some drama, return it, and move on to the next sale."

What next sale? Hello. We are closing! It is the last day of the pay period and Greasy's $2,000 return is about to make my sales a negative number for the day.

I feel like a hooker who gave a ten-hour blow job and was beat up and robbed by the john, just to have the police officer who witnessed it all say, "Oh well, better luck on the next blow job."

It's times like this at The Big Fancy when I could just freak out!

I'M DONE, PEOPLE! DONE WITH ALL OF YOU! I'M OUTTA HERE!

Maybe this is it. Maybe this is where I finally snap and jump the counter and start to handbag-whip the greasy fucking bitch. I'm like a crazy man. People have to pull me off her and take the Ferragamo away from me. I end up all over the news while I sit in the Los Angeles County Jail. The headlines read, "An Innocent Customer Receives Ferragamo Beating Instead of Service! What Kind of World Is This?"

But before the cops show up, I rip off my tie and walk out the mall entrance slowly, possibly stopping to get a vanilla latte at the Coffee Bar. Goodbye, Big Fancy. Outside the mall in the parking lot, it's raining. Pouring. My arms cinematically outstretched, I walk out from the sliding glass mall doors, welcoming the cleansing water, letting it wash away the heinous remnants of the store. The soundtrack to my dramatic exit is very John Williams and rises to a crescendo as I walk across the parking lot and never look back. The perfect ending. An Oscar-winning ending.

But not my ending.

I return Greasy's destroyed Ferragamo—she of course wants cash and holds up the store closing because she has to go to customer service to get it. On her way out, as I'm catching up on the department straightening I had to delay because of her return drama, she has the nerve to walk by and say, "You really should learn to give better customer service. You won't last here if you don't." I give her one of my famous shit-eating retail smiles and turn my back. The alternative is to cannonball a Dooney & Bourke barrel bag at her and hope its hardware knocks out her front teeth.

All the customers are finally gone, and the lights start to automatically shut off. It is almost 10:00. My feet feel like molten lava, I'm sweaty and disheveled, and I realize I forgot to set my DVR for *Dancing with the Stars*. Fuck. No mindless reality game shows for me. I have six bucks in my wallet for a Taco Bell dinner and twelve bucks in my checking account, which isn't enough for anything. I need gas to get home, all six of my credit cards are maxed out, I have a phone bill that's a week late, my rent is due in two days, and the new Adam

Sandler movie opens on Friday. Even if I want to quit, I can't. I need some kind of paycheck. No matter how small. The almighty dollar and the need for food and entertainment are keeping me engulfed in flames.

I should be on location somewhere rewriting lines for Julia Roberts and having drinks with George Clooney. But instead, I'm selling handbags at The Big Fancy.

Free-Spirit Personality

Although I don't really have any proof, I'm gonna stick my pitchfork in a galleria parking space and make the claim that I was the first man to sell handbags in Los Angeles. A friend once said I should try and get it in the *Guinness Book of World Records*. (Personally, I'd rather shoot for the record of eating the most Nacho Cheese Doritos in one sitting. Now there's a record to savor!)

Whenever I was forced to talk about what I did for a living, I often got strange looks from people. You'd have thought I told them I sold body bags, barf bags, or bags of pot. Regardless of how I defended myself to those who couldn't wrap their mind around the idea of a guy selling purses, it always hit me hardest when I was out at a bar trying to score and the conversation got personal:

HOT DUDE: "So, what do you do?"

FREEMAN: "I work in retail." (I always tried to be truthful at first, but vague.)

HOT DUDE: "Cool. Where do you work?"

FREEMAN: "Umm ... at The Big Fancy." (Here's where I'd place my prayer request to God and beg to let the "what I do" question end there.)

HOT DUDE: "Expensive store. What do you sell? (Prayer request denied. God went straight to my shit list.)

FREEMAN: "Umm ... handbags."

HOT DUDE: "What?" (They always said "what?" like I was speaking in tongues.)

FREEMAN: "Ladies' handbags. You know, like purses." (Humiliation ensued.)

HOT DUDE: "You sell purses to women?" (Laughing. They always laughed.) "That's fucking bizarre."

Handbag emasculation complete.

My balls had shrunk to my neck, where they proceeded to choke me.

(Handbags are not a topic of interest to a crowd of muscle men at a leather bar.)

Technically, I should have been telling everyone I was a screenwriter—and I did many times—but what always went down after that was, "Have you been produced?" followed by me saying, "Not yet," which usually led to the question, "What do you do for your day job?" And that would bring me back to dialogue that ended in handbag emasculation and ball shredding.

If I was drunk, horny, and wanted a fast hookup, I would completely lie; the job questions usually ended after I proclaimed myself a software developer, accountant, or veterinarian.

Early on at The Big Fancy, I also received my share of skepticism from women customers:

CUSTOMER: "How are you going to help me? What do you know about bags?"

FREEMAN: "That's what I've been hired to do."

CUSTOMER: "But men never work in this section."

FREEMAN: "One does now. And men have been selling shoes to women forever. No difference really." (This was always my big line for customers questioning my gender-based abilities.)

CUSTOMER: "I suppose you're right." (Of course I am. The customer is *never* right.)

Thankfully, society has moved past the shock of men selling handbags, just as they have with women being allowed to tackle and Taser some asshole on the run. Thousands of my brethren are out there right now helping women find trendy totes big enough to hold their Chihuahuas in. Handbags have become status symbols and fashion statements, and because of the truckload of techie gizmos we carry around on a daily basis, guys are also dragging them around. Those are called *manbags*.

But when I moved to Los Angeles, way back when, men weren't selling handbags. I didn't own a handbag—I mean manbag—and the word was no more a part of my vocabulary than the word menopause. I thought I was going to be selling screenplays. Not handbags.

Knowing only a few friends who were nice enough to let me sleep on their couches, I landed in the mid-Wilshire district just miles from Hollywood. Unfortunately, none of my friends were related to Steven Spielberg or knew Ron Howard.

Having a limited amount of money to start my new screenwriting life, I needed a Pay-the-Bills Job. Delirious for a new L.A. wardrobe, I didn't think twice about where to go first: a store where I could buy cool clothes, measure the inseams of hot men, and make loads of money.

The buzz around town was The Big Fancy. A large, upscale department store famous for customer service, The Big Fancy carried the trendiest brands and paid their salespeople commissions. The idea of getting commissions played out in my head like a scene out of *Indecent Proposal*, with me rolling around naked in a pile of money.

How amazing would it be to write my Million-Dollar Screenplay while driving my limited-edition Mercedes and living in Beverly Hills?

I'd never been to The Big Fancy before (we didn't have one in Reno), but when I stepped inside the Burbank store, I thought I had died and gone to heaven. The place was like a golden marbled, mirrored castle full of beautiful things everywhere I looked. We're talking four floors filled with everything from clothes and cosmetics to espresso machines and comforters. They carried the hippest trends from the world's top designers. As I wandered through the men's section, drooling over racks and tables of amazing clothes, my eyes went straight to a $50 designer tee emblazoned with a flying skull. It called out to me, "Freeman, you must buy me NOW!" The salespeople at The Big Fancy were smiling and looked happy and their customers were leaving with shopping bags packed full. *Who wouldn't want to work here while they write their Million-Dollar Screenplay?*

After flirting with a cute guy in customer service, I wasted no time filling out my application. Minutes later, I was sitting down with the H.R. manager, Two-Tone Tammy. Her name wasn't really Two-Tone Tammy. That's what I called her because she had two tones: Sicky Sweet and Fire-Breathing Dragon. One minute, she was the caring nanny who wanted to rock you to sleep; the next, she was a mean old ogre who wanted to eat you alive. Two-Tone was a blubbery woman in her mid-thirties with frizzy prematurely gray hair, bulging eyes like a bulldog, and style that could only be described as Uglier Betty. When I met her, she had on a thick navy blue cable-knit sweater, a gauzy pink gypsy skirt, and sparkly red ballet shoes.

"I'd really like to work in Men's Clothing," I told her as I tried not to stare at her red slippers.

"I'm so very sorry," Two-Tone said in her Sweet voice, "You have excellent experience and references, but we just don't have any openings in our men's areas. In fact there's a waiting list."

A waiting list to sell pants? What? Do you people advertise in the Gay Yellow Pages?

"Would you consider working in another area?"

Thinking Two-Tone might offer me something in one of the departments that sell Egyptian cotton sheets, overpriced blenders, ceramic mugs filled with candy, or maybe even a gig in Customer Service, I said, "Yes, I'm open to anything. I just moved to L.A. and I need a job."

Big mistake.

Never sound desperate and always hold out for what you want. If you want to measure men's inseams, don't stop until you get there. Stupidly I panicked.

I need a job. Must grab whatever job I can. I'm sleeping on a couch.

"We have an opening in our handbag department," she said.

"Handbags?"

At first, I wasn't sure what that was . . . the word sounded foreign. I know what a hand-job is. But hand-bags?

Was that something to do with the janitorial staff? Garbage? Cleaning bathrooms?

Then it dawned on me, "Do you mean women's purses?"

"We don't refer to them as purses here," Two-Tone said, "They're called handbags, and I think you would be great in that area because of your free-spirit personality."

"Sell purses?" I said, wondering what she meant by *free-spirit personality*.

"Well, we have men in Ladies' Shoes, Cosmetics, and even in Women's Designer. Our motto is creativity through diversity. We like to mix things up. I can see you working in Handbags."

Creativity through diversity? Diversity? I'm as white as the Pillsbury Dough Boy. What the hell is she talking about? I certainly didn't ask her if I could work in the purse department. All I want to do is measure men's inseams. Wait a minute. I know what this is all about.

Two-Tone had gaydar and she was taking advantage! It's well known in the retail world that women love to buy shit from gay men.

Free-spirit personality, my ass. She wants to exploit my gayness!

DON'T DO IT, DON'T DO IT, FREEMAN! DON'T SELL FUCKING PURSES!

What I should have said was, "Thank you very much, but no purse selling for me." An inseam-measuring job had to be available somewhere in L.A.

The problem was I didn't have the patience or the luxury of time to look for one. Filling out applications and going on interviews is laborious and time-consuming, and like so many other Hollywood Hopefuls, I just wanted to get started on my Million-Dollar Screenplay.

I could take the purse-selling job or walk out the door. The choice was mine. After a gulp I'm sure Two-Tone heard, I made my decision.

"Umm . . . okay."

The purse deal was sealed. My soul was about to be snatched from me, but the only thought running through my head was, *How can I get my hands on that T-shirt with the flying skull?*

"How soon do I get my discount?" I asked, hoping I could buy the shirt on my way out and wear it out that night in West Hollywood.

"After you've completed training," she replied, her bulbous eyes scanning me.

Damn. Not soon enough. I had to have that shirt.

Climbing Mount Fancy

After hiring me to work in the purse department and requiring me to sign a gazillion forms for God Knows What, Tammy handed me a pink flyer emblazoned with **Employee Parking and Entrance Instructions** and told me to report for training in the meeting room at 8:00 A.M.

What she didn't say was that I'd first have to climb a goddamn mountain.

If I had known about the mountain, I would have listened to my screaming intuitive mind and said, "No fucking way. Not working at The Big Fancy. Not climbing a mountain. Not selling purses. Thank you, but nooo."

But I didn't know about the mountain.

How could I have ever seen something that bad coming?

All this bitching has to do with the Employee Entrance.

Every store, big or small, has a so-called Employee Entrance—a designated area providing access into the building for all employees before and after each shift. It's a normal requirement.

However, The Big Fancy's Employee Entrance was anything but normal. Built out of solid steel and standing 50 feet tall, Mount Fancy was an architectural monstrosity capable of causing hearts to fail and bones to break.

Mount Fancy was eight flights of stairs.

That's right, *eight* flights of fucking stairs.

Eight flights of stairs up to work. *Eight* flights of stairs down from work. Up eight flights. Down eight flights. Up eight flights. Down eight flights.

Are you tired yet?

You think your commute is bad? Try climbing a mountain of stairs every day. If you happen to be seven-time Tour de France winner Lance Armstrong, it's a breeze. But for a 55-year-old overweight woman with varicose veins working in the plus-size department, Mount Fancy is sheer torture.

Each flight in the great mountain contained sixteen wide ledges for a total of 128 heart-stopping steps to the peak, where the actual entrance was located. The massive, unventilated stairwell connected these treacherous flights with nine platform levels that are supported by four floors of store. There was no assistance getting to the top of Mount Fancy. No elevators. No escalators. No ropes. No Sherpas. Not even a drop of goddamn water. Just stairs. Lots and lots of stairs that had to be climbed daily.

For my first ascent up Mount Fancy at 7:45 A.M. on Training Day, I was running on little sleep (due to first-day jitters), two cups of Mini-Mart coffee sloshed around in my empty stomach (causing me to feel shaky and nauseated), and I was wearing a full-on black suit (and my good-luck Hollywood Stars tie) with a pair of brand-new dress shoes (purchased at a Discount Store for $10).

Completely ill prepared.

Cheap shoes are not what you want to wear when climbing eight flights of stairs.

I followed the instructions on Tammy's flyer (which didn't say shit about any stairs) by parking on the roof of the mall's parking structure. Then I took an elevator down and went for quite a walk through the parking structure's underbelly, until finally reaching The Big Fancy's Employee Entrance. I entered a numeric code in the brown box next to the double doors. A clicking noise signaled. I opened the Employee In door.

Musty air hit my face, reminding me of a locked-up toolshed in the summer. Under fluorescent lighting, I stepped onto lifeless, turflike garage carpeting. My eyes were immediately drawn to a large yellow sign in the shape of a diamond with glittery green letters:

Welcome to The Big Fancy, the Jewel of Burbank. Home is where you make it. We're thrilled you are part of our family. —Suzy Davis-Johnson, Store Manager.

It sounded like something Tony Soprano would say right before he asks you to shoot your mother. A chill crawled up my spine.

Completely ignorant of what lay ahead, I looked around for a hallway or door leading into the store. Not finding anything, I figured it must be right up the first flight of stairs, which wouldn't be so bad if it was the only one on Mount Fancy. I grabbed the handrail and hauled myself up sixteen steps. No biggie. I slid a bit in my new cheap shoes on the garage carpet, but I figured it would be just a few short steps. Easily handled.

On the second platform there was a huge rectangular scratched mirror running across the entire length of the wall between the staircases. Above it hung a clear plastic sign with bold red letters: **THROUGH THESE DOORS WALK THE MOST IMPORTANT PEOPLE IN OUR COMPANY.**

At the time I didn't think much of these condescending words, but after having to climb Mount Fancy daily, every time I read them, I feel foolish and mocked. Day in and day out, my cloudy reflection wants to destroy the Important People mirror with a baseball bat.

If I'm so important why am I climbing eight flights of fucking stairs? How do the unimportant people enter the store? Through an underground sewer tunnel?

But back on my first day, I wasn't bitter yet. I just straightened my Hollywood Stars tie in the mirror and looked around, bewildered. No entrance next to the Important People Mirror.

Puzzled, I went to the side of the second landing and looked up.

Before me was a dizzying scene straight out of Alfred Hitchcock's movie *Vertigo*. Flights of stairs. Lots and lots of flights. Flights infinitude.

Where in the name of God is the store?

Hiking boots with crampons couldn't have prepared me for what happened next.

Mount Fancy consumed me.

I bumbled up the second flight, slipping around like a cartoon dog on black ice. The entrance had to be on the third platform. But the fucker wasn't, and I practically skated across the platform, my cheap shoes and the garage carpet not getting along. There was a massive multicolored sign swathed in balloons shouting: **Fling Your Sales into Spring! Open New Accounts.** I did not stop to read what else the sign had to say because I was afraid of falling. Plus I really didn't care. Holding on to the rail, I sidestepped my way up the third flight, skidding onto the fourth platform, where I found nothing. No entrance. No store. Just a few candy wrappers on the floor. The wall, however, was plastered with photos of salespeople and the departments they worked in. **These Are Your Service Superstars Burbank!** said the wall.

Whatever. Don't fucking care. Not stopping.

Halfway up the fourth flight, my right foot glided off a step like it was made out of grease. When I attempted to regain my footing, my shoe slammed into the step. Pain seared from my toes to my heel.

FUCK! SONOFABITCH! GODDAMN THIS SHIT!

At that moment I was over climbing Mount Fancy, and I hadn't even reached the top. But I didn't know there were four more flights as I muttered to myself, "This-had-better-be-the-last-fucking-one." I bumbled my way to the top of the fourth flight like a circus clown who had been shot in the foot. Still no store. And no hallway leading to a store. Instead I was greeted by three bikini-clad Headless Mannequins posing suggestively against the wall like eyeless gargoyles. They scared the shit out of me. I thought they were real people at first. Like some bizarre crime scene out of the TV show *Dexter.* I quickly passed them, looking over my shoulder, keeping an eye out. You just never know what mannequins without heads are capable of. Teetering and tottering up flight number five, my throbbing toes and burning feet screamed for mercy.

Get these torturous shoes off me and stop all this bullshit RIGHT NOW!

The air suddenly vanished. Just like on a real mountain. I couldn't breathe. Sweat peppered my temples and poured out from under my arms.

Am I in the wrong place? Is this a joke? Where is the goddamn store?

No sign of it on the sixth platform. Instead, a gallery of motivational signs awaited me there. Clichés and quotes from Big Fancy executives: **The people in our company are everything. —Cindy**

Billingsworth, Senior Marketing Corporate Credit Analyst Senior Advisor.

What the hell is a Corporate Credit Analyst Senior Advisor?

Expect to be the best and you will. —Mr. Michael, President, CEO, The Big Fancy.

I wonder if he has ever climbed these stairs.

Work is not all about work. —Diana Soon-Smith, Corporate Human Resources Director of the Southwest Division 2.

Evidently it's also about a workout! I almost vomited all over Diana Soon-Smith's quote.

I couldn't read anymore. Sweat dripped into my eyes. The rest of the signs were a blur as I hauled myself up step after hideous step, breathing like I was going into labor. By the time I reached the seventh flight after what seemed like an eternity of sweat and pain, I considered screaming for help. But I was alone on Mount Fancy. Just the Headless Mannequins and me. They weren't going to help. Death was imminent if I stopped. I considered turning around, but I quickly realized I'd have to go back down all the stairs I'd just come up. What if I found out after going down them that I'd have to go back up them all over again?

Not.

Happening.

I kept climbing. Lifting, stretching, pulling. Halfway up the seventh flight, my thighs felt as if they were being pulled on a taffy machine from all the lunging. I clutched the handrail like it was a life preserver. The eighth flight turned out to be a hot, sticky, breathless blackout.

Am I at 50,000 feet? When does the atmosphere give out?

My throbbing feet were on auto-climb-pilot: moving through the pain. When I finally heaved my sweaty, exhausted body up onto the ninth platform and saw the brown door with **Store Entrance** stenciled on it, I sighed with disgusted relief and said, "There is no fucking way I am EVER doing that again."

"No fucking way" are famous last words of just about every Retail Slave. For me, this was a defining moment. Little did I know I was about to find myself saying and doing many Big Fancy things after uttering the phrase, "No fucking way."

Although Two-Tone Tammy had failed to mention that I'd be climbing eight flights of stairs every day, she had made it crystal clear about using the entrance: "Not using the Employee Entrance can be grounds for termination," she had said, in Dragon tone. "Every employee is required to use the Employee Entrance upon the start of their shift and upon leaving the store."

Who in their right mind goes up and down eight flights of stairs for work every day? Why isn't there an elevator or escalator or sky tram here? It's a Big Fancy department store, for chrissake! I'd settle for a pack mule! Eight flights of stairs? I just don't understand it. How could someone have designed an Employee Entrance like this? I CALL BULLSHIT!!!

Mount Fancy has head injury written all over it.

Feeling like a contestant on *The Biggest Loser*, I attempted to pull my sweaty, out-of-breath self together on the steel mountain's ninth summit as I slid across the carpet toward the door. Next to it was a giant wall calendar with holidays, special events, and employee birthdays.

God, I hope my name never ends up there.

What The Big Fancy really needs to put on the ninth platform is a comfy rest area with couches, a big-screen TV with cable, and maybe a nice tropical fish tank. They also need showers. I'm sure many of us climbers end up smelling like eau de sweat by the time we reach the top. Lockers would be a good idea too. Then we could climb the mountain in workout clothes and tennis shoes. Massage therapy would be nice for our tired retail feet, and a full bar wouldn't hurt either. Watermelon margaritas can take away just about any pain.

Behind the heavy brown Store Entrance door is a small foyer area opening to a narrow hallway that runs by offices into Customer Service and, eventually, leads to the fourth floor of the store. Inside the foyer there are two electronic time clocks mounted on the wall, surrounded by a bunch of store reports hanging from binder rings. On the opposite wall are department mailboxes next to a window with a shelf. This is what The Big Fancy calls the Employee Check-In (ECI).

All employees (except managers) are required to check in any belongings larger than 5" × 7". This includes handbags, packs, coats, umbrellas, and store purchases. None of these items are allowed on the sales floor for fear we might load them up with merchandise. ECI is a pain in the ass, but I get it. We live in a world where people steal Halloween decorations off front lawns.

When I blundered through the Store Entrance door that first time, breathing as if I was having an asthma attack, I found a young, brown-haired, makeup-free woman who looked like she'd just woken up sitting behind the ECI counter.

"Can I help you?" she said.

"I'm here for training."

"Just need you to sign, since you can't clock in yet."

She pushed a clipboard toward me and I scribbled across it, still panting.

I could barely talk, but I managed to ask, "Is the meeting room around here?"

"It's in the basement."

My breath suddenly caught up to me.

"No fucking way. You've got to be shitting me," I said, throwing any concern about my first impression right out the window.

Luckily, Security Agent Girl didn't hold my language against me.

She knew why I was agitated.

"Don't worry," she said smiling, "You can take the elevator in the store."

Thank you, Jesus!

Sunshine from Satan's Ass

After you've had to climb eight flights of stairs at 7:45 in the morning, getting into an elevator is like being rescued by a helicopter from the roof of your car during a flood. My feet were still throbbing, my clothes wet with sweat, and my breathing still unbalanced, but at least I was in an elevator.

The Big Fancy's basement is the complete opposite of its sparkling, picture-perfect store.

Windowless and industrial, it resembles the cargo hold of a plane.

Metal pipes hold rows of clothes suspended from the ceiling and chain-link cages contain wooden shelves of everything from shirts and pants to coffeemakers and the purses I'd soon be selling. The basement's dimly lit hallway gave me the creeps; it was a place Hannibal Lecter could call home.

I quickly got myself to the meeting room.

Inside I found a stuffy room with beige walls and fluorescent lighting. Six-foot-long tables had been pushed together in the shape of a square horseshoe, with its ends facing the front of the room. A giant Post-It note sat on an easel displaying the words, **Welcome! We're glad to have you!** Next to it was a smaller, five-foot-long table holding stacks of colored collated paper, piles of pens, and a TV with a built-in VCR. I was the only one in the room.

As I sat down at a corner of the horseshoe wondering if I was in the right place, I noticed a bunch of posters similar to the ones on Mount Fancy:

Customer Service is our number-one priority!
Never underestimate the power of a smile!
Always show the customer the dessert tray and give her
more than one choice.
Greet every customer within 30 seconds.
A larger poster stood out. It had a childlike drawing of a sun below the title **The Sun of Success**. Inside the sun was the word **YOU**. On the lines representing the sun's rays were the words **Customers, Merchandise, Salespeople, Managers, Buyers, Board of Directors, Money, Career, Community, Self-Fulfillment,** and **Family.** Below that, it said:
You are the center of the sun.
How bright you shine affects everything.
I gazed at *The Sun of Success*. It was the biggest load of corporate bullshit I'd ever seen. I may be new to The Big Fancy, but I'm not new to department-store propaganda. I had enough of it shoved down my throat at the store in Reno to know the truth behind it all.
YOU are expendable. YOU are disposable. YOU are replaceable.
YOU aren't the center of anything in retail.
Everything from that point on went to a very dark, sunless place.

My fellow newbies were all women. Twelve of them. Various ages. I wasn't thrilled about being the only guy. Many jokes were had at my expense. "Looks like you're part of the Girls' Club now! You're outnumbered! Better hope we don't decide to do makeovers!"
The first part of my Big Fancy orientation was administered by Two-Tone Tammy, who bounced between her two extremes. She sweetly congratulated us on joining The Big Fancy family, and then seconds later she let out her Dragon, saying The Big Fancy had huge expectations and many people don't cut it. Some of us might not be the right fit for The Big Fancy.
Sicky-Sweet Tammy excitedly laid out the benefits package for health, vacations, and retirement. Then Fire-Breathing Dragon sternly went over all the things that weren't tolerated within the company: all the harassments, all the unlawful ringing methods, all the dress code mishaps. The endless list of decrees nearly blew my brain right out of my head.

Then we did something I absolutely hate.

We had to stand and do stupid introductions as if we were at a singles convention.

"Hi, my name is Hilary. I just divorced my jerk of a husband. Turned out he was a queer, so I took the bastard for everything. Now I'm working in the Kitchen Access department."

Oh, God. I better stay clear of her.

"Hi, my name is Cindy. I used to be vice-president of a bank, until it collapsed. I'll be at the MAC cosmetic counter doing makeovers. It's a change, but I'm ready for the challenge!"

Now she's pushing lipsticks? Damn, that's sad.

"Hi, my name is Barbara. My husband is a prominent lawyer in La Crescenta. I'm in Women's Tailored Clothing, just here for fun, something to do, I don't really need the money!"

Okay, that's just disgusting. Someone should examine her head.

When my turn rolled around, I said, "Hi, My name is Freeman. I just moved here and I've been assigned to the purse department."

They all stared at me like they were waiting for more, like I was supposed to name off all the people I'd slept with or present a Power-Point show of my life. *Fuck that.* I shot them my famous shit-pleasing retail smile, a smile that makes me look like I give a shit when I actually don't. It's my number-one viable retail asset.

But Two-Tone shot me back with what looked like her own shit-pleasing smile and then made us play ridiculous word-association games on the chalkboard with words like **Team Player, Courtesy, Follow-Through,** and **Service.**

"What do you think of when you hear the word 'service'?" Tammy asked. I so wanted to yell out "blow job," but I held back. The woman named Hilary with the queer ex-husband was nearby, and she might have stabbed me with her ballpoint pen.

Later, we were herded down the dreary corridor to another room called Register Training. Inside were rows of registers. Waiting to take over the reins from Tammy and teach the money handling side was Brandi, The Big Fancy's Store Operations Manager. Brandi was an annoying woman in her mid-forties who bore a frightening resemblance to TV's Marcia Brady. Only this Marcia Brady did a baby-talk routine, as if her audience was composed of preschoolers. "GOOD MORNING, NEWBIES! How are we all this morning?" chanted Baby-Talk Brandi, "I see bright new shiny faces! Are we happy to be here? I know I'm happy to be here and meet all of you! LET'S ALL HAVE A ROUND OF CLAPPING!"

She cannot be fucking serious. Where am I? Sesame Street?

Twelve women and one man stared at her.

"COME ON EVERYBODY!!" shouted Baby-Talk, "GET THE BLOOD FLOWING! CLAP! WE HAVE A LOT TO LEARN IN A SHORT AMOUNT OF TIME AND I NEED YOU PUMPED UP!! IT'S SUPER-FANTASTIC TIME! WOOHOOOO!"

The twelve women and one man clapped. I wanted to super-fucking kill myself.

Like a chipmunk on speed, Brandi chattered uncontrollably about handling money, fraud, credit, pricing, ticketing, and new accounts. "Did everyone get that okay?" she asked to vacant stares, "Do you understand? Great. Perfect. Super-fantastic. Moving on. Onward and upward, class!" And just like that, we were at the registers.

The Big Fancy's sophisticated computerized registers were supposed to be simple, but to some, operating them ended up being more complicated than learning Chinese. I caught on easily because they were similar to the ones I'd worked with before, but the Lawyer's Wife had major problems. Her register beeped in error so many times I thought it might explode.

"SUPER-FANTASTIC!" Brandi screamed in my ear after I figured out how to do a Charge Send properly.

Finally we were released for lunch. I wanted to get a salad at this French Café place, but then I saw half my fellow Female Newbies standing in line. I went to Carl's Jr. instead.

Man food. No Female Newbies there.

The afternoon was off to a lobotomizing start as Tammy began showing us Big Fancy movies that threatened to knock me out. We endured the history of The Big Fancy with some old dude yapping on and on about how lucky we were to have been hired at a *Fortune 500* company devoted to customer service. Didn't hear half of what he said; the man food had sent me into a food coma.

We were forced to watch something on inventory and the importance of accuracy, and then some nonsense about returning everything for the customer, and finally a canonizing masterpiece delving into the seedy world of stealing employees and what happens to them when they get caught.

I slept with my eyes open.

That is, until Baby-Talk Brandi scared the shit out of me by yelling, "TIME TO WAKEY-UPPY, WE ARE GOING TO HAVE SOME SUPER-FUN RIGHT NOW! AND GET THIS PARTY BACK TO LIFE!"

The super-fun was having us draw slips of paper out of a fishbowl with scenarios printed on them about subjects like opening new accounts, multiple selling, approaching customers, and handling returns. We were to take turns role-playing in front of the class.

Did I mention I *loathe* role-playing games?

My slip of paper had me playing the part of a woman wanting to buy lipstick.

Hilary, with the gay ex, played my Cosmetics salesperson. The look she gave me when I asked her if she had anything in Candy Apple Red made me want to ask Tammy if I could take out a restraining order.

Suddenly the meeting room door flew open, and a woman stuck her head in and shrieked at a pitch that made Brandi's cheers sound tame: "WOOO-HOO! WHAAAASSSUP, BURBANK NEWBIES??!?!!"

I nearly jumped clean out of my chair.

The owner of this shrieking voice was Suzy Davis-Johnson, the store manager. I call her Suzy Satan because she rules The Big Fancy Underworld like a Disney witch on Ecstasy. "NEWWWBIES! NEW, NEW, NEW, NEWBEEEEEEEEEEEEEEEES!" Suzy Davis-Johnson sang out, making my ears beg me to cover them. *American Idol* rejects have nothing on her.

I didn't know whether to laugh or scream. Suzy Satan had orange and blond stripy highlighted hair cut into a pageboy, and thick black rectangular glasses.

"MY NAME IS SUZY DAVIS-JOHNSON!" she screamed, "I'M YOUR STORE MANAGER! THE CAPTAIN OF THIS FABU-LOUS SHIP! I WANT TO WELCOME YOU TO OUR MAGI-CAL STORE. THE BIG FANCY IS THE GREATEST PLACE TO WORK EVER!!"

Satan fired off a laundry list of expectations: No cell-phone conversations in the store. No chewing gum on the sales floor. No standing around. No frowning. No. No. No.

With tears in her eyes, she told us what customer service means to her and how it can change the world. "If we love our customers, they love us, and they keep coming back."

A confusing lecture about sales requirements came next. If we didn't sell more in commissions than our hourly rate, we ended up doing something they called Misfire. Apparently it was the equivalent of committing murder at The Big Fancy, and if we did it three times in a row, we were viewed as "Ineffective Sales Associates" and considered "not a right fit." Termination was initiated. Suzy Satan announced all of this with a smile that had to be hiding something wicked.

Positioning herself in front of the *Sun of Success* poster and framing it with her arms, à la Vanna White, she gushed: "The Sun of Success is our most prized and cherished philosophy. Each one of you has the ability to be a beautiful, radiating sun at this store, full of tremendous warmth and light. When you excel at what you do, you grow brighter, and all of those around you shine even more. The rays of your bright shining sun affect everything!"

Somebody get me a paper bag! The Gay Guy is going to barf.

Brandi passed out sheets with suns drawn on them so we could fill in our own Sun of Success to present to the class.

I cringed. In sci-fi movies people are killed by the sun. Could this day get any worse?

Before we could start, Tammy announced we were out of time and we'd have to sadly forgo that part of orientation.

I was so happy I almost yelled, "SUPER-FANTASTIC!"

Suzy Davis-Johnson continued, "I hereby welcome all of you to our close-knit family. We are highly dedicated individuals and are motivated to win! ROCK ON! Now that you have completed training, I have a fabulous tool I want to give each one of you. IT'S THE OFFICIAL EMPLOYEE HANDBOOK!"

Oh. My. God. NO! Not a fucking handbook. Studying and tests go with that word. I don't want to study. I need to go home and write. What have I gotten myself into?

"IS EVERYONE READY TO GET THEIR EMPLOYEE HANDBOOK?" she yelled.

A half-assed "Yessss," answered back. Satan's face went sour.

"NOW, THAT'S NO GOOD!!!" she cried, "REMEMBER, YOU ARE ALL SUNS!!! BRIGHT, BRILLIANT, RADIANT SUNS! YOU ARE THE LUCKY ONES, BEATING OUT HUN-DREDS OF OTHER APPLICANTS TO WORK IN THIS STORE! I WANNA HEAR HOW EXCITED YOU ALL ARE TO BE WORKING HERE!!!"

"YEeeAAaaH!" responded all the women and one man, sounding like a broken accordion.

"What do you think, Tammy?" Suzy Davis-Johnson asked, deflated.

"I think they're ready, Suzy," she said, looking haggard from the day's training events.

Baby-Talk Brandi walked up to the front with a large box. I held my breath. If she took out anything bigger than an old *TV Guide*, I was going to bawl.

To my surprise she pulled out a stack of glossy 4" × 6" cards and gave them to Satan, who went around the room handing one to each of us and shaking our hands as if we had just graduated. "Congratula-tions, here is your official employee handbook, shine on!" she said.

On the front of the card there was a photo of an old black book that said EMPLOYEE HANDBOOK in gold lettering. On the back it read:

Welcome! Congratulations on joining our team! Our number-one goal is to give excellent customer service above and beyond the norm. Remember, you are the center of the sun. Store rules: Use your best judgment with everything. There are no more rules. Have fun!

I stared at the Employee Handbook, relieved that it wasn't the size of *Gray's Anatomy*, but I was confused by the message.

This did not make sense.

*Have fun? Are they fucking kidding? No rules? Where are Satan's expec-
tations about not chewing gum, not misfiring, and not using cell phones? What
about everything Tammy said that isn't tolerated? What about Brandi's threats
regarding what would happen to us if we didn't carefully inspect every credit
card and hundred-dollar bill? What about the fucking eight flights of stairs we
have to climb every day? What about? What about? What about?*

The Big Fancy's Employee Handbook was as bogus as one of the
computerized personal checks Brandi told us to watch out for.

When I looked around the room, I saw the blank faces of my
Female Newbies.

Not a peep. Not even a frown.

Today the mice were going to be quiet and take their drugs.

This included me.

I wanted the hell out.

Finally we were excused, and everyone quickly rushed the door.
Before I could even get close to it, Suzy Davis–Satan lurched toward
me and started yammering inches from my face: "I've heard SOOO
MANY GREAT THINGS ABOUT YOU! We finally have a DUDE
working in handbags! RIGHT-ON! HIGH FIVE! ROCK AND
ROLL! I expect GREAT things from you! This is SOOO EXCIT-
ING! I'm totally excited! You must be excited? Are you excited?"

*What a crazy-ass freak. Who is this woman? What have I done getting a
job at this place?*

Moments later, I stood at the top of Mount Fancy looking down the
eight flight of stairs.

*Now I have to go down them? How the hell will I do this every day?
I am so screwed.*

I felt like I had been shot into the center of the sun naked.

Completely fried. Char-broiled. Burnt to a crisp.

All the Noxzema and aloe-vera gel in the world would not be able
to save me.

But in moments of great duress, the human mind can find ways to
protect its body from the most severe conditions.

My cheap dress shoes came off.

And I didn't care who saw me.

The P-Word

Climbing Mount Fancy was not the only obstacle I faced at The Big Fancy in my early days as a newbie sales associate. I had to learn not to say the p-word.

Purse.

I know many of you women out there still refer to the piece of backbreaking luggage you drag around all day as your purse, but at The Big Fancy and in the fashion world, saying the word purse is akin to calling a day spa a beauty parlor.

When I arrived in the handbag department on my first morning an hour before the store opened, I was like an Ohio farm boy stepping off a bus into New York City for the first time.

I was in over my head.

There had to be millions of different sizes, shapes, and colors of purses. They looked like lumps of wild, exotic, sleeping animals and if any of them woke up, I was sure they were going to eat me alive.

How the hell am I going to sell these things? I don't know shit about purses.

The place suddenly felt like Bikram Yoga class. I thought it was leftover heat from my stairwell workout coupled with my purse nerves and the fact that I was wearing a suit, but I found out later the AC didn't kick on until 10:00 A.M. Suzy Satan didn't think air-conditioning before the store opens was cost effective.

I *so* wanted to take off my sport coat, but the dress-code requirement called for all men to wear a dress shirt, tie, slacks, and sport coat. "Everyone must be the epitome of fashion professionalism," said Two-Tone Tammy during training.

Nothing about that in the Employee Handbook!

Since I had no budget for a closet full of suits when I started at The Big Fancy, I pulled together a suit look with a black sport coat and black slacks.

I did not feel like the epitome of fashion.

I felt like the epitome of Discount Store.

Because that's where it all came from, including a pair of new dress shoes for Mount Fancy, with thick hiking-boot soles.

The only fashion fun we Retail Slave men got to have was with our ties. I took full advantage of this, and I own quite the collection. Picasso, Monopoly, the Tasmanian Devil, hundred-dollar bills, sunflowers, Homer Simpson, pizza, billiard balls. You name it. If it's weird and on a tie, I'm wearing it around my neck.

For my first day in the purse department I wore a new black tie with a screaming white alien; apropos considering the circumstances. (Mom gave me that one. From one Retail Slave to another.)

While wandering around the sweltering compound sweating in my suit and checking out the purses, a strange thing happened. I found myself wishing I could carry some of them. The Big Fancy had cool purses. They had unusual locks, hooks, buckles, and weird shit on them, like charms, chains, and pom-poms. Many were covered in letters, and a few had phrases like "Juicy Girl," "Crazy For Couture," and "I'm As Mean as I Look." They were made out of astonishing leathers, colorful fabrics, shiny plastics, and exotic animal skins and came in every shape imaginable—from slouchy-looking sacks to clunky-looking gym bags. I even saw one resembling a bowling-ball case. I couldn't help but touch and play with them, feeling their textures, moving their zippers, pushing their locks.

The plethora of intricately designed purses blinded me and impressed me at the same time. It was as if each one was trying to outdo the other. I suddenly realized why women get so hooked. Already I wanted a $1,300 black leather Marc Jacobs because the heavy silver zippers and push-locks looked like my motorcycle jacket.

Perfect for the leather bar.

And I thought the $800 Isabella Fiore with a painted pirate skull was beyond cool. Perfect for Disneyland!

When I picked up a zebra-print sack with gold medallions hanging from it and saw the $4,000 price tag, I almost fainted.

Holy fuck! I could live off that for almost three months!

"Versace," said a woman's voice, "the It Bag for spring."

I almost dropped the $4,000 Versace It Bag for spring.

"Hi, you must be Freeman. I'm Judy, the handbag manager," said a skinny woman in all black with short, dark red hair. Her hardened face reminded me of a dried-up lake bed. "Tammy and Suzy have told me so much about you. I'm expecting great things. You're the first man we've ever had in Handbags. We've been looking for a while now. All the designers have men selling handbags in their boutiques. Women love it."

If one more person tells me how much women are going to love me, I'm going to scream. Not to mention she's treating me like the latest breakthrough in technology.

"Umm . . . thanks . . . nice to meet you, Judy," I said.

Judy's black eyes sized up my screaming alien.

"Interesting tie," she said in a monotone.

Judy wasn't one for fun and games. As far as she was concerned, we were at war in The Big Fancy—at war to win sales and have department increases. Judy was a tense, stressed-out Retail Droid, always dressed in designer black from head to toe. She drank coffee at all hours of the day, but I've never seen her eat actual food. I know little about her personal life because Judy was not one to chit-chat or talk about the latest movie. I heard she was married with no kids and lived somewhere in the valley. It was all about business with Judy. Getting the sale. Having increases. Taking care of the customer. Making the department look Big Fancy perfect. She was constantly on the move. Edgy. Jittery. Terse. And at times completely unhappy. I'm not sure who came up with it, but we had given our stoic bitch of a handbag manager the nickname General Judy. Or the General. When she began barking orders, the handbag troops scrambled.

"You have had full training and I saw from your app you are retail-experienced, so I expect you won't need any babysitting," said General Judy. "I will give you a quick tour of the department and the handbags. Then we will go to Customer Service and get the money for the registers. I need to meet with Suzy about the Charity League fashion show, so you'll be alone for the first hour. You should be able to handle it."

Alone? In the purse jungle by myself. For an hour? I am fucked.

I started to timidly protest about the being alone part, but the General was on the move, not interested in what I had to say. I followed her to a long, glass, case-like island similar in shape to a place where cows are rounded up to be slaughtered. I called it the Corral. The phones and two registers were embedded inside it, and there was barely enough room for us to walk. This was our counter; the place where all the transactions occurred, the place where all the blunt-force drama went down.

Judy quickly unleashed a long list of procedures. She did it so methodically and so fast, I barely retained anything. Work the phone console like this. Answer the phone like that. Handbag repairs work this way. Handbag claims work that way. Clean handbags like this. Do handbag repairs like that. Straighten handbags this way. Display handbags that way.

After each thing she said, "Got it?"

I gave her my best shit-pleasing retail smile and said, "Got it," back.

Then General Judy dragged me over the handbag floor with an arm-waving introduction.

"The Fendi shop is there. The Coach shop is there. The Kate Spade shop is there. Juicy Couture, Isabella Fiore, Kenneth Cole, and Betsey Johnson shops are all over there."

Judy called everything a shop. I didn't see any shops. I saw sections, shelves with purses. She fired off more designer names: Dooney & Bourke. Gucci. Marc Jacobs. Burberry. Monsac. DKNY. Fendi. Dolce & Gabbana. Hobo International. Furla. Botkier. Kooba. Perlina. Some I had heard of because they make men's clothes, but most of them may as well have been names yanked out of a Swedish phone book.

How will I remember all of these? Half of them sound like drag queens. What the hell is a Kooba? A Japanese Anime monster? And what about Hobo International? Sounds like a creepy motel.

"Umm . . . Judy, I'm a little nervous about all of this. I've never sold purses before."

Her pitted, worn face tightened.

"They are not purses. They are handbags. You wouldn't call a flight attendant a stewardess and a color stylist a hairdresser, now, would you?"

"I guess not."

"You guessed right. Always say handbag instead of purse."

Handbag instead of purse. Sounded easy enough. But until that point I'm pretty sure the word handbag had never come from my mouth. In my world of ignorant maleness, the clunky contraptions women stuffed full of whatever were called purses. Not handbags. When I was a little boy, my Grandma had a *purse*; a big brown, monster of a *purse* with double straps and what seemed like hundreds of compartments and zippers. I believed Grandma's Big Brown Purse had to be another door to the kingdom of Narnia and its contents nothing short of treasure. The need to know what was inside consumed me. I remember one time around the age of eight, giving in to this fantastical urge. When I thought I was alone, my hands found themselves rummaging around, deep inside the Big Brown Purse like I was on an archeological dig. Then Grandma walked in and caught me.

"LITTLE FREEMAN! GET OUT OF MY PURSE!" she yelled.

Whenever an older family member said the word little in front of my first name, it usually meant I was in some sort of trouble.

"Sorry, Grandma," I said, feeling like a criminal, "I just wanted to see what was inside."

Grandma laughed and then sat me down next to her.

"A woman's purse is private. It's not a place for boys. You never go inside a woman's purse. The things inside are not for you to see. Do you understand, Freeman?"

"Yes, Grandma."

She then reached into one of the many pockets in her Big Brown Purse, and gave me a piece of Bubble Yum, my favorite. I never went inside Grandma's purse again.

My mother also echoed Stay-Out-of-My-Purse sentiments, further convincing me the inside of a woman's *purse* was no place for a man, but instead a sacred vault only to be entered by those of the female persuasion. This conditioning was so embedded in my psyche that even when my Mom asked me to get something out of her purse, it felt as if I was breaking the law.

And now I was selling them.

"I'm totally on board with the handbag thing," I said to Judy, ready to overcome my childhood purse conditioning, "I'm just curious, though. Why is it a handbag instead of a purse?"

The General simultaneously rolled her eyes and released a tired sigh. "A purse is a cheap, plastic discount store thing. A handbag is what contemporary, fashion-conscious women carry. And that's what we sell. Expensive designer handbags. An assortment of the latest trends and must-have famous names. They are *handbags* and you need to refer to them that way. You can say bag for short, but never, ever, ever say the word purse. It's an insult to the exclusive designers we carry. Got it?"

"Got it."

But I didn't really get it. The whole thing sounded kind of snooty and stupid. Say handbag instead of purse. As a writer, I'm well aware of word transformations. Some like to say hot dog instead of wiener, photo instead of picture, and adult film instead of porno. Who am I to judge? The names of things are constantly changing. If the word purse has been thrown into the dumpster of past terminology, so be it. Handbag instead of purse. Whatever.

Judy went back behind the Corral, opened a drawer by the register, and handed me a hundred-page packet titled **A Guide to Handbags at The Big Fancy.**

The Employee Handbook is a card and the Handbag Guide is the size of a screenplay? How can this be? It'll probably put me to sleep, but at least it will help sell the $4,000 Versace.

"You can read this in between helping customers, but it has to stay in the department."

"Can't I take it home and study it?"

"It's the only copy I have. You need to read it here."

What? How am I going to read all of this while trying to sell purses . . . I mean handbags?

Judy noted the apprehension on my face.

"Don't worry. It's trial and error. Even women are intimidated at first. You'll catch on."

You and Suzy expect GREAT sunshiny things from the Gay Guy. I'd better catch on.

"Is it okay if I take my jacket off? I'm really hot," I said, wiping my forehead.

"I'd rather you didn't. The dress code for men is a coat and tie. The air will kick on any second and the rally should be starting soon."

Before Judy could explain the rally, Suzy Davis-Satan's voice detonated from the store's PA system like a chalkboard-fingernail-scratching bomb: "GOOOOOOOOD MORNING, BURBANK!!! TODAY'S RALLY HAS BEEN CANCELED. HAVE A ROCKIN' DAY, EVERYBODY. HIGHLY DEDICATED AND MOTIVATED TO WIN! WIN! WIN!"

Somewhere glass must have shattered. I was glad this rally thing had been canceled.

Minutes later, the General marched me up to Customer Service, where the money bags were. We had to recount the cash in each bag. Twice. Judy said it was in case of mistakes. I didn't quite understand why we were checking to make sure someone else hadn't made a mistake, but The Big Fancy was all about perfection.

As soon as we were done, Judy left for her meeting. The next thing I knew, I was in the handbag department, alone in the Corral. I had managed to open the registers without a problem. Then a voice came over the PA: "The Big Fancy is now open for business. Have an awesome day, everybody!" I didn't know whose voice it was, and I didn't care. A short distance away a dude in a suit pulled back a curtain that blocked the mall from our store. Right next to it was The Big Fancy's coffee bar. I salivated. An iced mocha latte would sure hit the spot. Suddenly a woman was at my counter.

"Hi. Can you help me?" she said, "I need to find a metallic silver rhinestone evening clutch."

I had no idea what the fuck that was. Judy never mentioned this clutch word. Did Big Fancy sell designer car parts? I frantically flipped through the guide searching for the word clutch.

I saw other strange names like satchel and hobo, but no clutch.

"What are you doing?" asked the Customer.

I stopped looking for the clutch word. It was no use fooling her.

"Umm ... I'm new. I don't know what that is, but I could help you look around for one."

"They really shouldn't have men working in this department," she said.

I thought the women were going to love me?

The next hour was complete estrogen hell. Nervous sweat seeped from my underarms and I did not move from behind the Corral. I was too afraid. The phone rang every thirty seconds. Women asking for other women I did not know and questions I did not have the answers to. I had to return three different bags, and every time I had to look at the slip of paper to enter my ID, 441064, into the register. "Why are you taking so long?" one of the women returning asked. "It shouldn't take this long." Then a lady wanted to buy a gift card for $84, but I could not remember how to do it. "I'm new. Maybe you should go to another counter." She stormed off. Another woman wanted to see handbags that were in the Corral cases. I pulled out an Isabella Fiore, a Burberry, a Marc Jacobs, a Gucci, a Michael Kors, and a Kate Spade. She tore out stuffing and threw it all over the counter, asked me which ones I liked, fingered them all, and then left. Then a woman wanted to know the price of a Fendi. I couldn't find a ticket. "I'm new. My manager will be back soon," I said. "Forget it," she replied, "I'm in a hurry." She left. This is how it went. Total craziness. The phone rang nonstop, and customers got pissed at me for not knowing shit. By the time Judy returned, I'd only sold one small wallet for $55, and it looked like a tornado had hit. Bags and stuffing were lying on the counters and floor surrounding the register. You could tell I'd decided to take up residence in the spot like some kind of sales-floor squatter.

"OH MY GOD!" she bellowed, "What happened? Was it busy? Why didn't you page me?"

"You didn't say I could page you."

"Freeman, I expect you've had enough retail experience to know to call for help if it gets out of control. Here at The Big Fancy we pride ourselves on customer service. This is . . . unacceptable, but it's your first hour here, so I'll let it slide."

"Sorry, Judy. Next time I'll page."

If there ever is a next time. What the hell am I doing here? What have I gotten myself into?

"Why are these bags piled up over here?" she said.

"Those purses were all returned. I didn't know. . . ."

"Freeman, I told you. They're handbags, not purses," Judy said calmly while picking up the Fendi off the floor.

Like a fucking moron, I added, "Oh and that purse is missing a price tag."

"FREEEMAN! HANDBAG! NOT PURSE," the General yelled.

SHIT! HANDBAG, HANDBAG, HANDBAG!

"I can see you are going to need some work," she added bringing her voice down.

Over the next few days I was babysat, and frankly, I didn't mind. I grew more comfortable with the register and the merchandise. But no matter how hard I tried, the p-word continued to fall from my mouth. The other handbag salespeople tried to help by telling me horror stories of how they had to splurge for a department pizza party or pay $10 if they said the p-word. I hadn't even been paid yet at The Big Fancy; no way could I afford pizza parties or coughing up $10.

Despite the warnings, one morning I stupidly used the p-word twice with a customer and General Judy came at me faster than the runaway bus from *Speed*.

"FREE-MAN!" she shrieked, splitting my name in half, "You PURSE your lips, but you SELL handbags! We sell HAND-BAGS here, NOT purses."

Purse my lips? I don't purse my lips. You purse your lips. Not me. Go fuck yourself with a purse. Whatever. Handbags vs. purses. Stupid as hell.

"Yes, okay, thank you, Judy," I replied while my customer stared at me like I was a freak.

I should have learned my lesson there, but I didn't. Hours later, I was reporting to the General after I had finished colorizing the clearance table. I spoke before thinking. My vow to change my pursy ways went west.

"I arranged all those purses just like you wanted."

Judy's black eyes seared into me.

Uh-oh. Pizza Party, here we come.

"FREE-MAN! How many times do I have to tell you! HAND-BAGS, not PURSES! Remember, purses equal lips, handbags equal keeping your job."

"Yes, Judy, I'm sorry. Handbags."

For the next several days I became a total purse-aholic. I could not control myself, even after saying a handbag mantra over and over before I went to sleep at night. Every time I was around Judy, my mind turned to nervy mush, and I thought of nothing but purses. Although she never mentioned cash fees, Judy continued to yell at me every time I said the p-word:

"FREE-MAN! I'VE HAD IT! YOU'D BETTER START SAY-ING HANDBAG."

"FREE-MAN! IT'S HAND-BAG. NOW, REPEAT AFTER ME FIVE TIMES!"

Finally one morning she flipped out.

"FREE-MAN, IF YOU DON'T STOP USING THE P-WORD, I'M GOING TO WASH YOUR MOUTH OUT WITH LEATHER LOTION!"

I think I'd rather pay ten dollars, thank you very much.

I distinctly remember the moment I thought I was going to get attacked with a bottle of leather lotion by the General: I was ringing up a $250 Kenneth Cole and told the customer, "Let me just wrap your purse in tissue for you, ma'am."

Judy stood just inches away from me as I committed the verbal crime.

I winced, expecting a nuclear explosion.

Surprisingly, Judy said nothing, although I did feel her laser stare as I finished up with the customer. Trying to backtrack and save my ass, I awkwardly asked the woman if she'd like a wallet to go with her new Kenneth Cole HANDBAG? She didn't, and left.

I waited for the outburst, but it never came. The General was thinking.

A few seconds passed and then she said softly, "Okay, Free-man. I'll make you a deal. If you NEVER say the p-word again, I'll let you work here without wearing the suit jacket. But only when the buyers and executives aren't visiting. Then you won't sweat so much either."

What? No pizza party? No cash fees? How lucky am I? I'd better not screw this one up. You have yourself A DEAL, Judy! I'm hitting the red button and slamming down the cover. I'm taking the Banker's offer. I'm done! The sweatsuit is coming off! Hurray!

Like magic, handbag became my best friend. I thought of it as an air conditioner.

I never said the p-word again.

Angels and Demons in My Head

EXT. ARGONNE FOREST—MILITARY TRENCH—DAY

Explosions. Machine-gun fire. A sky filled with
smoke. The battalion is burrowed deep in the hole,
surrounded by barbed wire and heavy artillery. A
metallic-sounding ROAR shakes the forest.

>   CAPT. OSWALD
>   What the fuck was that?

>   PVT. JONES
>   The Germans are getting closer.

>   MAJ. RITTER
>   That was no German.

>   CAPT. OSWALD
>   Hey Dave, did you get a reading?

>   PVT. DAVE
>   Ritter is right. It's no German. I don't even
>   think it's human.

An EXPLOSION hits too close for comfort. The men huddle.
Another deafening animalistic ROAR shreds the air.

>   MAJ. RITTER
>   Jesus, it's close!

                    PVT. JONES
We can't stay here.

                    CAPT. OSWALD
We don't have a choice.

                    MAJ. RITTER
You *chose* to steal my sale.

                    CAPT. OSWALD
You weren't helping her.

                    MAJ. RITTER
Barbara is my personal! I called her.

                    CAPT. OSWALD
You say everyone is your personal.

                    PVT. DAVE
And you steal everyone's sales!

                    CAPT. OSWALD
I do not steal sales.

                    PVT. DAVE
Last week you snaked that $3,000 Marc Jacobs
from me.

                    CAPT. OSWALD
I did no such thing. You lie.

                    PVT. JONES
Hon, I saw you do it.

                    GENERAL JUDY
I WANT YOU ALL TO SHUT IT RIGHT NOW! We need
to move on and talk about what's coming in
for spring. Fuchsia is the must-have color.
AAAARGH! DAMMIT! SONOFABITCH!

My World War I Million-Dollar Screenplay adventure thriller, where *All's Quiet on the Western Front* meets *Jurassic Park*, had been infiltrated by the cast of saleswomen at The Big Fancy's handbag department, and I could not get them out of my head.

Women's voices coming out of soldiers' mouths. I am so seriously screwed right now.

The weeks following my training were a blur as I moved from my friend's couch to a studio apartment in an area called Beverly Hills Adjacent (a friend of mine used to call it Scratching to Get into Beverly Hills). My new home next door to BH was considered furnished, consisting of a single bed, desk, and a kitchen table. Not pretty, but clean, and my landlords were wonderful people, a rabbi and his wife. The compact size of the studio didn't matter; all I needed was a place for my computer, TV, and PlayStation. After settling into my room, I quickly fell into the mindless day-to-day go-to-work grind of climbing Mount Fancy as 441064 and selling handbags, not purses.

On this day of my character soldiers suddenly talking like cat-fighting saleswomen, I desperately needed to be touched by the screenwriting gods, but they were nowhere to be found.

And this was due largely in part to events that happened earlier in the day—much earlier, in fact.

Like 6:45 in the fuckin' morning early.

This was the time I had to attend my first department meeting.

On my day off.

As anyone who works in retail will tell you, your days off are not your own, and they are not immune to ruin by boring meetings. For anyone attempting to pursue another career and claw their way out of Retail Hell, these store demands do *not* work in your favor.

When I tried to get out of Judy's big department meeting, she jumped down my throat: "The Department Meeting is mandatory. If you are going to be a part of this team, the expectation is that you attend. There will be many other times when you have to come in on your day off. It's part of being committed to the success of this company. Got it?"

Oh, I got it, all right.

I got pissed about having to drag my ass out of bed in the middle of the fuckin' night at 5:00 A.M. to get to The Big Fancy on time. Why can't we have night meetings in retail? Why do they always have to be at an hour reserved for paperboys and crack addicts? Screenwriters don't get up before the sun rises. We like sleep. And lots of it.

Besides General Judy, there were six other women selling with me at The Big Fancy handbag department. They also had to get their asses up early.

I had met all these women on my first day in the jungle. Shortly after Judy had deserted me, I found myself in the presence of an Americanized Armenian woman in her forties with beady black eyes. She had outdated feathered black hair and wore a conservative white pantsuit. She reminded me of John Travolta in *Saturday Night Fever*. When she told me her long, unusual first name, I couldn't make it out—something, something "oush" at the end. But that doesn't matter here, as I've decided to call her Douche. Because that's what she was. A giant, horrible douchebag. You see, Douche was the Shark—a salesperson who steals sales. She wasted no time in proving that to me during my first moments with her. Douche took three of my first big sales: a Gucci, a Burberry, and a Ferragamo, claiming I wasn't yet ready to ring them (even though I'd been through Brandi's annoying register training). I may have been a newbie, but I wasn't an idiot. The fucking douche was stealing my sales, and when I brought it up to her, she'd do her signature, "Aagh . . ." phlegm-like grunt, followed by a wave of her hand saying she had no time for confrontation.

Things got even worse when a young woman named Tiffany arrived. Tiffany was a chubby black girl in her late twenties with a model's face, a pig's mannerisms, and a blind person's wardrobe. Sounding as crisp as a newscaster, she wasted no time in telling me that the General considered her "the Assistant" and she was in charge when Judy wasn't around. Drunk with her "I am the Manager" power, Tiffany immediately pulled me off the sales floor and assigned me all the department shit jobs: answering the phone, cleaning, taking empty boxes to the trash, getting supplies, taking transfers, and sending packages to the store's receiving area. I did all this while Tiffany and Douche hogged all the sales for themselves.

An hour later, a petite Italian-looking woman with bobbed black hair and a huge nose, was in my ear talking a mile a minute. Another handbag seller. Her name was Marci, and she unleashed a torrent of mind-numbing chatter. For fifteen minutes, Marci yapped about her plans to make a chili-cheese casserole recipe she saw on the Food Network. She then scrutinized my every movement as I cleaned the glass shelves. "You're wiping in the wrong direction," she said, "Dust is flying everywhere. You need to wipe front to back, left to right." I wanted to stuff the cleaning rag in her mouth and beat her with the Windex bottle.

If ever there was a Demon Squad, I was surrounded by it.

Feeling like Kirsten Dunst at the end of *Spiderman 3* when she's dangling by a finger high above New York City, I actually considered quitting. There was no way I could work with these bitches. The General was bad enough, but to be thrown into a retail lifeboat with a bossy droid, a lying shark, and a whiny talker was more than I could take. I'd rather jump out and start swimming. I would take my chances with hypothermia and becoming fish food.

Lucky for me, however, the closers soon arrived.

Charlie had his Angels fighting bad guys, and I quickly discovered I had mine.

The Handbag Angels.

Defenders against demon saleswomen.

Suddenly the shroud of darkness in the Handbag Jungle lifted, and my job-hunting thoughts did as well. The first one I met was Cammie, a sexy-hot Orange County blond in her mid-twenties with a hip fashion style I related to. Cammie's infectious, fun-loving personality could make a room full of depressives want to get up and dance. Her potty mouth, love of music, and dream to become an actress bonded us instantly. That night we were out drinking, and I vowed to write a script for her. We've been buds ever since. The blond Will and Grace.

When I met Jules, she was so easy to talk to I knew instantly that I'd like her. A Seattle transplant in her mid-forties with amber hair, an hourglass figure, and classic style, Jules instantly got my respect when she told me she was married to a jewelry salesman, they had two little girls together, and she juggled her family and The Big Fancy while studying to get a real estate license. I was blown away. I couldn't imagine attempting to be a screenwriter while being married with kids. What I could imagine was Jules selling ten-million-dollar homes. The woman had the ability to sell someone a wad of chewing gum she had pulled off the sidewalk.

My third Handbag Angel was Marsha, a young-at-heart native Angelino in her late fifties. She was well known for her crazy laugh, spicy outbursts, and use of the endearment "Hon." Marsha had big brown hair, oversized lavender glasses, and a penchant for colorful, funky fashion. Having slaved at the store for more than twenty-six years, Marsha was gossip @ Big Fancy. com! She held the lowdown on everyone. She had been divorced three times and had no kids, and the loves of her life were four cats: Mr. Butters, Tire Track, Putz, and Shania Twain. They were bizarre cat names, but Marsha's left-of-center approach was what I loved most about her. Having worked at The Big Fancy for so many years, Marsha dreamt of her retirement day and moving to Hawaii with her cats.

After our casual introductions, my Handbag Angels grilled me about how the morning had gone. Not holding back, I truthfully exposed the antics of the Demon Squad. The Angels weren't surprised by the treatment. Seconds later, they burst into the stockroom and had it out with the General. I don't know what was said, but when I got back from lunch, Tiffany had backed off, Douche was no longer taking my sales, and Marci wasn't talking to me, which was fine by me.

The lines had been drawn in the Handbag Jungle.

And even though I love wearing black, listening to alternative music, collecting skull art, and watching horror movies, I quickly decided it was time to hang with the angels.

When I arrived for my first Big Fancy department meeting, it was so early the track lights had not yet come on. Spotty fluorescent lighting made the store look dim and shadowy. It made me want to go back to sleep. Inside the Handbag Jungle, several fixtures had been moved aside to create a clearing for a small scattering of chairs. Angels Cammie, Jules, and Marsha huddled together in one group while Demon Marci was a few feet away, and to the far right, a body-length's space away, sat her evil counterparts, Douche and Tiffany.

I moved my chair next to the Angels. Would I sit anywhere else?

"Is there any coffee?" I asked Cammie.

"Are you fucking kidding?" she replied.

"Hon, they're too cheap for coffee," said Marsha, "We had to buy ours at the Coffee Bar."

I was just about to go find the General to ask if I could make a latte run when the stockroom door flew open. She marched up to us and let loose:

"I'm holding this meeting because we have a lot to work on here, people. We missed our month twice in a row. There was a 22% decrease in January, a 13% decrease last month. You know how Suzy feels about third strikes. I absolutely cannot allow this department to miss another month. The unemployment rate in Los Angeles is at an all-time high, and I'm sure I can find plenty of hungry people to sell handbags and get me increases."

They'll also break every rule in the Employee Handbook.

For the next half-hour Judy continued to rag on us for everything. Misfire. Not selling enough. Returns. Not sending thank-you notes to customers. Rag. Rag. Rag. Holds. Opening new accounts. Insufficient cleanliness. Rag. Rag. Rag. Not approaching customers properly. Failing to capture clients. Rag. Rag. Rag.

When the General started barking about customer service, things went sour. The once-silent group of six women was now not so silent, and a fight erupted. The Handbag Angels and Demons tore into each other.

"Great service isn't possible when *some* people in this department refuse to acknowledge the doubling up policy, and they wait on more than one person at a time," said Jules.

"Amen to that," said Marsha.

"Oh hell yeah," said Cammie, slapping palms with Jules in a high-five.

"I don't think that's really the problem here, it's about paying attention," said Tiffany.

"When it's busy, *some of us* don't have a choice," said Douche.

"You chose to steal my sale yesterday," said Jules.

"You weren't helping her," said Douche.

"Barbara is my personal. I called her," said Jules.

"You say *everyone* is your personal," said Douche.

"And you steal everyone's sales," said Cammie.

"I do not steal sales," said Douche.

"Last week, you snaked that three-thousand-dollar Marc Jacobs from me," said Cammie.

"Aagh! I did no such thing. You lie," said Douche.

"Hon, I saw you do it," said Marsha.

"She was not helping that woman. I know for a fact," said Douche.

"If I knew Cammie was waiting on her, certainly you must have known too," said Marsha.

"Douche doesn't pay attention on the floor half the time," said Jules.

"That doesn't make her Cammie's customer," said Douche.

"Excuse me, Douche, but *it does* make her my customer," said Cammie.

"We really need to set some boundaries," said Marci.

"Some people are always out for themselves," said Marsha.

"I think people are just jealous of Douche because she's at the top of her game," said Tiffany.

"Jealous? No we're sick to fucking death of it," said Cammie.

"We all have personal customers, Douche. So do you," said Jules.

"I'm not talking about my personal customers," said Douche.

"Then what the fuck are you talking about? This is bullshit," said Cammie.

"I don't appreciate the awful language, Cammie," said Marci.

"There are more professional ways to express yourself, Cammie," said Tiffany.

"Is your mother happy that you talk like that? Aagh!" said Douche.

"I should kick your mother-fucking ass right now, you sharky whore," said Cammie.

"THAT'S IT! I WANT YOU ALL TO SHUT IT!" yelled the General.

Cammie and Douche were about to hit the carpet for a hair-pulling wrestling match. Being the newbie and the only man, I stayed out of it, though if called to duty I would have definitely cheated for Cammie and smacked Douche on the back of the head with my chair.

Judy finally got things settled down and redirected her meeting toward merchandising and the new handbag lines that were coming in. Tempers cooled, and so did my interest as she went into a lengthy discussion about what was going to be hot for spring.

I nearly went to sleep.

Even though the department meeting had been some thirteen hours earlier, I couldn't get it out of my head. The handbag haunting was in full force.

"That was my Coach customer!"

"You say everyone is your customer!"

"We need to get the sales up in this department or shifts will be cut!"

The voices of Angels and Demons snipping away at each other.

A fate worse than writer's block.

So I did the only thing any writer would have done at that point. Turned off the computer, started guzzling beer, and flipped on *Reno 911*. The soldiers of the Argonne Forest would have to wait another day to meet their monster. I had to get rid of mine first.

Can I Interest You in a Dead Animal Hide Hobo Named Lucifer?

"Freeman, do we have a Dolly in red?" Jules called out to me from the Corral.

The place had been a morgue, so we were all on cleaning duty. I had the Allure shop. The Big Fancy's own brand. Marsha had Juicy Couture, Cammie had Coach, and Jules had the Corral's countertops. When the phone started ringing, Jules was closest, so she answered. It turned out to be a check from another Big Fancy store. A salesperson wanting this Dolly thing in red.

I stared at Jules like she was speaking in Arabic.

"Well, do we? I can't see from here?"

No clue what the hell she was talking about. The only person I know named Dolly is the fabulous singing legend, Dolly Parton, and I certainly did not see her in red sitting anywhere in The Big Fancy handbag department.

"It's an Allure satchel," said Cammie from the Coach shop.

"What's a satchel?"

Cammie said, "What the fuck?" and Jules dropped her bottle of glass cleaner. Cammie quickly came over to where I was, reached over on the shelf behind me, and grabbed a red, two handled, midsized Allure handbag off the shelf. "This is a fucking SATCHEL, and its goddamn name is DOLLY. Dude, you should know this!"

But I didn't.

"Hon, you don't know what a satchel is?" asked Marsha.

"Umm . . . no . . . Judy never told me about satchels. Is that something in the Handbag Guide?"

"Shit on a stick," exclaimed Cammie, "He's screwed unless we help him."

"You got that right, hon," agreed Marsha. "Poor thing doesn't even know what a satchel is."

"That's it. We are just going to teach you ourselves," announced Jules.

My official handbag training began at that moment. I didn't really give a shit what a fucking red Dolly was, but it was time to start using handbag lingo. The General had been pressuring me. She kept asking how my Guide studies were going. "Suzy doesn't like cashiering. You need to improve your sales by selling, not waiting for customers. You NEED to find the TIME to READ the Guide."

Sorry, General Judy, What I NEED is to hurry up and write my Million-Dollar Screenplay and quit The Big Fancy!

I'd found Judy's so-called Guide completely useless, reading it was like reading a legal deposition written in Latin. There were no pictures, just a list of companies, their uninteresting histories, and a bunch of bizarre handbag terms that sounded like an inventory sheet for a military weapons arsenal: roll bag, drawstring feedbag, tote, crossbody, demi pouch, barrel, hobo, mini, messenger, carryall, duffle, and convertible bucket.

Convertible bucket? Are we selling cars? Drawstring feedbag? Does it come full of apples and oats? Roll bag? Who invented that? Cheech and Chong?

"Every handbag silhouette has a name," said Jules, "They may sound strange, but many shapes and designs are actually taken from the names of bags in other industries. Dooney & Bourke once copied an old ammunition bag and made it in three sizes, and it was the hottest style for several years."

"Did they call it the Ammo Bag and fill it with bullets?" I asked, teasing.

Jules laughed and replied, "No, but it was heavy as hell. Dooney called it the Spectator."

"Spectator sucks," I said, "I would have called it the Bullet or maybe the Uzi."

Then Marsha jumped in on the trip down Handbag Memory Lane: "What I remember about the Dooney & Bourke Spectator is how much I hated merchandising them. They wouldn't stay standing up. Fell over constantly like dominos. They were always a mess and I pulled a muscle lugging those bastards out of the stockroom. Sold a lot of them, though."

Jules was on the move in the leather jungle. She grabbed a pink medium-size structured bag with a single handle. "This is one of my favorite handbag shape stories," she said, "They call this shape—with the single rounded handle—the Kelly bag. It was created by the famous French fashion house Hermès. Then in the '50s Grace Kelly was photographed wearing it because she wanted something stylish to cover her pregnant belly. Next thing you know, everyone goes nuts and women around the world had to have it! Any bag made in this shape is now called the Kelly bag. The Big Fancy makes this one on our private label and they call it Amanda."

I was mesmerized by the Grace Kelly story because I love so many of her films, but then I realized Jules had called that Big Fancy brand Kelly bag Amanda. Handbag names 101 was getting complicated.

"Wait," I said, "Are you telling me they have silhouette names AND people names?"

"Afraid so, hon," said Marsha, "Just like my plants and cats!"

"And my dog, Ginger," added Jules, "She's a Yorkshire Terrier. Absolutely gorgeous."

Cammie tossed a slouchy-looking bag over her shoulder, "This motherfucker is named Rodan. How fucking stupid is that?"

"A satchel named Rodan?"

"Umm . . . Freeman, that one is a hobo," said Jules.

"Hobo? I am so fucked. I'll never remember all this. Maybe I should leave right now."

Marsha's arm went around me. "You'll do no such thing, hon. We love you! It's been a breath of fresh air having a guy around here for a change."

With the Handbag Guide in tow, the Angels went over every shape, showing me what was what. Turned out a demi pouch was small with a short strap, a roll bag looked like a giant Tootsie Roll with a strap, and a drawstring feedbag was definitely something a horse could eat out of.

In my mind a hobo was a vagabond, a shoulder was a body part, a clutch was a car part, a tote was a crate in a warehouse, and a satchel was the name of some four-legged, tree-hugging creature in a rainforest. Not so in the Handbag Jungle.

A clutch was flat and carried in the hand, a tote was usually square-shaped with two handles but sometimes had straps, and a satchel had two short handles and has been around since the Middle Ages.

"A hobo is a large, rounded, unstructured, slouchy bag designed to be worn on the shoulder," said Marsha while Cammie modeled a variety of different hobo styles.

"It's called a hobo because the shape sort of looks like the bundle at the end of a stick that hobos used to carry way back when in movies and cartoons," added Jules.

I couldn't believe one of fashion's hottest handbag shapes came from bums on skid row.

What's next? Traffic-cone hats and bedpan shoes?

Learning the basic shapes wasn't too difficult, but the stuff that really annihilated my brain cells were all the feature add-ons: triple-zip satchel, push-lock satchel, hand-held satchel, east-west shoulder satchel, zip-zip satchel, and multifunction box satchel.

"I don't get it. Why don't they just call it a satchel?"

"I know it's confusing, hon," Marsha said, "But you'll get the hang of it with practice. Just remember, there are five basic handbag shapes: satchel, shoulder, tote, clutch, and hobo."

I felt like Audrey Hepburn's Eliza Doolittle in *My Fair Lady* struggling over the "rain in Spain" phrase, except that my nightmare of words was north-south oversized satchel zip-top.

It only got worse after that.

"Do you know anything at all about leather?" asked Jules.

"Umm . . . I have a leather motorcycle jacket and lots of shoes."

The Handbag Angels stared at me.

"But dude, do you know about the different kinds of leather?" asked Cammie.

"Not really. Can't I just say it's leather and looks cool?"

"Hon, that will *not* fly in here," said Marsha.

My Angels taught me that Napa leather feels buttery soft, mock-croc is embossed to look like crocodile, and washed leather has an aged, crinkly, wrinkled look. They gave me the rundown on all the different fabrics, from jacquard to wool to terry cloth. I discovered handbags are made out of just about everything but sheet metal and drywall. Could it be possible that one day women will actually be able to live in their handbag satchels named Dolly? I think so.

The list of leathers mentioned made my head hurt: vachetta leather, distressed leather, patent leather, silk-screened leather, metallic leather, glazed leather, and washed leather.

What the hell is washed leather? Is it preferred over dirty leather? Do they use a really good detergent like Tide when they are washing the leather? How long does it stay in the rinse cycle?

And the skins all these handbags were made out of? Calfskin. Lambskin. Buffalo skin. Deerskin. Snakeskin. Goatskin. Ostrich skin. Croc skin. Rabbit skin. Oh my God . . . I could feel the ghosts of dead animals staring up at me.

Should I call PETA? Do they know about Big Fancy's House of Handbag Horrors?

"Is any of that making sense, sweetie?" Jules asked in her breathy Marilyn Monroe voice.

I groaned. "Dead animal hides everywhere."

Cammie agreed. "It's a fuckin' dead-ass zoo in here." Then she held a bag from the clearance table that looked like suede with white fur around it. "You know what this bitch is made out of?"

"No clue. A cow?"

Jules smiled. "Shearling. Real shearling. From the skin of an unborn lamb. Obtained after a pregnant adult sheep has been slaughtered for meat or skin or died from a disease."

Holy shit! That's way worse than bunnies and goats. I might throw up.

"But NEVER say that," she warned, "It will turn customers off big-time. Always be casual and just say, 'Oh it's a type of leather.'"

"That's so fucking disgusting. A baby lamb! All for a look!"

"Fashion can be cruel. Take a look at this GORGEOUS Isabella Fiore handbag," Jules said, picking up a large burgundy bag with two short handles and a frame opening. "This is what we call a framed doctor's satchel. Feel it. Simply gorgeous."

From a distance it resembled an intricately detailed woven tapestry, but when I touched it, I felt little hairs in the swirling design.

The kind of little hairs found on the hide of a dead animal.

"I'm afraid to ask," I said, wondering what poor mammal gave its life up to be a satchel.

"Read the tag," she said, showing me the inside of a small folded card attached to the bag.

I read a short flowery story about how the handbag was Arthurian inspired, but it was the last sentence that grabbed me: **Handcrafted Italian laser-cut calf.**

Laser-cut calf.

Three words that should not be put together. "Omigod."

Jules smirked. "You need me to tell you about it?"

My head filled with screaming calves being laser tattooed against their will.

"Sweet Jesus, no. That's so gross."

"Exactly, my friend. Not a pretty sight," she replied, "Ignorance is bliss. That's why you can never go wrong by saying Italian leather for just about anything."

"Unless it's a snake," Marsha said, "Women hate snakes. Turn them all into handbags and shoes for all I care."

"You got that fuckin' right," added Cammie, "Snakes creep the shit out of me."

Once the ladies felt they'd covered everything, it was testing time. Cammie modeled a black, wrinkled, rounded, sack-looking Francisco Biasia on her shoulder and I had to figure out what it was.

After a few seconds I came up with, "Washed leather hobo."

Jules gave thumbs up. "Now look closer. Add on the features."

Cammie prominently displayed the zippered closure.

"Zip-top hobo?"

Marsha high-fived me. "You go, boy!"

"What else, Free? There's more," said Jules.

I noticed the shape of the Biasia was quite tall, very vertical.

"A north-south zip-top hobo?"

The girls cheered, but Jules pushed me further. "Now what's on the front?"

Cammie ran her fingers over two mini pockets mounted on its face.

After a moment I nailed it: "Double pockets . . . north-south double-pocket zip-top hobo!"

You would have thought I'd just won *Jeopardy*. My triumph was applauded, followed by hugs all around. It was the first moment in the Handbag Jungle where I thought I could survive as a salesperson.

Marsha's lavender fingernail pointed directly below the words north-south double-pocket zip-top hobo on the bag's tag. "And don't forget the name, hon. This one is Anastasia."

I felt a scream coming on. No way in hell was I going to remember their birth names.

"Don't worry about the stupid fucking names," Cammie said. "We can't remember most of them either. Usually they're printed on the tags or we just look them up in the catalogs."

"The catalogs?"

Marsha, Cammie, and Jules eyed each other, heads shaking in disbelief.

"Judy didn't show you shit, did she?" said Cammie.

They led me into the Corral, where Jules pulled open a drawer jammed full of color catalogs: A treasure trove of dead animal hide information. "If you need names, colors, and prices, you'll find them in here," she said opening one and showing me a photograph of an Allure shearling bag. Underneath was everything a man selling handbags needed to know: **Mia. $1,765. Authentic Italian Shearling. Large Cross-body Double-Pocket Drawstring Shoulder. Available in Cocoa, Shell, and Onyx. Features include two roomy outside pockets, a back zipper pocket, magnetic tab closure, an internal zip pocket, and an open cell-phone pocket banded in leather.** I couldn't believe it. All the info was right there. Along with fucking pictures.

"Why didn't Judy tell me about this?"

Cammie rolled her eyes. "Because she doesn't like us showing them to customers."

"Even though we all do it anyway," said Marsha.

Jules nodded, adding, "They want us selling what's on the floor. Not special ordering. And even though we do transfers, it saves the company money if you sell what's in front of you."

"Why didn't you guys just show me the drawer?" I said, pulling out the Coach book and opening it to a full-page photo of an east-west single-pocket tote in purple signature jacquard.

"None of it would have made sense without a basic knowledge of handbags," said Jules.

Cammie grinned. "Dude, you didn't even know what a fucking satchel was."

"And now you know what a double-pocket zip-top hobo is!" added Marsha, "You are no longer a newbie! You're an official Handbag Connoisseur!"

Handbag Connoisseur.

Not exactly something I'd ever thought I'd become.

But what choice did I have at that point? It was a good thing I had Angels in the Handbag Jungle. Otherwise the $3,000 glazed anaconda-skin multipocket satchel named Brutus would have eaten me alive.

Instead I sold it to a woman after I told her it was this year's It Bag on the Paris runways.

Falling Down Mount Fancy

One afternoon, I happened to arrive in the parking structure at the same time as Marsha, who was my fellow closer for that day. We walked together, talking about everything from her cats to my screenwriting. Our lighthearted chitchat ended when we reached the brown door where Mount Fancy waited silently, ominously.

"Sweet mother of God, here we go," sighed Marsha.

I entered the security code, waited for the click, and we both entered leg-lifting hell.

Then our jaws hit the floor.

I didn't hold back. "What the fuck?"

The steel carpeted mountain had been transformed into a birthday party.

Apparently it was The Big Fancy's fifty-second year in operation, and Suzy Davis-Satan had spared no expense in reminding us as we climbed. The entryway was awash in ugly yellow and purple balloons with green and white crepe-paper streamers strung everywhere. Suzy's welcome sign had been replaced with an oversized cheesy party store Happy Birthday card. A huge yellow banner covered the Important People sign: *Happy 52nd Birthday, Big Fancy! We Rock!* The walls were painted a putrid pea green color, the very same color Linda Blair released all over the carpet in the first *Exorcist*, with party-themed yellow and purple signs: *What can you celebrate this week? Make it a Big Birthday with Big Sales! Have a Cake Walk with Client Capture!* The Headless Mannequins were swathed in cheap Happy

Birthday wrapping paper and wore pointed yellow party hats where their heads should have been. And at the top of the mountain stood a giant fake cake with fake lavender frosting and a *52* on top.

As we climbed, I was dumbfounded by the amount of decorating work involved. "Seems like they went to a lot of trouble to do all of this. They could have spent the money installing an elevator."

Marsha let out a cackle as we trudged up the third flight of stairs. "Hon, that will never happen. This company is too cheap to spend money on something to make our lives easier. It's been this way ever since the store opened."

"I just don't understand it. How could they have designed an employee entrance full of stairs? Shouldn't this be against the law? Why haven't they been reported to OSHA?"

"Ha! OSHA! That'll be the day. Did you know that nearly all The Big Fancy Stores have stairs in the employee entrances?"

"You're shitting me."

"Nope," said Marsha gripping the handrail. "This store has the most. Almost all Big Fancies have them. It's because of Mr. Lou."

I figured she was talking about one of The Big Fancy's executives. For some ridiculous reason they like to be called Mr. with their first name after it. Kinda creepy if you ask me.

"Who is Mr. Lou?"

"Hon, don't you remember the training video?"

"I think I slept through most of it."

"Freeman, he's the founder of The Big Fancy."

"Oh. Right. Yeah."

On the fifth platform, we passed the birthday-paper-wrapped Headless Mannequins with their yellow party hat heads, and Marsha let out a gasp, "What the hell are they supposed to be?"

"Party Animal Mannequins, I guess. I hope they don't start dancing."

"You got that right," said Marsha as we lumbered up the sixth flight. "Anyway, Mr. Lou is an absolute pig. He was visiting the store once and came into the handbag department pretending to look for something for his wife. The scumbag asked me if I wanted to go to dinner in his hotel room. You believe that? Dinner in his hotel room! Sleazy sonofabitch! His wife had just given birth in Des Moines, to Mr. Michael."

"CEO, President Mr. Michael?"

"That's the one. I'm dating myself now," she said, wheezing and white-knuckling the handrail. "His father, Mr. Lou, was a walking hard-on. He had mistresses at all the stores. I could tell you stories. . . ."

When we got to the seventh platform, Marsha stopped for a moment to catch her breath before resuming.

"Are you okay, Marsha?"

"This is my bad spot. Two more flights. But I'm a tough old broad. I'll make it." Marsha steadied herself with the railing while trying to regain her composure. "All these damn stairs were Mr. Lou's idea," she gasped, "The bastard had builders install stairs in all the Big Fancy employee entrances because he felt the employees needed to get a little exercise each day before our shifts to work off our fat."

"Work off your fat? No way!"

"Yes way, hon. His exact words at an employee meeting. I'm afraid so."

"What an ass. It's not like we can wear workout clothes and tennis shoes to work!"

Marsh wheezed as we started up the seventh flight. "Apparently, he wasn't happy with the way many of The Big Fancy's salespeople looked. He felt most were out of shape and needed to work off a few pounds. Mr. Lou was really into fitness, a big lover of Jack LaLanne. Before Mr. Lou dropped dead of a heart attack, he made his sons swear they would keep building Employee Entrance stairs. They built this store a short time later, and his sons wanted to pay tribute. Mr. Michael christened these very stairs Lou's Big Workout."

"What an evil bastard," I said, panting like a golden retriever tired of fetching, "I'm surprised there isn't a sign when you walk in that says LOU'S BIG WORKOUT!"

"Funny thing about that! There used to be one! Suzy didn't like it. She felt it was too uninspiring so she replaced it with that fake feel-good-family-jewel garbage."

"Does Mr. Michael do Lou's Big Workout when he visits?"

"You kidding? That wussy? Comes in through the mall like all the other executives."

"He should go up and down these godforsaken stairs a couple of times. See how he likes it."

Marsha dragged herself up the eighth flight with a grunt.

"Darlin', if I had the chance, I'd make that smug little prick carry me up on his back, and I'd use a riding crop on his ass the entire way."

As Big Fancy Salespeople continued to exercise our allegedly out-of-shape bodies on Lou's Big Workout, pulled muscles and cardiac arrests were not the only hazards we had to worry about on Mount Fancy.

There was the incessant danger of tumbling down it.

The possibility of broken bones or falling to our death was far greater. If you hit your head just right, the floor of the seventh platform could turn into a tunnel of white light.

I don't think anybody ever died falling down Mount Fancy, but plenty of people took spills down the mountain. Marsha told me about Elsa, an older lady from Alterations, and Trina, a young twenty-something girl from Cosmetics. Apparently they toppled down the stairs within weeks of each other. The news of their falls traveled fast, but details were sketchy. Elsa and Trina took a dive down Mount Fancy and disappeared. That's all anyone knew. They were never heard from again. I desperately wanted to know what happened to Elsa and Trina!

Did they end up wheelchair bound?

On life support?

Were they keeping quiet via their lawyers because of large medical settlements?

Not even Marsha could find out.

The medical claims on Mount Fancy must have been staggering. I can't say I never thought about taking a nosedive off Mount Fancy and becoming a part of those staggering medical claims. But, while going out on workmen's comp might sound like a perfect way to create a paid writer's retreat to finish my Million-Dollar Screenplay, with my luck, my typing fingers would be the body parts to break, leaving my brain to sulk and lament.

One day at the top of Mount Fancy where the handrail began its descent downward on the eighth flight, they attached a laminated yellow sign with black lettering:

Caution, hold on to the handrail.

No fucking duh. How stupid do they think we are? Look, Ma! No hands.

Although, I don't think I ever saw anyone intentionally freestyle their way down Mount Fancy, it was nice to know the store truly cared about my safety as I rappelled down their steel edifice. Still, I couldn't help but wonder if this safety propaganda had anything to do with the disappearances of salespeople like Elsa and Trina.

One night after closing down the store and having to stay late by myself cleaning and straightening because the jungle was a fucking mess, I lumbered across Mount Fancy's top platform like a zombie. The **Caution, hold on to the handrail** sign beckoned me to perform its command. I reached out and grabbed the rail like a good Mount Fancy Climber.

Unbeknownst to me, some kind of greasy shit had been slathered all over the metal railings of Mount Fancy, and my hand slid down and off the rail, causing me to careen forward and flail my arms out for balance like Charlie Chaplin on a tightrope.

After a few seconds, I was able to bring my body back from the ledge, saving myself from a horrible accident. I had nearly plunged down sixteen steps.

My brain was not happy.

YOU SEE THAT? YOU ALMOST FUCKING KILLED US! Once our head smacks a step, it's lights out. And our legs and arms . . . don't even let me get started about what would have happened to them. No million-dollar screenplay or Oscar for you, dude. What kind of fucking moron puts grease all over the handrails of a 50-foot, eight-flight, 112-step Employee Entrance? Are they trying to kill everyone?

After the rant, my brain also told me to march back into the store and complain to someone that the rails of Mount Fancy had been tampered with. But then I realized there was no one to complain to in the store, except for Security and a few people in Customer Service. I further realized there was no other way to leave, as all the other doors were locked. The only way out was down the slippery slope of Mount Fancy.

My brain was pissed.

I'm not kidding. If you don't fucking be careful, I swear to God, we'll end up in a coma.

So I went down Mount Fancy without holding on to the handrail.
I went down so slowly you would have thought I had vertigo.
Each step was taken with full in-the-moment concentration. It must
have taken me fifteen minutes, but I got to the bottom safely.

My brain was relieved.

Thank god that fucking disaster is over. Your nerves are now demanding
cocktails. I suggest you comply. And they don't want just beer or wine, they
want something that will make them forget this horrible incident with a full-
on blackout.

Luckily, I had two days off after that. When I returned to The Big
Fancy and prepared to climb the great mountain, either the stairwell
rails had dried or someone had wiped them down. I wondered if anyone died or ended up on life support in the hospital. Would there be
enough healthy salespeople left to open the store? In my Screenwriter
Mind I saw it as a disaster movie—all the salespeople grabbing the
slippery rail and tumbling down the stairs. One after the other, like at
the end of *Titanic* when the ship goes upright.

I later found out from Judy that housekeeping had been prepping
for Clean It Up Day the evening I worked, and they had polished the
railing with some sort of greasy metal cleaner polish or some shit. She
said it was a one-time deal, and their hours had been cut. They were
no longer cleaning the stairwell.

While this was good safety news, not cleaning the stairwell at all
left me concerned. What about growing stairwell cooties, like dust
mites? What about bird flu?

I stormed up to HR, where I found Two-Tone Tammy at her desk
analyzing reports. I passionately suggested that housekeeping keep
cleaning the stairwell. All she needed to do was make a new sign:

Caution, handrail slippery when wet. Carefully crawl
downstairs.

Unfortunately, she didn't like my idea.

Guns and Toilets

Fresh out of Handbag School, I was eager to make as many sales as I could, so I stopped at nothing in my attempts to find bags for women. One of my early selling techniques was to simply take customers on a tour of the jungle, show them as many bags as I could, talk to them in a fun way, and find out what they were looking for in a handbag.

I found women bags that were expected to be transformed into mobile doghouses, gym lockers, makeup stores, junk food pantries, office supply rooms, and medicine cabinets. Every handbag has a unique purpose, depending on what the woman carrying it puts inside it.

One of my most unusual requests came from a toothpick-skinny chick with massive curly blond hair. She resembled one of those scary shiny dolls they sell on QVC late at night, but after probing, I found out she was actually a sweet, friendly prostitute who worked at Wild Horse Ranch outside of Vegas.

The first words out of her mouth upon seeing me were: "Hey there, Sugar, why you are just the cutest little thing. I love your spiky blond hair."

How could I not want to help someone who said that?

"Why thank you, I love your hair too," I replied.

"I need something for going out," said The Prostitute, "Something small that is classy, sparkles, and is completely waterproof."

Waterproof? Is your whorehouse underwater?

When I asked her why, she said, "More times than not, it falls in the toilet, and I hate it when my money gets wet and everything inside is ruined." I could visualize several reasons why her evening bags were falling into toilets, but I decided not to dig deeper.

The Prostitute and I had a great time. Her dirty mouth and mind kept me laughing as I found her a $400 Whiting & Davis ornate evening bag completely made out of metal mesh and nylon. Totally waterproof. I told her it could withstand a hurricane.

Thrilled out of her mind, she pulled out a wad of cash and paid me in $20 bills. She promised to tell all the girls at the ranch about me and said she'd come back and buy a fashionable overnight bag for her upcoming trip to wine country.

Some days after that, my handbag-searching talents were needed on the other side of the law. I waited on an attractive woman who reminded me of Mariska Hargitay from *Law and Order: Special Victims Unit*. She confessed right away that she was a detective in a quandary.

"I hate shopping for clothes and I hate shopping for bags even more," said The Detective, "If I could, I'd rather not carry anything at all."

"I understand," I replied, "I hear that from so many women." (I was fast becoming the Dr. Phil of handbags. Bring it on, ladies. I'll find the answers to all your bag-carrying woes.)

The Detective told me she wanted something that was trendy and fashionable but was also small and could be used for going out at night.

Unlike The Prostitute, she wasn't concerned about its falling into a toilet.

"It's got to be big enough to hold my gun and handcuffs," she said.

She proceeded to pull her gun and cuffs out and try them in every bag I showed her. I had won the handbag-helping lotto! This was beyond cool. We tried the gun and cuffs in several different bags before she decided on a pink signature Coach Demi Pouch with embroidered butterflies. At first she was concerned it was too girly, but I reminded her that just because she was a detective, it didn't mean she had to be unfashionable!

While The Detective stood in front of the full-length mirror modeling the bag she would be taking home, I asked her if I could pose with her gun in front of the Coach shop and have Cammie take my picture for Facebook.

Unfortunately, she said no.

But she did leave telling me that many policewomen have trouble deciding on handbags, and she'd tell the other women on the force to come see me.

I smiled and thanked her. I hoped they didn't come in at the same time as the prostitutes.

I'm Not Ready to Rumble

9:10 A.M. The Big Fancy felt like Death Valley in July. I'd been there for fifteen minutes, and already my no-name dress shirt had sweat rings.

But that wasn't from lack of air conditioning.

The perspiration flowed as a result of the twenty boxes of handbags Cammie and I were unpacking. When we arrived, they were stacked up on the Handbag Jungle's edge, overflowing onto the hard aisle floor. We couldn't even see Women's Shoes.

Everything in the wall of boxes needed to be taken out, unwrapped, and merchandised, and then the duplicates had to be put away in the stockroom. All before the store opened and without a stock person.

As much as we all bitched to Judy about the stock-work–sauna situation, Suzy Davis-Johnson stood firm. Stock people and morning air conditioning just weren't affordable.

Neither were box cutters.

The only tool available to open the wall of sealed boxes was an old pair of dull scissors with one of the blades broken off. My dull, broken scissors had managed to unseal ten boxes of Coach, Kate Spade, Kenneth Cole, and DKNY. The bags were all still layered in plastic and tissue, but at least they were unpacked.

As I threw an empty box onto a mound of cardboard and tissue that looked like kindling for a really good fire, sweat dripped into my eye, forcing me to wipe my eyes with my shirtsleeve.

I looked down and saw my no-name dress slacks covered in dusty dirt from moving the boxes.

At 9:20 I continued to open boxes, dump out handbags, and unwrap, while Cammie sorted and lugged everything to the stockroom. We were nowhere close to getting the entire shipment unpacked. Ten boxes still barricaded the front of the handbag department.

No matter how understaffed we felt, The Big Fancy morning expectation remained the same.

Everything had to be unpacked and displayed on the handbag floor.

"You can't sell it if it's in a box," Suzy Davis-Satan once said to me after I ran out of time and pushed several unopened boxes to the stockroom.

"We are all taking on more, doing more with less," she said, "You need to jump a little higher and move a little faster. The expectations do not change."

Morning stock-work duties did not end at unpacking, merching, and putting away extras. As Judy had informed me on my first fateful day at The Big Fancy, it was our responsibility to dispose of all the tissue, plastic bags, and boxes.

The image of the Perfect Department Store must be maintained at all times.

At 9:25 we were anything but perfect. The place was in total shambles.

I had managed to get everything out of the boxes, and Cammie had put away a few things, but there were still piles of plastic-coated handbags and wallets scattered all over. The mountain of empty cardboard boxes waited to be hauled away.

If only I had some kerosene and a match. Or maybe a magic wand.

Cammie and I looked as if we'd climbed Mount Fancy ten times; our faces were slick and our clothes damp. I began to sweat more, throwing boxes into a pile as fast as I could.

I looked at my watch. 9:29.

I stared at the jumble of handbags and trash all over the main aisle.

We were in trouble.

It was too late.

Before I could come up with some sort of emergency plan that involved using one of the larger cardboard boxes as a bulldozer, the sound of a bell clanged across the store, followed by the sound of stomping and marching, and then the voice of famous boxing-event announcer Michael Buffer bellowing, *"LADIES AND GENTLEMEN. WELCOME TO THE MAIN EVENT! LET'S GET READY TO RUUUUUMMMMMBBBLLLLE!!!!"*

My skin crawled.

Then came an electronic DUN, DUN, DUN, DUN, DUN, DUN, followed by fast-paced techno music. Nightclub/workout techno music. Blasting out of huge speakers in Cosmetics.

We scrambled like chickens before the slaughter.

As the rumble music continued to pulsate, a female voice pierced the air: "OKAY, EVERYBODY, IT'S RAAAAAAAALLY TIME! COME ON, EVERYBODY! COME ON OVER TO COSMETICS. WE'RE GONNA PUMP IT UP! WHOOHOOOOOOOO!"

It was Big Fancy Rally time.

I wanted to slit my wrist with the broken scissors.

One of the most hateful things The Big Fancy does to keep our Retail Slave angst alive and angry on the selling floor is to constantly inject us with the Cheerleading Virus, using nerve-shredding, eardrum-shattering pep rallies.

I've never liked the whole pep-rally thing.

Not even in high school when we were all marched into the gym, segregated onto bleachers by our grades, and forced to clap and cheer for two hours about school spirit.

We've got spirit, yes we do! We've got spirit, how 'bout you!

My spirit is exactly where it should be at 9:30 A.M., thank you very much: sleeping.

It does not need whooping and clapping to wake it up.

Maybe some coffee or hot sex, but definitely no whooping and clapping.

Unfortunately, there is no way to avoid the Morning Rally. All salespeople are required to attend, per Suzy Satan. No excuses. Doesn't matter how slammed you are with department work. Doesn't matter who calls in sick. Doesn't matter if there is only one opener because the store is cutting hours. Doesn't matter. Doesn't matter. You'd better get your ass to the Morning Rally and clap and cheer like you're sitting next to Jack Nicholson at a Lakers game.

As soon as Cammie and I arrived in Cosmetics, we faced the body belonging to the wall of sound.

Stephanie. The store secretary.

"OKAAAAAAAAAY, PEOPLE," she shrieked. "HOW IS EVERYBODY THIS MORNING? WOOOOOOOOOOOO HOOOOOOOOOOOOOO!"

I wanted to rip my ears off.

Stephanie had android-green eyes screwed tight into a perfectly sculpted Barbie doll face, with shiny blond shoulder-length hair and a fake white-teeth smile. I called her the Stephanator because she reminds me of the T-X model Arnold fought in *Terminator 3*.

"WOOHOOOOOOO!" Stephanator screamed again. Her rally war cry was so loud, I'm sure dogs were starting to bark down the street. "I'VE GOT CANDY FOR EVERYBODY! YAAAAAY!"

Without warning, Stephanator had reached into a shopping bag, and mini boxes of Hot Tamales candy rained down like stray bullets.

"WE'RE GOING TO HAVE A RED-HOT DAY!!!" screeched Stephanator into the microphone. "HOT, HOT, HOT, HOT TAMALES WILL GIVE YOU A FIERY SUGAR RUSH AND GREAT BREATH TO APPROACH OUR BIG FANCY CUSTOMERS."

For the next several minutes Stephanator turned herself into a Hot Tamales skeet launch. She managed to hit the Women's Shoes manager in the back of the head, and one box landed in the large bosom of a woman from Home Goods. Boxes flew everywhere, hitting people who weren't paying attention. I caught two boxes, but only to stop them from smacking my face. Cammie took one and threw it back, clipping Stephanie in the shoulder. She didn't even notice.

The little square boxes were all over the floor, being stepped on, kicked, and crushed. A Hot Tamale massacre.

"COME ON, PEOPLE! WAAAAAAAAAKE UP!!!" wailed Stephanator. "I WANT TO HEAR YOU. LET'S CLAP! HOW GREAT IS OUR STORE?"

Quite a few people followed her command, but many more of us were going deaf from pulsing techno music and needed our hands to save our ears.

Stephanator nailed me with a disapproving green-eyed glare. "FREEMAN!" she shouted, "DON'T BE SUCH A FUDDY DUDDY! COME ON, CLAAAAAP!!!"

I gave her a gun-to-the-head, shit-pleasing smile and slowly started clapping.

What else could I do?

I had to clap, just like all the other Retail Slaves.

It was one of those store moments when the Stephanator exerted her managerial power over everyone, even though technically she wasn't anyone's boss.

"CLAP, EVERYBODY! KEEP CLAPPING! THAT'S IT! WOOHOOOO!!!"

I continued clapping, but not without praying she'd slip on a box of Hot Tamales and break her neck.

Please, God. Make it happen. I'll owe you! I promise.

Suddenly Suzy Davis-Johnson surged through the crowd, sporting a purple-and-green plaid poncho, denim skirt, and red cowboy boots. She looked like a pint-sized country drag queen about to do a number from a low-budget community theatre production of *Annie Get Your Gun.*

"GOOOOOOOOOOOD MORNING!" Cowgirl Suzy blurted out into the mike. "HOW IS EVERYONE THIS MORNING?"

I'm still sweating, my ears hurt, my palms are turning red from clapping, my clothes are dirty and wet, my heading is pounding, and I'm actually thinking about opening the box of Hot Tamales. That's how I am, Suzy, thanks for asking.

A few claps and grunts greeted her back. She was not thrilled.

"OH, COME ON, PEOPLE! SOMEBODY DIDN'T TAKE THEIR POSITIVE PILLS TODAY! I KNOW YOU CAN DO BETTER THAN THAT! GIVE ME SOME NOISE. EVERYBODY WAAAAAAAKE UUUUUUUP!!!"

How can she think we're not awake after techno music and the Stephanator forcing everyone to clap? I am so awake right now I could jump off the roof and pretend to fly. I'll never sleep again.

As if an applause sign had lit up, the studio audience obeyed instantly, clapping and whooping. My eardrums pleaded with me to take them away from this bad, bad place.

"THAT'S MORE LIKE IT!!! HOW ARE Y'ALL TODAY?" asked Suzy Satan.

"Well let me just tell you how *I* am! *I've* been to spinning class this morning and I am OVERFLOWING WITH ENERGY! WOOHOOOOOOOO!!! Today I want to talk about SMILING! Smiles are the motivating essence in life. You are never fully dressed without a smile. You should never leave the house without smiling and always come to work with a smile. Smiles are contagious! Today I want everyone to SMILE! And I want you all to think about smiling and what it does for you. Smile at people walking by your department. Smile at your customers. Smile at each other. Heck, just SMILE! THAT'S WHAT IT'S ALL ABOUT, PEOPLE! LET'S SEE SOME SMILES OUT THERE!"

What the hell? Where did all this smiling bullshit come from? Her Chicken Soup for the Soul desk calendar? She makes it sound like we can grab one at the 7-Eleven on the way to work.

Nevertheless, Satan had made a command. I smiled so hard my face felt like it was going to split in half. Cammie looked like Elmo.

"THAT'S WHAT I'M TALKING ABOUT, PEOPLE!" she gloated into the mike, with an oversized, eerie cartoon grin, "DOESN'T IT FEEL GREAT! DON'T YOU JUST LOVE SMILING?"

Around the room, everyone smiled, from ear to ear. We were all smiling happy faces. Cammie and I turned to each other with our huge, unnatural, fraudulent smiles. Through her clenched-teeth smile, she uttered, "I can't ucking elieve this!" Through my own clenched-teeth smile, I responded, "She is ucking insane!"

For the next twenty minutes we were in Big Fancy Retail Rally Hell.

We had to listen to Satan complain about the figures and service. (She wasn't smiling.)

Then Stephanator yelled out the names of The Big Fancy's Top Ten Salespeople and the Top Departments with increases—it was a list that never seemed to stop, and we had to clap for each one. My palms hurt.

Then Satan went back to lecturing us about multiple sales, approaching customers within thirty seconds, blah, blah, blah. During the entire rally, all I could do was look over to the Handbag Jungle in the distance. It looked like a designer cargo plane had crash-landed.

Finally, at 9:55, Satan belched out her closing address:

"I WANT TO MAKE SURE EVERYONE IS HIGHLY MOTI-VATED AND DEDICATED TO WIN! I know I am! I want to see lots of bright, shiny SMILING faces today! HAVE A RIP-ROARIN' ROCKIN' DAY, EVERYBODY!"

Cammie and I bolted for the Handbag Jungle.

"JUST THROW ALL THE SHIT INTO BOXES AND WE'LL PUSH IT BACK," she shouted in a panic, "I have no fuckin' idea where any of it is going."

The store doors opened. Customers poured through, making their way down the main aisle, awkwardly sidestepping over handbags and boxes. One lady bent over, picked up a Dooney bag and said, "Are you guys having a special sale today?"

Suddenly, the Stephanator appeared out of nowhere and screamed, "FREEMAN! MY GOD! WHAT ARE YOU DOING? THE STORE IS OPEN!"

I just stared at her.

Did the Megatron monster think I was unaware of that? WOO-FUCK-ING-HOOOOOO!

"Dig in Stephanie, there's plenty to go around," I answered.

Her fiber-optic eyes seared into me as she snapped, "If you and Cammie had gotten your work done before the rally started, you wouldn't be in this position. I'll be having a conversation with Suzy about it."

"GO RIGHT AHEAD," Cammie shouted from behind her, "And while you're at it, tell her we need a stock person, LIKE A NORMAL STORE!"

I turned a box on its side to scoop up a bunch of DKNY wallets and stacked five boxes in two rows. Then I bent over and pushed them, like a broken-down car, down the aisle leading to the double doors that opened into our stock area.

My face flushed red. Stephanie pissed me off.

If we had gotten our work done before the rally! She has no fucking clue what we have to go through every hateful morning here. I think I'll go accidentally spill coffee all over her desk when no one is looking.

When I came out of the stockroom, it was a freakin' retail riot. Cammie, along with salespeople and managers from Women's Shoes, scurried around, picking up handbags and wallets. The Stephanator had taken command and barked orders: "THE STORE IS OPEN, YOU GUYS! WE HAVE TO GET THIS DONE!"

I watched with a sigh as they haphazardly threw handbags and wallets behind the Corral and behind the door of our stockroom. It would take all day for us to clean up the mess.

In her whirlwind to control, Stephanie violently snatched up a bunch of Coach bags and heaved them over the counter with bionic force. A $698 black leather Coach satchel flew through the air without wings. The Coach went airborne, sailing across the Corral, eventually hitting the top of the register, bouncing down it, and smacking the tape dispenser before disappearing from sight.

The Stephanator ran down the aisle, hysterical, head completely up her ass.

She had no clue about the murder she'd committed.

I rushed behind the Corral. The $698 Coach bag had fallen in the metal trash bin under the register. A horrible deep scrape marred the front leather flap above the buckle.

Ruined. The Coach was dead. Caught in the destructive path of a short-circuiting Retail Droid. No woman would want it now. Not even marked down.

Killed by an out-of-control store secretary and Scotch tape dispenser.

Before I could decide on how to handle the burial arrangements for the deceased $698 Coach bag, a customer ambled up to the counter and scrutinized it.

"Oh my," she said, "that beautiful bag has an awful scratch on it!"

I tossed her my shit-pleasing retail smile and said, "How may I help you this morning?"

She put a shopping bag on the counter and said, "I want to return this." I looked inside. A $1,500 Marc Jacobs stared up at me. One that I had sold.

Sonofabitch. Now I'm starting the day in a financial hole.

Around me the Handbag department churned like a stormy sea.

Another customer asked one of the helping managers about a bag thrown behind the counter.

Another customer needing help hailed me from the end of the Corral.

Suzy was now on the scene, and Stephanie yapped at her wildly about the handbag mess.

Cammie got pissed and jumped into the fray, yelling at Suzy.

The phone started ringing.

A trickle of sweat slid down my forehead.

My clothes were damp, dirty, and disheveled.

My ears were ringing.

My palms had turned bright red.

My stomach felt like it was housing an alien.

Techno dance music banged away in my head.

And my Rip-Roarin' Rockin' Day had only just begun.

Polly Wants to Talk

My first official Big Fancy Shopper Stalker was a woman I never met. She did all her shopper stalking over the phone.

"Hi, Mr. Freeman, how are yooou?"

That was how every single phone call started with Polly.

Polly was a Crazy Lady who loved to call me Mr. Freeman and ask, "How are yooooou?" like she was some kind of freaky ghost.

My unwanted hella-communication with her started because I was the unlucky idiot who picked up her call. Abiding by Big Fancy Customer Service Phone Etiquette, I happily assisted her for a good hour as she interrogated me about the brands we carried, the styles, and what was new.

Fresh out of Handbag-Selling School with Jules, Cammie, and Marsha, I was eager to nail as many sales as possible—over the phone or otherwise. In Polly's case, she decided on Fendi because her coworker had one and she loved my story about the Fendi sisters, so she had me put five handbags on hold.

That was the first night.

Every night after that she continued to call, wanting to know what was new and wanting me to describe the bags I had on hold for her over and over. I tried to get her to come in or buy them over the phone, but Polly told me she didn't have a car or credit card and she liked to pay only in cash. I thought this was strange because Polly also told me she was a nurse at a big hospital in downtown L.A. Nurses make fairly good money, way better than Retail Slaves, and she was telling me she was a nurse without a car or credit card? Something wasn't right.

I smell a bored bloodsucker with Mr. Freeman as her evening entertainment.

POLLY: "Mr. Freeman, are yooou there?"

ME: "Yes, Polly, I'm here."

POLLY: "Do you still have my five Fendi bags on hold?"

ME: "Yes, Polly, they are all on my hold shelf, and I've extended it until Saturday."

POLLY: "Wonderful, Mr. Freeman. Could yooou go and get them; I have some questions."

ME: "Polly, when can you come into the store? I've had them on hold for two weeks now."

POLLY: "I'm not sure. It's very difficult for me."

Every time Polly called, I wanted to fucking scream. Right into the phone! But I didn't. Giving Excellent Customer Service is our priority. When Judy bitched at me for holding the Fendis for so long, I told her the situation, and she snapped, "You need to get her in here to buy, or I'm putting the bags back, and I better not get any calls from Suzy about this woman being upset. This is your customer and I want you to take care of it. Got it?"

Yes, General. I got it.

ME: "My manager keeps asking me when you're coming in, Polly."

POLLY: "My hours at the hospital are long, and I don't drive, and I live in downtown Los Angeles. I told yooou last week I don't drive, Mr. Freeman. Now please go get my bags. I'm not sure about the pockets. I'd like yooou to measure each pocket, tell me their dimensions, and describe what they are made out of, whether or not it's the Fendi material or tan leather. After that I'd like yooou to tell me the story again about the Fendi sisters. Did they have any children or pets? Find that out for me please, Mr. Freeman."

I'M GONNA FIND OUT WHERE YOU LIVE AND GET A COURT ORDER TO HAVE YOU COMMITTED, YOU FUCKING CRAZY BITCH!!!

ME: "Yes, Polly."

As I put her on hold, I saw Douche ringing up a $1,700 Burberry, Marci selling a $435 Signature Coach, and Tiffany showing a $600

Isabella Fiore with a matching $200 wallet. For the next hour I would be talking to a ghost over the phone. No sales for me.

The best I could do was pray that a track light fell out of the ceiling and knocked me out.

Ring. Ring. Ring.

CALLER: "Hi, Mr. Freeman, how are yooou?"

Polly had called so many times, I was afraid to answer the fucking phone.

ME: "Hi Polly. I'm fine."

POLLY: "Did you get anything new in today?"

ME: "No, I'm sorry, Polly, we didn't." (I lied.)

POLLY: "Do yooou still have my Fendi bags?"

ME: "Yes, Polly. When are yooou coming into the store?"

POLLY: "I don't know, Mr. Freeman. I'm working on it, like I told yooou, it's hard for me to get to your store. Perhaps I can catch a cab or something."

I wanted to scream. The crazy phone-calling loon had told me over and over again she was going to come into the store.

Judy went on the warpath and yelled at me for ten minutes because I wasn't able to push Polly into buying the Fendi bags crowding my hold shelf for the last month. "I WANT THEM GONE, FREEMAN! GOT IT?"

Tiffany suggested that I talk to Security to see if they could do anything about my phone stalker. They said unless she'd made violent threats, the only thing I could do was continue answering the phone.

I asked the Customer Service manager how I should handle Polly, and he said, "I'm not touching that one with a twenty-foot Fendi! Ha-ha!"

I don't know what was so funny.

Jules suggested I go to the head honcho for advice. Suzy Satan smiled like she related to my plight as I bitched about holding everything and losing sales. But when I asked her how I could nicely get rid of Polly, she cast me a worried look and said, "We don't get rid of any potential customers here at The Big Fancy. We are all about giving the best customer service possible. Sometimes you have to give to the community without expecting anything back. Just go with the flow. I'm sure this lady will get bored and stop calling eventually."

After my powwow with Suzy, Cammie said, "Why the fuck did you go to her? She makes us wait on homeless people! What you need to do is to tell the bloodsucker to leave you the fuck alone or you're going to burn down her motherfucking house." As usual, Cammie had the best advice, but the question was how could I tell Polly to get lost without her complaining to Suzy Davis-Johnson that I had burned down her house?

POLLY: "Mr. Freeman? Are yooou there?"

ME: "Yes, Polly, I'm here."

POLLY: "Great! I want to talk about wallets. What kind of wallets do you carry? I'll need to know exactly how many pockets each wallet has. Does Fendi have matching wallets? Anything new? What kind of wallets do yooou like, Mr. Freeman?"

ME: "Yes, Polly, we have matching Fendi wallets."

I felt a smack on the back of my head.

Compliments of Cammie.

Big Nightmare #1

Even though The Big Fancy had me by the neck with a leather shoulder strap, I knew that if I wanted out of Retail Hell, I'd better get my ass in gear and write that Million-Dollar Screenplay. Writers are supposed to write.

That's easier said than done when you work retail.

Every week my schedule felt like a vomit-inducing thrill ride at Magic Mountain amusement park, except that I was anything but amused. I'd open, then close, then open, then work a mid-shift (11-8), then open, then close. Which shifts and days I worked would change at the drop of a handbag, based on whatever drama was going down in the department. More times than I could count, Judy begged me to stay late and come in early, and then demanded I attend all meetings and seminars on my days off. Just like during my days in Reno, the Store was taking over my life.

One afternoon, my good Retail Droid behavior paid off. Judy said I could leave at 4:00. The plan was to go directly home—as fast as I could—and channel the writing genius of Stephen King.

Unfortunately, my plan and The Big Fancy's plan rarely matched up.

At 3:55 I found myself all alone while chaos ensued. Tiffany was still at lunch. The phone rang nonstop. Customers were everywhere. A woman demanded to have her old Coach handbag repaired. A young girl wanted to return a Burberry tote that I'd never seen before. (Of course she had no receipts.) And an elderly lady insisted I call Big Fancy stores to locate five identical $38 evening bags because she needed them for a wedding in two days. The firestorm of handbag hell consumed me.

Until 6:30.

Although I was pissed off at not being able to leave early and cursing the fact that I had to stay late, as I descended Mount Fancy's fifth flight, I made a vow not to give up.

"I'm still going to write," I shouted down the hollow stairwell of Mount Fancy.

"I'm still going to write," I mumbled to myself repeatedly as I got into my car.

"I'm still going to write," I said out loud as I hit a road closure for a movie premiere at Hollywood and Highland and was trapped in traffic for an hour.

"I'm still going to write," I bitched through clenched teeth as it took twenty-five minutes for me to get my dinner at a Jack in the Box drive-through because the car in front of me was an SUV holding twelve people.

"I'M STILL GOING TO WRITE, YOU FUCKERS!" I yelled out my car window while circling my apartment building for fifteen minutes trying to find a parking space.

By the time I opened my front door, it was 8:30. I could have screamed.

But instead, I calmly said, "I'm still going to write!"

A half-hour later, after gobbling down my Ultimate Cheeseburger and checking e-mail, I opened the screenwriting program.

All ready to write.

It was three hours later than planned, but hey, I had faced retail adversity in the eye!

Ha ha, Big Fancy. You did not get all of my energy.

"I'm still going to write!" I said out loud and proud.

Within seconds my script appeared on the screen, awaiting my creative brilliance.

But it never showed up.

Twenty minutes later, I slumped in my desk chair almost to the point of falling out. There was not a single word or vision in my brain. It had been deep-fried by The Big Fancy, and I couldn't find the backup generator.

Maybe I just need a break. A short, little break. I'm not giving up. I'm still going to write!

To relieve my writer's block, I listened to Green Day and played AstroPop on my computer, mindlessly blasting bricks to make points. After reaching 70,000, I figured I'd better write. But then I had the munchies. After eating half a bag of Nacho Cheese Doritos and watching several episodes of *Scrubs*, it was after midnight. Time was quickly slipping away.

But I held firm to my dream.

I decided at that late hour, *I was still going to write, dammit*, even though I was getting sleepy. I took a deep breath and forced my fingers into typing position on the keyboard. My eyes focused on the white screen, and I told myself to write.

So I did.

I finally wrote:

EXT. ARAGONNE FOREST CAVES—NIGHT

No clue what comes next.

Where is the monster? Where is Captain Oswald? What the fuck does the nest look like?

So many unanswered questions swirled in my head. Then the mind wandering started.

I wonder which movie premiere was happening that closed the streets on my way home. I should call Cammie and see how her video shoot went. She's probably hanging out with the band getting drunk. I wonder if I should buy that new Ben Sherman shirt I saw in Men's Trend. Sales were bad today. I can't afford any shirts. My paycheck is going to suck. I wonder what that customer was so upset about that had to talk to Judy. And there was that other customer who wanted me to call all The Big Fancy stores to find five matching cheap evening bags for her stupid wedding—FUCK—I forgot to call, she is going to be pissed!

Too many thoughts. Too many words and images. All blurring together.

My eyelids drooped. Everything went black. Then white.

A blank page appeared. Black words in Courier font magically typed across it. A script!

Polly the Phone Poltergeist

An original screenplay by Freeman

Down at the bottom, in the left corner, it said:

Revised final draft.
April 12, 2020.
Rewritten 253 times.
Represented by CIA.
Produced by NBA.
Authenticated by FDA.

Then those famous screenplay words appeared.

FADE IN:

Followed by a screenplay magically writing itself. (Now that's my kind of screenplay!)

EXT. BIG FANCY DEPARTMENT STORE—ESTABLISH

INT. HANDBAG DEPARTMENT—NIGHT

Track lights flicker. A wind picks up. The department phone RINGS.

A shrunken CAMMIE looks just like the little girl from the *Poltergeist* movie. Blond bangs and white nightgown. She answers the phone and does her Handbag Department GREETING. Listens. Covers the mouthpiece.

> CAMMIE
> The crazy bitch is heeeeeeeeeeere!

She hands the phone to a terrified FREEMAN.

> POLLY'S VOICE
> Hi, Mr. Freeman, How are yooooou?

Freeman looks as if he is going to cry. He starts
sweating.

                    FREEMAN
          Umm . . . Hi, Polly.

                    POLLY'S VOICE
          Are you still holding my five Fendi handbags
          and three wallets, Mr. Freeman?

                    FREEMAN
          Yes, Polly.

                    POLLY'S VOICE
          Which ones do yooou like for me, Mr. Freeman?
          I want you to gather all of my Fendi bags,
          measure each one, and tell me their details
          so I can imagine what they look like.

He goes pale. He is speechless. Cammie yanks the phone
from him.

                    CAMMIE
               (Speaks into phone)
          Look, you crazy psycho, get a fucking life
          and stop calling here!

The Corral shakes like an earthquake is hitting it.
Handbags fall. Glass shatters. Cammie's body goes
transparent pink and swirls into the shape of a tornado.

                    CAMMIE
               (Yelling over the wind)
          YOU FUCKING BITCH! NOOOOOOOOO!!!

Freeman tries to hang on to her. But she dissipates in
his hand. The phone console inhales the pink smoke like
a genie returning to its bottle.

FREEMAN
(Screaming over the wind)
CAMMIEEEEEEEEEEEE!

The wind and shaking abruptly stop. Freeman grabs the phone.

FREEMAN
Where is she, Polly?

POLLY'S VOICE
Talk to me about the Fendi handbags, Mr.
Freeman! Tell me which ones have the most
zipper pockets. If you don't, there's no
telling what will happen to your little
friend. Do yooooou understand, Mr. Freeman?

Freeman gulps.

INT. HANDBAG DEPARTMENT—DAY

JULES and MARSHA wear lime green jumpsuits emblazoned
with **Handbag Ghostbusters.** They have a large purple
machine that looks like an industrial floor shiner.
A long green hose is attached to the phone console.

JULES
We'll get Cammie back. Polly will regret the
day she haunted our phone line!

MARSHA
I don't know why it isn't working. Wal-Mart
said this was the best Evil Phone Spirit
Remover they had. I paid fifty bucks for it.

FREEMAN
You need to plug it in, Marsha.

MARSHA
Oh, yes, you're right, hon . . . oops.

She plugs it in and the machine begins to spark and make weird gurgling vacuum noises.

The phone starts to ring and Jules hits speaker-phone. Polly is screaming.

                         POLLY
          WHAT ARE YOOOU DOING, MR. FREEMAN!? WHAT
          IS THIS? I WANT MY FENDIS!

                         FREEMAN
          GIVE US CAMMIE BACK! OR I'LL SELL THEM ALL TO
          SOMEONE ELSE, POLLY! I SWEAR I WILL!

                         POLLY
          NOOO . . . MR. FREEMAN . . . NOOO!

Flashes of light blind the room as hot pink smoke erupts from the phone console like a volcano. There's an explosion. As the air clears, Cammie appears, lying on the 50% off clearance table. Covered in thick pink slime, she sits up, dazed and confused.

                         CAMMIE
          What the fuck is this shit?

                         MARSHA
          She slimed Cammie!

                         JULES
          We need to get her to the Chanel counter, stat!

Suddenly GENERAL JUDY yells from the stockroom.

                         GENERAL JUDY's VOICE
          WHAT THE HELL IS THIS! FREEE-MAAAAAN!

Freeman runs for the stockroom and opens the door . . .

INT. STOCKROOM

A pissed-off GENERAL JUDY stands there, holding
armloads of Fendi bags.

ANGLE—EMPLOYEE HOLD SHELVES—FREEMAN'S HOLDS—TOP SHELF

Hundreds of Fendi handbags and wallets are on the
top shelf, stacked into a wobbly, unstable pyramid
stretching all the way to the ceiling.

> JUDY
> FREE-MAN, I TOLD YOU TO PUT ALL THESE FENDIS
> BACK!

> FREEMAN
> I tried, Judy. I think she's gone now. I'll
> get right on it—I promise!

But before Freeman can move, hundreds of Fendi straps
appear from the stockroom depths like tentacles. They
engulf Judy and drag her away kicking and SCREAMING.

The phone begins to RING, its wail so loud, it's like a
siren. Polly's laughing rises above the ringing.

> POLLY'S VOICE
> YOU WILL NEVER GET AWAY FROM ME, MR. FREEMAN!

The pyramid has amassed to thousands of Fendis. It's
swaying ominously.

> POLLY'S VOICE
> I DEMAND YOU TELL ME THE ENTIRE STORY OF THE
> FENDI SISTERS! NOW! AND START FROM THE VERY
> BEGINNING.

Suddenly there's a rumble. The mountain topples like a
rock slide. Handbags and wallets come crashing down.

Freeman SCREAMS.

FADE OUT TO BLACKNESS AND RINGING.

My eyes opened to the stunned face of Eric Cartman from *South Park*—a plastic wind-up toy that sits on my desk. His molded face wanted to tell me something.

Seriously, dude, that was so fucked up. You are totally hella-screwed.

As I lifted my head from my keyboard pillow, I saw that the computer screen had gone dark.

Fucking nightmare.

Yet I could still hear ringing.

Because it's not a dream. It's your real phone, dumbass!

I jumped up out of my desk chair, fumbling for the phone, bleary eyed and dazed. Polly's ghostly voice echoed in my head.

"Yooooou can't get away from me, Mr. Freeman!"

Dazed, I pushed the talk button, and barely got "Hello?" out of my mouth.

"Freeman?" a woman's voice asked, "It's Tammy from Big Fancy. According to the schedule, you were supposed to have been here over an hour ago to open. Is everything okay?"

I looked at the black digital skull-shaped clock next to my bed. 10:20 A.M.

SHIT!!!

"Umm ... Hi, Tammy. I've been really sick all night. I think it was food poisoning from Jack in the Box. I was just going to call. I'm better."

Dead silence.

Tammy wasn't falling for my lie about Jack.

Two-Tone knows I've overslept. She'll fire my ass for sure!

"Judy has been in a meeting all morning. I'm watching your department because there is no one else to do it. Can you please get here as quickly as possible? I have my own work to do."

"Yes, Tammy. I'm on my way out the door right now."

"Oh, and by the way," she said in her Sicky Sweet voice, "A customer named Polly called for you. She wants you to call her as soon as you get in. She said you were holding Fendi bags."

I was too stunned to respond.

The Big Fancy had invaded my dreamscape and creative mind. Writing my Million-Dollar Screenplay was going to be a lot harder than I'd thought.

Sinners, Serpents, and the Craziest Crazy-Lady Customers

Bubble, bubble, toil and trouble, get me a JD on the rocks and make it a double.

Queer-Eye Handbag Guy

"What's a man doing in the purse department?"

She brought up the man thing and said the p-word all in one sentence.

A cranky old lady customer. The Big Fancy was crawling with them.

This curly-red-haired granny had on a white kitten-emblazoned sweatshirt, black poly stretch pants, and tan orthopedic shoes. Worst of all, her rumpled, misshapen handbag looked no better than a plastic supermarket bag.

I just sighed, taking in the question I'd heard a thousand times.

During one of those thousand times, I actually corrected an old hag's usage of the p-word. This ended up getting me my first Big Fancy complaint letter, "He told me that purses were no longer called purses. He corrected me and said they are called handbags. I do not appreciate his rudeness. I have been carrying a PURSE for fifty years! What does he know? You should not have men selling purses."

Well, guess what, Grandma Moses, hold onto your Aqua Net, 'cause the future is here and men are selling handbags!

Of course Suzy Davis-Johnson took it upon herself to have a little chat with me about the complaint. Satan didn't berate me or sentence me to the stockroom chain gang, but she strongly suggested that even though the word handbag is proper by industry standards, it was probably best if I did not correct customers who hadn't adopted the term. In those cases, it was perfectly okay to use the p-word.

Well I hope you told the General, because she'll shit green satchels if I say the p-word!

Suzy assured me she'd tell Judy not to get upset if I said the p-word, but truth be told, I had sort of started to hate the word purse. It sounded so white trash and cheap. I was selling Coach, Kate Spade, and Gucci *handbags*. Ferragamo designed handbags, not purses. And Marc Jacobs does not introduce a fall purse collection—he introduces a fabulous fall handbag collection! Purses were back in the dinosaur times of dime stores, not the fashion free-for-all times of now.

Regarding Curly in the cat sweatshirt, I decided to let her have the truth straight up.

"A man in this department is no different than a man selling shoes, and I'm sorry to inform you, but we don't call them purses anymore; they're handbags."

So there. Take that. Go complain to Satan. I'm sure she'll massage your ancient purse-lovin' ego.

The woman looked at me like she was going to smack me and then she burst out laughing.

"What an idiot I am," she said, "You are so right. This isn't the '50s! I'm glad there are men selling purses—I mean handbags! Good for you!"

I didn't know about the "Good for me" part (measuring men's inseams would have been good for *me*), but the fact that she had opened her eyes to the times so quickly impressed me.

"I guess it's as good a place as any to be working," said Curly, "but don't try and sell me another handbag. I need another handbag like I need a hole in the head. Got a closet full of 'em."

"A woman can never own too many handbags," I responded, having learned the line from Jules, who had told me it was a good comeback for the whole "closet full of handbags" excuse.

Jules had said it was up to me to convince women that changing handbags with their outfits made a statement about who they were and how they dressed. "An old, worn-out bag or one that's outdated can completely ruin a gorgeous outfit," she had said, adding, "And then the fashion police are called in."

I guess this was a good philosophy to brainwash customers. If women who were addicted to handbags suddenly had the revelation they should never, ever, ever need to buy a new handbag so long as they lived, I'd be out of a job. Then Two-Tone Tammy would have sent my free-spirit personality somewhere really scary, like hosiery.

I was all for women owning too many handbags. It paid my rent (sometimes).

Hell, I've got too many ties.

And clothes. Way too many clothes.

"Do you have a pink handbag?" I asked Curly, who was eyeing an Isabella Fiore collection just in. They were quite sparkly works of art, constructed out of pink floral tapestry embellished with embroidery and crystal beading.

"Of course not, why would I want a pink handbag?" asked Curly, smoothing out her kitten sweatshirt.

This was my in. I knew what to do next.

I've sold so many pink handbags I could turn into a pink elephant, sprout some pink wings, and fly off in search of the land of pink vodka lemonade.

After being taught the technical terms in the world of handbags, over time I had learned a slew of other helpful selling techniques that got my customers to the register.

The first one was "bags and shoes don't always have to match any-more." Although it's kind of a given in today's fashion environment, many women still have the hardest time letting go of matchy-match dressing. This anything-goes attitude was awesome for handbag sales-people like us, giving us free rein to show the customer anything we wanted!

That purple fringe suede bag looks amazing with your Stuart Weitzman rhinestone shoes! It's high fashion!

Okay, so it may not have worked with everything.

Jules also taught me to point out every zipper, compartment, pocket, and doohickey on the bag. "You won't remember every thing about every bag," she said, "But you can PRETEND you do. Just touch everything—unzip the zippers, stick your hand in the pockets, undo the straps, whatever. Talk about features as if you already knew they were there."

The bag blind leading the bag blind!

She also helped me get over my aversion to an important visual method to selling handbags.

Modeling the way a bag is worn.

At first I was like, no fuckin' way am I putting a woman's handbag on my shoulder! But Jules quickly pointed out that men wear backpacks and messenger bags instead of briefcases. My balls slowly grew back to regular size, but I still felt weird modeling a Juicy Couture slouchy hobo covered in dangling pompoms and heart-shaped charms.

The women, however, loved it.

Seeing a man emasculate himself was often what closed a sale!

The other handbag-selling problem I had to conquer was inviting customers to try their things inside a style they were considering. Marsha told me this was a major weapon in the fight against having bags returned for not adequately holding everything.

"Hon, you're selling them now," she said. "Your grandma would understand."

I've now seen the insides of so many handbags, I could write a book about the psychological and emotional connection women have to the crap they carry around with them all day.

Sorry, Grandma! Don't kill me. They made me go inside women's purses, er, I mean handbags.

As my handbag comfort and confidence grew, I developed a few selling tricks of my own. With greedy sharks like Douche and Tiffany swimming alongside me in the Jungle, making sales was do or die. So I resorted to going totally over the top:

"That bag is *fabulous!* SO hot! If I were a woman, I'd wear it myself!"

"I have to say the aubergine Coach carryall really compliments your hair color."

"Did you know the Marc Jacobs Sophia was named after director Sophia Coppola?"

"That Isabella Fiore pirate bag will stop traffic! Men will comment and women will be jealous!"

"My friend's Kate Spade messenger bag got totally soaked on the Jurassic Park water ride at Universal Studios and it dried perfectly! No stains at all! Completely clean!"

"This Juicy Couture bowler just came in this morning. We already sold three. It's the last one!"

"Suitcase bags are all the rage. It doesn't matter what size you are or how little you carry!"

"Last night on *Access Hollywood*, Gwyneth Paltrow had on that very same grass green hobo! It's SO unbelievably hot!"

Most of my phrases I pulled directly out of my ass. Some were true, some not. But one of my most favorite handbag-selling lines I learned from the iconic handbag designer Kate Spade.

Well, she didn't teach me personally, but it would have been really cool if she had.

"Kate says that a woman should use a bag to accessorize her outfit like a man does with his tie."

This magical handbag-selling anecdote from Kate often held the key to a customer's buying a bright yellow satchel *and* a hot pink clutch!

"See, it's like what I've done. I'm wearing a black suit, but I have on this festive red tie with Hershey's Kisses all over it. Doesn't it just add something to my all-black look? I don't look so menacing now, do I?"

My newly acquired selling skills had me quizzing customers like I was Anderson Cooper on a mission to end world handbag aggravation for women everywhere. Sloped shoulders, weak backs, wrists with carpal tunnel—you name the ailment, I found the handbag. I helped women accessorize for weddings, business meetings, luncheons, concerts, and dates. I assisted them in deciding on bags for carrying their workout clothes, medical books, kid's toys, laptops, carpet samples—whatever their heart's desire! I even located bags big enough to tote their dogs and cats.

After romancing hundreds into carrying striped Kate Spade, signature Coach, trendy Isabella Fiore, bold Marc Jacobs, and classic Ferragamo, the transformation happened.

I became Queer-Eye Handbag Guy.

And the women of The Big Fancy ate it up.

My *free-spirited personality*, cool ties, and hip handbag lingo set me apart.

I found myself saying the words "fabulous" and "gorgeous," modeling handbags on my shoulders, quoting famous designers, and rummaging around in bags against Grandma's wishes.

I had my own stack of Big Fancy business cards that said *Freeman Hall, Handbag Sales Associate*, and within a short time, women started coming into the department and asking for me.

If they didn't know my name, they'd ask, "Is that blond guy here?" followed by a whispered, "You know who I mean, I think he's gay."

Whenever Jules mentioned this, she'd glow like I was her third child. "I remember when you thought a cross-body messenger was a buff UPS driver!"

Marsha was also like a proud mother: "You sell handbags better than I do!"

And Cammie loved to tag-team customers with me. She'd model for my customers, and in return, I gave her customers Queer-Eye Handbag Guy punditry: "That bag is so unbelievably hot! It will give you a whole new edgy look!"

I even had one customer tell me every time she got a compliment on her handbag, she'd reply "I got it from Freeman!" Then the complimenting person would say, "Freeman? Is that a new boutique on Montana Street?" My customer would reply, "FREEMAN AT THE BIG FANCY! Let me give you one of his cards."

The experience for Curly, with her kitty sweatshirt, stretch pants, and hideous shoes, was no different. After romancing her on the artistic look of the Fiore, I modeled it, showed her the features, had her try her stuff in it, and told her it was featured in *Vogue*. I guided her into taking it for a test drive in front of the floor mirror, and told her it was wearable art, a collector's item.

Curly was sold. Within fifteen minutes she was handing me her Visa card.

It also helped that I was wearing one of my silly ties that happened to have Garfield the cat on it. When I fed her Kate's awesome philosophy about a woman wearing her handbag like a man wears a tie, Curly took a gander at Garfield, and it hit her where she lived.

Not only did she buy the Fiore bag, but I convinced her it was so fabulous she should ditch her black trash bag and put her things in the Fiore and wear it out!

There have been many customers of Queer-Eye Handbag Guy who walked into The Big Fancy as ugly purse-wearin' frumps but left as gorgeous handbag-carryin' fashionistas!

And Curly was one of them.

Not ten minutes had passed when Curly returned, glowing and full of life. She looked ten years younger. Was this a new selling tactic for me to explore?

Forget Botox! This bag will make you look younger—and without needles!

"I was just leaving the store," Curly said excitedly, "But I had to come back and tell you a woman just stopped me in Cosmetics and told me my handbag was stunning! That has never happened to me before. Thank you so much! I sent her to you. I hope you have another one!"

I did, and I was ready for her.

It was a scene repeated countless times, as I ended up outfitting the shoulders of thousands of women all over Southern California and beyond. With all this excitement surrounding my sales, you'd think I'd become rich or snagged my own reality TV show on Bravo.

Move over Carson Kressley; there's a new Queer-Eye in town!

But the dark side of selling handbags kept anything like that from happening.

Being adored at The Big Fancy came at a price.

Shoposaurus Carnotaurus

Shopping till you drop is old-school, Shopaholics are *so* ten years ago, and Shopzillas have already used up their five minutes of fame, thanks to an overblown website whose logo is a shopping cart with fire coming out of its ass.

But let me introduce the Shoposaurus Carnotaurus.

Hungry to shop and hungry to buy, they show up with insatiable appetites capable of devouring piles of merchandise without ever returning a single thing (which is a major difference from Shopaholics). For commissioned Retail Slaves, the Shoposaurus Carnotaurus is a wet dream come true.

And lucky for me, I had caught the biggest, most badass one of them all.

When I first saw the towering 6'2" fifty-something woman (who looked like a thin version of Tracy Turnblad's mother, Edna, in the movie *Hairspray*) brutally interrogating handbags on the clearance table, the first thought that came to my mind was . . . tranny.

That woman has to be a transvestite. Or a tranny in training. Or a man in drag.

She had chestnut-dyed bouffant hair in sort of a '50s Jackie O style and a pasty, green-eyed face sporting painted brown eyebrows and reddish-orange lips. Her attire was dressy: a colorful Mondrian print silk blouse, navy stretch wool slacks, and expensive navy Ferragamo

leather shoes with grosgrain bows. If it hadn't been for a new Fendi signature satchel dangling from her forearm, I'd have never gone near her.

The '50s Time-Warp Tranny looked anything but friendly. As it was,
the girls I was selling alongside that day—Tiffany, Marsha, Marci, and
Douche—were all avoiding her like they knew a deadly secret. None
of them approached Time-Warp Tranny, even though The Big Fancy
maintained a thirty-second-greeting rule toward all customers, regardless of how they look. Did the girls know something I didn't? Was this
giant woman a psycho or bloodsucker? Maybe they were just freaked
out by her scary white basketball-player-in-drag look. Nevertheless,
when I spied that Fendi signature satchel, I figured she might just have
a designer fetish. I hadn't sold much all day, and even if Time-Warp
Tranny turned out to be an annoying sale shopper and bought something on sale, it was better than nothing. I needed to get my volume up.

As I approached her, I noticed that although she was built like a
linebacker and her nose and mouth were huge in a masculine way, she
had no Adam's apple and her hands were not as large as a man's. The
woman indecently groping the sale bags wasn't a tranny or a man in
drag at all. She just had a major case of the uglies.

I made my move, positioning myself directly across from her at the
clearance table.

"Hi! How are you this afternoon?" I inquired.

Time-Warp Tranny didn't even look at me.

She was too busy fondling the insides of a gold croc-embossed
Michael Kors tote.

"I can't find the fucking price. Where is the motherfucking cocksucking price tag on this fucking whore? GODDAMN IT! I hate it
when this fucking bullshit happens. Jesus fucking Christ!"

Not in my wildest dreams would I ever have expected to hear the
word fuck drop from this conservative-looking lady's mouth, let alone
cocksucker.

Looks like Edna Turnblad has a potty mouth! My kind of woman!

I spied the tag dangling from the bottom of the strap and couldn't
resist communicating back in her language: "The motherfucking
price tag is right there on the strap."

If I got in trouble for saying that, the plan was to point a finger and
say, "She said it first!" But I never got in trouble.

That was how I met Lorraine Goldberg, my very own Shoposaurus Carnotaurus. What happened next blew me away. The perfect
storm hit: a combination of my Angels training, my Queer-Eye persona, and her hunger to buy.

I decided to give Lorraine the full tour and go over every designer
and every bag: new and old, on sale and regular price, casual and
dressy, trendy and classic. I covered it all.

After *motherfucking* and *cocksucking* many bags and wallets, Lorraine
had fallen in love with a bunch of brands: Coach, Kate Spade, Juicy
Couture, L.A.M.B., Michael Kors, and Marc Jacobs.

While she looked at a new quilted Marc Jacobs satchel, a customer
unknowingly picked up the Michael Kors tote Lorraine had momentarily set down.

Lorraine revealed big, white-yellow, tobacco-stained teeth,
threatening to eat the world as she roared, "DON'T YOU DARE
FUCKING TOUCH THAT! IT'S MINE! THAT FUCKING
MICHAEL KORS BAG IS MINE, BITCH!"

The woman ran off like a scared little bunny rabbit while Lorraine
turned to me and said:

"Don't let anyone touch any of my fucking bags. I HATE it when
people touch my fucking shit. I was here first. ALL THESE MOTH-
ERFUCKING BAGS ARE MINE, GODDAMN IT!"

It was an outburst that caused everyone in the department to gawk
and stare. And I didn't care. I thought it was hilarious. She swore like
a truck driver, and nobody would say shit because she was spending
$8,890.

That's right. $8,890.

Marsha congratulated me, Tiffany helped me pack everything up
(Lorraine demanded gift boxes to store all her bags in), Marci couldn't
stop talking about who has that kind of money for handbags, and the
best part was Douche's sneer with raised eyebrows. She was jealous as
hell, and I loved it!

I had bagged my own Shoposaurus Carnotaurus! *Take that, Douche!*

In a few short days Lorraine and I were on a first-name basis. She
called me on the phone and said, "Freeman, I want another fucking
Juicy Couture cherry tote. Find me one in perfect condition!" As the
fucks and cocksuckers flew, Lorraine ordered things over the phone

and then dutifully came in to pick them up on Saturdays, smelling of cigarettes and Chanel No. 5 perfume after spending the morning in the "beauty parlor," as she called it.

I always knew when my freshly coiffed, tobacco-perfumed Shoposaurus was about to arrive, because she'd give me her ETA the day before. Moments before her big entrance, I'd be overcome with a sense that Lorraine was nearby. It would play out in my head like the scene in *Jurassic Park* when the water in the plastic cup starts to ripple right before the T-Rex stomps out of the jungle.

But before I actually saw my Shoposaurus Carnotaurus, I could hear her ear-scraping wail from fifty feet away. She sounded like a champion hog caller, her voice booming from the aisle:

"FRAAAYMAN! FRAYMAN! FRAYMAN! FRAAAYMAN!"

Heads turned. Customers stopped shopping. Salespeople stopped selling. A handbag fell over.

"What was that?" said a Customer I was helping one Saturday.

"It's my personal customer calling for me."

The customer wrinkled her nose. "Does she always yell out your name like that?"

"It's her way of announcing she's arrived."

"Where is she yelling from? I don't even see her?"

Seconds later Lorraine loomed behind her, looking wild-eyed and shampoo-fresh. "FRAYMAN! I'M HERE! I'VE JUST COME FROM THE BEAUTY PARLOR! I WANT MY FUCKING FER-RAGAMOS! I HOPE THOSE COCKSUCKERS IN THE SHOE DEPARTMENT DIDN'T TOUCH THEM. I'LL BE FUCKING PISSED IF THEY DID!"

Lorraine began to eye my customer and the new L.A.M.B. satchel she was looking at.

"Is that L.A.M.B. bag new?" she cooed, "I ADORE Gwen Stefani's bags! Frayman, why didn't you tell me there were new L.A.M.B.s? I told you I collect them!"

"We just put them out," I replied, "I was going to show them to you first thing."

"Get me a new one out of the back!"

"We only got one of each, but I can always call another store if you want."

Lorraine's full focus turned to the L.A.M.B. She stared at the bag as if she wanted to eat it or would die without it. When she set her mind to devouring something in the store, whether it was a fancy blouse, Ferragamo shoes, or another handbag, she stopped at nothing until it was going home with her.

The other customer stared back, fearful and completely unnerved: "I don't want this. You can help her, I'm gonna look around some more."

"I WANT IT THEN!" howled Lorraine, "I'M NEXT IN LINE, YOU HAVE TO LET ME HAVE IT. I'M FUCKING NEXT IN LINE, GODDAMN IT!"

The rattled woman huffed, handed it to her, and walked off.

"Fucking slutty bitch," Lorraine whispered to me. "She wasn't gonna buy shit anyway. Fucking Lookie-Loo cocksucker."

Lorraine was right.

I'd been helping the lady for twenty minutes with no sale or interest. She was a total Lookie-Loo.

"I'm taking this motherfucker," said Lorraine, "That little cocksucker can't have it back. This little L.A.M.B. is mine now. Hold on to it, and don't fucking let go of it. And I want a goddamn wallet. You know I have to have a fucking wallet to match!"

I thanked my lucky retail stars.

The Shoposaurus had run off the Lookie-Loo.

I loved riding on the back of the most powerful animal in the Handbag Jungle.

When Lorraine came in to pick up merchandise, it typically went like this: "Hi Lorraine!" I'd say with my shit-pleasing retail smile, "I got your navy Ferragamo shoes."

"All THREE pairs? I wanted THREE pairs in navy," she'd respond, as Eau de Goldberg (powder plus ashtray) wafted over me.

Lorraine was constantly worried about things she loved being discontinued. She feared waking up one morning in the future and discovering there was no replacement for her worn, scratched-up, beloved Ferragamos in navy. So she took on the Costco approach and bought in bulk. Even when we're talking Ferragamo shoes at $350 a pair. It's a very Shoposaurus Carnotaurus thing to do.

"Yes, Lorraine! All three pairs are here!" I'd announce excitedly, "I've got them on hold in the shoe department. The manager said they just came in."

"FRAAAAAYMAN!!!" she'd bawl at me, "SONOFABITCH! I don't want those fucking asshole cocksuckers touching my Ferragamos with their filthy fucking fingers! And you know how those idiot bastards are in the shoe department; what doesn't get lost gets stolen. FRAYMAN! GO GET MY FUCKING FERRAGAMOS OUT OF THERE!"

Whenever Lorraine got slightly riled up, sounding like she was born in a battleship on the high seas during wartime, I did my best to put out her fire, "Cool your jets, Lorraine, Your fucking Ferragamos are fine."

I quickly learned early on that when Lorraine mouthed off, it wasn't directed at me personally; it was only her tribal way of communicating. The words that flowed from her massive hot-lava mouth just happened to be football locker room style.

Her favorite potty-mouth phrase was "fucking asshole cocksucker." Months after meeting Lorraine Goldberg, I wondered how this could be. She wore Ferragamo shoes with bows on them, bought Fendi handbags, and went to the beauty parlor every Saturday to pouf up her hair. How could a woman who looks like this actually use the word cocksucker in a sentence?

Why was everyone a fucking asshole cocksucker?

An insight into this eccentricity of Lorraine's revealed itself gradually as I began to know a little bit more about her background over the years. Lorraine had never been married or had a boyfriend *or girlfriend* that I've ever known of (and believe me, I prodded), so it was quite possible Lorraine Goldberg might just have been a fifty-year-old virgin. Her only companion was a nine-year-old French poodle named Mitzy.

Lorraine was born an only child into a family that owned a successful warehousing business in Los Angeles. When she was in her twenties, her father died and she became responsible for her aging mother, who lived across the hall in their high-rise condo. After her father passed, Lorraine did what any good, strong-willed, big, tall, young girl with unpleasant looks would do.

She took over her father's warehousing business.

One day Lorraine called me for an update on the status of my quest to find her a Nicole Miller silk blouse with playing cards on it in size XL because the size L that I had sold her was too small.

Her mood was feisty and dark as she began complaining about one of her managers. Moments later she blamed the entire male race ("Except for you, Frayman") for all of her problems. She confessed that the men in the warehouse pissed her off continually and tried to take advantage of her because she was the boss. Apparently no other women worked in the Goldberg warehousing business. Lorraine was the only one.

Bingo! You don't have to be Dr. Phil to see the writing on that bathroom wall. For me, being surrounded daily by a bunch of men in a warehouse would be a porno fantasy come true. For Lorraine, it ended up being the absorption of a lot of bad language.

At that moment I understood why she shopped so hard, buying boatloads of cosmetics, Nicole Miller silk blouses, and Italian shoes with bows on them.

They made her feel feminine.

Surprisingly, there were times when Lorraine could control her cocksucking and fucking and actually live up to her Jackie O drag-queen look. This usually happened when she met other people who had an air of importance or authority, like managers, buyers, or celebrities.

For instance, whenever she'd chat with Suzy Davis-Johnson on the aisle in front of handbags as she often did, Lorraine Goldberg transformed herself into a complete lady and became Big Fancy Customer Royalty.

"I just absolutely *adore* the new Kate Spade handbag collection. They are stunning! Her most beautiful yet. I bought three of them from Frayman. I don't know what I'd do without him. He calls me the minute something fabulous arrives! I just spent Two thousand dollars!"

"I'm so happy to hear that, Lorraine," Suzy would reply with a gleam in her eye, "We appreciate your business, and Freeman is certainly one of our best! You know, Lorraine, I'd love for you to have lunch in our restaurant on me."

Lorraine would blush like a schoolgirl.

"Why, thank you so much, Suzy. That is so kind and thoughtful. I just *adore* this store. I don't shop anywhere else. This is absolute heaven for me."

Lorraine could play high society with the best of them, but there were times certain people or situations ruffle her scales, causing an eruption of the language gore that I love so much.

"I never want that fucking bitch girl at the Estée Lauder counter waiting on me again," Lorraine barked one day. "She's a little smart-mouthed, fucking asshole cocksucker! She can suck my dick, the little blond whore."

"Lorraine, it's okay," I said, attempting to soothe her while trying to hold back the tears of laughter that would pour out of me later in the day, "You just call me and I'll get your eyeliners."

"It's Free Gift time and I'm buying six eyeliners in cobalt and I expect to get three gifts. Can you get me the extra gifts? Sometimes they won't give out extra gifts."

"It's okay. I'm friends with the manager, Melinda. She'll give them to me."

All Shoposaurus Carnotaurus types are hungry for free gifts, but Lorraine is never satisfied with one free gift. She wants as many as she can get her claws on.

"I'm buying five handbags and five wallets, I should get ten gifts!"

I've learned over the years to get Lorraine "extras" of anything that's free. If the handbag department was giving away a gift-with-purchase necklace, or Fendi had a gift-with-purchase bath set with perfume, I would hoard as many as I could when no one was looking and then give them to Lorraine, telling her, "Don't worry, I got you extras." I always did whatever I could to make sure my Shoposaurus Carnotaurus was well fed.

Though Lorraine thrived on playing the part of high roller and spending as if she owned an oil well, her shopping expeditions were not always easy grab-and-buy situations.

Every item needed to be probed closely for flaws.

Lorraine would immediately reject any merchandise that had the slightest scratch, dent, or thread missing. If something was a little off, a little not quite right, a little shop-worn, Lorraine Goldberg, Shoposaurus Carnotaurus, roared louder than King Kong.

"AAAAAAAAAAAAH DO YOU SEE THAT?? THERE'S A CREASE ON THE BOTTOM OF THIS KATE SPADE HANDBAG! I don't want it. Take it away. Get me a new one!"

Yes, everything Lorraine bought needed to be pristine, in mint condition.

If I was able to fulfill her neurotic need for perfection by finding a brand-new Kate Spade in the stockroom that was still wrapped in the plastic and tissue it was shipped in, she glowed like a child about to unwrap a pile of birthday presents.

One time Lorraine dragged me to the Clarins Cosmetics counter to stock up on ten jars of foot-soothing cream during a Clarins free-gift promotion. She wanted enough cream to last her for five years. Or maybe it was for Mitzy's paws.

The Clarins salesgirl, who looked like a timid ten-year-old, was completely astounded when Lorraine announced she was buying ten jars of foot-soothing cream. She quickly added that I was her personal shopper and I'd be ringing them up in handbags.

"You want ten jars?" the Clarins Girl said, her eyes growing wide.

"Did I stutter?" said Lorraine, all bitchy, "I want ten jars of foot-soothing lotion and four free gifts and gift bags."

The Clarins Girl raised her brows over her wide eyes.

"We only give one free gift with a purchase of one hundred dollars or more. . . ."

I cut Clarins Girl off before Shoposaurus Carnotaurus bit her head off. "The four free gifts have already been approved by your manager, Melinda. Ms. Goldberg is one of The Big Fancy's best customers, especially in cosmetics."

No longer talking, the Clarins Girl quickly began putting stacks of boxed creams in a bag. Lorraine stopped her immediately, "Hold on a minute there, princess. I need to check every jar. I've had fuckin' problems before. Some of these bitches have a sinkhole in the middle. They should be filled to the fuckin' top, with a swirl."

We all began opening jars of foot cream. To our amazement and disappointment, Lorraine was correct. Many of the jars had slight dips in the center.

"YOU SEE THAT!" Lorraine howled, "SINKHOLE! SINK-HOLE! SINKHOLE!"

We opened twelve jars of soothing foot cream between the three of us. Only two passed inspection.

Lorraine found the first perfect one.

She fondled the jar as if it was a scientific wonder.

"You see," she said softly, pointing her shiny red fingernail at the cream inside, "It has a fuckin' swirl that peaks. There is no dip, no sinking. It's completely fuckin' full. All the rest of these are defective and should be sent back. Every single motherfucking one of them has a sinkhole! They're all shit!"

Lorraine looked up at the girl while screwing the lid on the jar of foot-soothing cream that had passed inspection. "You need to go in the back and bring out more. Each one must be checked."

The Clarins Girl jumped to the task, quickly realizing it was best not to anger a Shoposaurus.

"Absolutely. I'll be just a moment, ma'am."

"I know she thinks I'm a fuckin' nut job," Lorraine leaned in and said to me. "But if I'm buying ten jars of foot-soothing cream at sixty-five dollars each, every goddamn cocksucking jar had better be filled and have a perfect fuckin' swirl at the top."

"Right you are, Lorraine; I couldn't agree more," I said, chuckling at her lunacy.

Lorraine was correct in her assessment of what other people at The Big Fancy thought about her. They thought she was a nut job.

I had customers and fellow salespeople both exclaim, "How can you wait on that woman? She's awful! She's treating you so badly!"

I just smiled at them and replied, "Her bark is worse than her bite. She's actually one of my best customers."

Most didn't know that sometimes Lorraine turned into a ferocious prehistoric beast with other salespeople just to entertain me because I found it wildly amusing.

Yes, I will burn in Retail Hell.

As the proud owner of one of the most ravenous Shoposaurus Carnotaurus in all of Los Angeles, I had no choice but to tame or be killed.

Several months after I started waiting on her, Lorraine and I had our Survival of the Fittest Death Match.

The showdown was about Spring Green bath towels.

I'd already sold her five of them. But because Lorraine *adored* the color and brand so much, she feared they would not last the next nuclear blast and panicked, wanting me to secure her five more.

They were sold out at all The Big Fancy stores, and the buyers refused to order just five towels. I hit a wall. No more Spring Green towels. Anywhere. And Lorraine would not let up. Her need for more Spring Green towels had gone beyond the level of shopping junkie. During a department rush one afternoon, she went full-on Shoposaurus Carnotaurus crazy over the phone as I watched Douche and Cammie ring up sales.

Lorraine screamed in my ear, "I'VE GOT TO HAVE THOSE FUCKING SPRING GREEN TOWELS YOU FUCKING ASS-HOLE COCKSUCKER!"

That's it. No more. I've listened to this Shoposaurus Carnotaurus roar long enough. Time to let her have it.

The foul mouth of Lorraine Goldberg began pouring out of me!

"You know what Lorraine," I replied heatedly, "I am NOT one of your fucking asshole cocksuckers. It's totally fucking busy in here and I'm losing sales listening to you bitch and moan about getting more stupid fucking Spring Green towels when you already have five. I've had enough of your shit! I can't fucking take it any more! You OBNOXIOUS FUCKING BITCH! FUCK YOU!"

I hung up on her.

Shaking with anger, I retreated to the stockroom. At any second I expected a call from Suzy Davis-Johnson. I planned to tell Satan I could no longer wait on Lorraine. Enough was enough. I sat and medicated myself with Ruffles potato chips.

Then Cammie called on the stockroom phone.

"Lorraine's calling and she's really sorry. Talk to her. Give her a second chance," she said, sounding like a marriage counselor.

Minutes later, Lorraine and I were back to normal. Shoposaurus and greedy Retail Slave.

"I'm sorry I called you a fucking asshole cocksucker," she said.

"And I'm sorry I called you an obnoxious fucking bitch," I replied.

After that pinnacle moment, Lorraine was in the palm of my hand and I could do no wrong. By confronting her in her own dirty-mouthed way, I'd won her over.

But the name-calling didn't stop.

It transcended bitchiness and became our unique way of showing friendship for each other.

"Lorraine, you're such a backward fucking whore!" I would say after watching her terrorize a new salesperson in the Kitchen Access department.

"Fuck you times two, Freeman, and get that deluxe Crock-Pot down off the shelf so I can see it better, you cocksucker," she would respond, not even looking at me.

Having Lorraine Goldberg as my personal customer may have caused me perspiration, exhaustion, and agitation at times, but there was always a sale at the end.

Not only did she drag me all over the store, grabbing everything from bras to bedding, but she would buy duplicates of things she loved, sometimes spending thousands of dollars. I guess a lonely woman in her fifties with a successful warehouse business has a lot of extra cash to burn.

Another perk to being Lorraine's little Retail Slave was that she rarely returned anything I sold her. This was a tremendous advantage because some of the other crazy customers The Big Fancy threw at me didn't keep what they bought. There was nothing worse than being deep-fried by a lunatic shopper for several hours just to watch her return everything two days later.

The Big Fancy's Once a Year Sale was Lorraine's favorite time of the year. She'd call me on the phone, so excited it sounded as if she'd just won the lottery.

"FRAYMAN, FRAAAAAYMAN! I GOT THE SALE CATA-LOG! ARE YOU READY! I'VE GOT MY LIST! THERE'S A CRAPLOAD OF STUFF I WANT!"

Within minutes she'd dictate a list to me that was three scratch-pad pages long and included clothes, shoes, bedding and bath products, cosmetics, kitchen products, and, of course, handbags.

Though I was blessed by the retail gods to have my very own Shoposaurus spending so much without returning, helping her during a sale would nearly kill me when I went to retrieve those three pages of Big Fancy merchandise.

Countless phone calls turned my ears sweaty as she pondered what she wanted next: "I just *love* the royal blue blouse on page six, but on page seventeen they're showing a similar blouse in cadet blue? What do you think? Should I get both? What's the difference between royal and cadet, anyway? Why the FUCK are they showing two blouses so close in color?"

After scouring the catalog, Lorraine made several trips into the store. I'd drag merchandise out of one stockroom after another all over the store so she could preview all the sale merchandise from different departments. After hours of deliberation, Lorraine picked out enough sale crap to dress half the women at the Los Angeles Mission shelter.

Judy always got slightly aggravated with me because a large section of the handbag stockroom had to be cleared to accommodate the mountain of clothing, cosmetics, and shoes Lorraine wanted to have held till the sale, but what could she say? Nothing. It's all for Lorraine Goldberg. One of Big Fancy's high rollers. A friend of Suzy Davis-Johnson.

On sale day, Lorraine returned to the store in full-on Shoposaurus mode. She was ready to shop and thrilled out of her mind. "FRAAAAAAAAAYMAN! FRAAAAAAAAAYMAN! I'M HERE FOR THE ONCE A YEAR SALE! I'M READY TO BUY!"

She'd gaze upon her loot like she was looking at it for the first time. Then the shopping would start all over again, with Lorraine covering every inch of the entire store. Hard-core.

Looking for *more* bargains. Looking for *more* stuff to buy.

Several hours later, after the Shoposaurus had plundered, all of her treasures had to be rung up. By me.

And ringing up Lorraine during the sale was always a confusing, exhausting mess. Prices were wrong. Tags missing. Loose threads found. Stains discovered. Lorraine also demanded that every single item be boxed in Big Fancy gift boxes and wrapped in tissue, and the clothing put neatly in plastic garment covers.

"I'm spending two grand, I want the fucking works!"

I came to know more about Lorraine than possibly any other person on earth, including her doctors. I knew every size she wore: 12 wide in shoes; 12–14 long in slacks; L or XL in blouses; 42B in bras; 9 in panties; and L in gloves. She hated dresses, cheap fabric, and tight fits. She wasn't big on fine jewelry but preferred gold to silver. I knew the details of all the cosmetic products she used from six different lines. Lorraine's handbags had to be roomy with handles, and she rarely bought shoulder styles (unless one was an It Bag of the moment). Wallets had to be checkbook-style. Her favorite colors were green, blue, and RED! Lots and lots of red. Lorraine loved scarves and blouses in bright colors with loud, unique designs and bold prints. She had a fetish for ultra-soft bath towels, 1,000-thread-count sheets that don't wrinkle, and the newest kitchen gadget, though she rarely cooked. And the woman would buy anything with a French poodle on it because it reminded her of Mitzy.

With the bounty of goods I sold to Lorraine Goldberg day in and day out, I did wonder how one single woman could buy so much stuff.

Where did it all go?

She couldn't possibly wear or use everything she bought.

Lorraine once told me there was a room in her condo for all of "Freeman's Things." This is what she called everything I sold her. Freeman's Things.

Yes, that creeps me out.

Because she bought more than she needed and it was impossible for her to actually wear or use everything, it all ended up in this so-called special room. I never saw the Freeman's Things room, but she used to tell me it was piled high with gift boxes and bags of stuff I've sold her. It often made me nervous to think that one day, she could just flip out and decide that it all needed to go back to The Big Fancy.

Back up the U-Haul truck, Lorraine Goldberg is returning Freeman's Things. Somebody call an ambulance! 441064 is going into cardiac arrest.

Although she spent tens of thousands of dollars with me and had a room overflowing with Ferragamo shoes and Fendi handbags, the most dramatic thing Shoposaurus Carnotaurus ever did for me at the Store had nothing to do with her need for designer feed.

It had to do with a Nasty-Ass Thief—my term for the scummy, no-good, shoplifting fraudulent customers who streamed into The Big Fancy on a daily basis.

One afternoon, while Lorraine was in the throes of seeing a new group of Ferragamo bags, a short, skinny, young druggie girl so strung out that she was shaking stumbled up to the Corral.

The Druggie Nasty spoke incoherently, wanting to return a $900 Burberry tote that she had no receipt for. The Burberry bag wasn't from our store, and the style wasn't in any of the recent catalogues or the Store's POS system. It had to be fake, jacked from another store, or stolen from someone's closet.

After telling Nasty several times there was nothing I could do, she turned ugly and screamed:

"I'm not going anywhere until I get help . . . here at this store . . . with this bare-berry purse . . . you have to do it . . . NOW!" she said, swaying like a willow.

I felt the heat of Lorraine's stare, as she watched Nasty and me argue about her not being able to return the bag.

When Nasty got bitchy and said I didn't know my merchandise, Shoposaurus moved in.

And stood in front of her.

"Miss, he SAID, he can't fuckin' help you any further," Lorraine said looking down at her. "You can fuckin' leave now. I'm next in line and I need him to help me."

The Nasty-Ass Druggie Thief sighed and looked up to the heavens. The several-foot difference between them did not seem to bother her in the least.

"Was I talkin' to you, grandma? Stay out of it, you wrinkled old saggy BITCH."

Believe it or not, at least twenty seconds passed before the Shoposaurus Carnotaurus began to roar. In those twenty seconds, I watched Lorraine's pale skin turn a heated pink while the lids over her brown eyes began to flutter. Her orange lips snarled, and her hands tightened around her Fendi. Then she unleashed on Nasty like a meteorite hitting the Earth:

"LOOK, YOU DIRTY LITTLE COCKSUCKING WHORE, DON'T EVEN TRY FUCKING WITH ME, SHITBAG! I HAVE THE MOTHERFUCKING MALL POLICE ON SPEED DIAL, AND I'LL TAKE YOUR BITCH ASS OUT FASTER THAN YOU CAN GET YOUR FUCKING PIECE-OF-SHIT CAR STARTED, YOU SKINNY LITTLE FUCKING CUNT!"

Nasty-Ass Druggie Thief was stunned. Speechless.

And maybe a little scared.

Lorraine had to be at least three of her. She would have squashed Nasty flat into the carpet with her size-12-wide Ferragamo-clad foot.

Lorraine glared at Nasty, breathing hard, "I SUGGEST YOU GET THE FUCK OUT OF HERE BEFORE I REALLY GET FUCKING PISSED OFF!"

Shaking like an A-bomb about to detonate, Lorraine quickly opened her Fendi and began digging for what I guessed was her cell, while unloading one swear word after another.

Nasty-Ass Druggie Thief swayed a few times and then stuffed the Burberry back in her tattered shopping bag. She zigzagged away without a single exit word.

"Lorraine," I said, "I really appreciate you coming to my defense, but you have to be careful with some of these people. You never know what they'll do."

She rolled her eyes, let out a Shoposaurus cackle, and replied, "Fuck that little gang-banging crack whore. I've got a fucking can of pepper spray in here and a forty-five in the glove compartment of my car. I'll blow her scrawny ass to kingdom come. Fucking asshole cocksucker, she can suck my motherfucking dick."

Still bubbling with adrenaline, seconds later my badass Shoposaurus Carnotaurus found what she was digging for in her satchel.

"HERE IT IS!" Lorraine yelled out, holding up a little can of pepper spray like it was air freshener. "I'm fully licensed and trained. I know how to bring anyone down to their fucking knees, shoot it right in their cocksucking motherfucking eyeballs!"

"Lorraine, you continue to shock the shit out of me!"

"C'mon" she said, dropping the pepper spray back into her Fendi, "Let's go get a latte, I'm buyin'. And I need a goddamn cigarette."

Monique Jonesworthy, Nasty-Ass Thief

Like handbags, Nasty-Ass Thieves come in all shapes, sizes, and colors. There are men, women, teenagers, children, white, Black, Asian, Latino, Russian, Middle Eastern, European, and yes, even Alien. They are fat, skinny, young, old, gay, straight, ritzy, trashy, pretty, ugly, poor, and yes, even Warren Buffet rich.

The faces of Nasty-Ass Thieves are many. There's no discrimination on their wretched bus bound for Retail Hell's sinful abyss.

In fact, this melting pot of evildoers could easily form their own worldwide coalition and call it United Nasty-Ass Nations. They would hold "conventions" next door to malls and Big Fancy Stores, and offer in-store training seminars on how to pilfer like a pro.

Monique Jonesworthy was a member of the United Nasty-Ass Nations. A black woman in her thirties with a gap between her two front teeth, Monique Jonesworthy was a potpourri of bogusness, deemed one of Big Fancy's Most Wanted Nasty-Ass Thieves by many throughout the store. If she wasn't shoplifting, she was buying with stolen credit cards or bad checks. And all of her returns were problematic, with no receipts, wrong receipts, missing receipts, tampered receipts, or torn price tags.

"I want to return this purse," Monique always said, not knowing or caring that a thirteen-hundred-dollar Fendi satchel is not a purse, it's a fucking handbag.

What she'd say after that depended on the "character" she'd adopted for the day.

Monique Jonesworthy had completely eluded The Big Fancy security team by cleverly changing her look every time she showed up at the store. Using hats, wigs, sunglasses, and clothes, she had more disguises than Jennifer Garner in *Alias*.

When she came up to the counter, at first we almost never recognized her.

One time I saw her approach Judy as Church-Going Monique, dressed in her Sunday best. A big pink frilly hat sat atop her head while a revolting green-and-purple striped dress wrapped around her fat body. She looked like a walking Easter egg—a rotten one.

"I want to return this purse," said Church-Going Monique to Judy, "I just came from church and *Lawd*, what a service, God bless. I am filled with the love of Jesus! And I got me this Kate Spade purse to go with my dress, but you can see it ain't a good match. I lost my receipts, but I'm sure you can take care of me. What a beautiful Sunday. I am sorry you have to work on a beautiful day like today."

Judy did not look like she was having a Jesus kind of day as she did Monique's bogus return.

Another time I waited on Monique after she had disguised herself as a movie producer. Wearing sleek black sunglasses, short black hair, and a black pinstriped suit, she ambled up to the counter holding a phone and talking into a headset loudly enough that I would hear every word before she had any contact with me.

"I'm at the store right now returning the purse we don't need for the movie," said Movie-Producer Monique into her mouthpiece, "Should be back on the set in about twenty. Yeah girl, I know what you're talkin' about. Hell no! He said that? Girl, that Marlon is the shit. Hey, I'm at the counter now. Hold on."

Movie-Producer Monique put a shopping bag on the counter and said, "I want to return this purse and I'm in a hurry. I have to be back on the set. I'm one of the producers for the new Wayans Brothers movie and we bought this purse to use in the movie and we ain't using it, so I'm bringing it back."

I almost burst out laughing right in her face.

Even before I realized it was Monique behind the sunglasses and headset, I knew something was up with that story, so I played along.

"How cool! I love the Wayans brothers. What's their new movie about?"

"Oh, I can't tell you that," said Movie-Producer Monique, "It's top secret. I'm not allowed to talk about any of that. There are contracts and shit. Hold on . . ." said Movie-Producer Monique, raising a finger and then pretending to go back to a call that I was quickly beginning to think didn't exist. "What'd you say, girl? I'm at the counter returning the purse. Yeah. Uh-huh. Yeah. Ain't nothin' you can do about it. They just gonna have to git it right. Yeah. What? Marlon wants to talk to me? Put sweet lips on. Hey, Baby, what's up? Yeah, I'm almost done here. Doin' the purse return. What's that? Yeah, they takin' care of it right now. I'll tell 'em to hurry, I know you got a scene to shoot, Baby."

Movie-Producer Monique was not one of her better roles.

"No problem, tell Marlon I said, hey, and I suppose you'll be needing cash for this return?" I asked her, unable to resist the sarcasm.

Monique didn't even tell her star to hold. My question got priority. "Hell yeah, the movie studio paid cash and they want cash back, I'm sure."

Movie-Producer Monique got her cash for Marlon.

Another memorable disguise of Monique's was Trailer-Park Monique. She sported a bright green scarf around her head like a pirate and wore square white sunglasses and an oversized T-shirt displaying a map of all the subway stops in New York City, and said, "I want to return this purse. My man got it for me and it's ugly as sin. He ain't got no taste. I told him he shouldn't be buyin' me no purses. Women git their own purses."

But, whatever clever persona Monique attempted to conjure up, it always wore thin when she revealed some problem with the transaction: She didn't have all her receipts, they never put a proof of purchase sticker on the tag, or the tag was torn when she bought it.

And then she'd smile, exposing the gap between her two front teeth.

The gig was up. We all knew who it was.

If Monique Jonesworthy didn't get her money back, she'd start to scream as if she was being physically assaulted. "I GOT MY DAMN

RECEIPT. WHAT'S Y'ALL PROBLEM HERE? HUH? IS IT CUZ I'M BLACK?" Regardless of her disguise, if Monique was refused, the first card she played was always the race card. She tried this with Tiffany, who calmly replied, "I'm sorry, but have you not noticed the color of my skin?" Monique stared at her unfazed and then said, "Yeah, well, you sound like a cracka, might as well be one, givin' a sista a hard time." Tiffany was pissed. Monique had to get her refund in Customer Service that day.

If Monique got denied by everyone in the store, it was well known that she was not afraid to call Big Fancy CEO Mr. Michael. Somewhere along her lengthy list of bogus returns, she must have called him to complain and gotten her way. And against our pleas not to, more often than not, he approved many Nasty-Ass Thief returns. All in the name of customer service. I'm convinced Mr. Michael would probably let Monique return everything in her closet if she wanted to. Even her nasty-ass underwear.

After one of Monique's appearances in our department, Stories circulated for days:

"Monique just returned a twelve-hundred-dollar Marc Jacobs with a torn ticket and no sticker on the back."

"Did you hear? Monique returned three Coach wallets yesterday with no receipts!"

"Monique just wrote a bad check using a driver's license with someone else's name!"

"Cammie just saw Monique shove a Coach clutch down her pants and walk out!"

In spite of her frequent visits to our store, Monique Jonesworthy never got caught by Big Fancy's security. For anything.

Why? Because they were lazy, moronic losers most of the time.

They'd tell us they needed more evidence. They needed to catch her in the act. They needed to have her on camera. They needed this. They needed that. They just couldn't arrest her until they had everything they needed.

So because of that, Monique Jonesworthy screwed me and all the other Big Fancy Retail Slaves over plenty of times. Once when she was cleverly disguised as a hip-hop fashionista, wearing a trendy pink workout suit, New York Yankees baseball cap, rhinestone-covered sunglasses, and some serious bling around her neck, I didn't even know it was her until it was too late.

Hip-Hop Monique knew exactly what she wanted and bought a $3,000 Bottega Veneta hobo from me, paying in cash with a wad of $100 bills. Not believing who this hip-hop princess was, but also believing that those girls have an insatiable appetite for All Things Designer, I wasn't suspicious in the least.

That is, until I handed her the wrapped-up Bottega in a shopping bag and she grinned at me, unveiling two big front teeth with a space in between.

Monique Jonesworthy? Oh NO! Please God, NO! Don't let it be her.

All of the past split-teeth smiles Monique had flashed while committing offenses played through my mind like a training video for Dental Reconstruction School.

I'm fucked! Totally fucked! Hip-Hop Monique is going to do something nasty with this three-thousand-dollar Bottega Veneta hobo and my fucking employee number is on it! Holy shit!

"Isn't your name Monique?" I said, feeling nauseous.

"Monique?" she replied coyly, "Nah, y'all got me confused with some other girl. My name is Shatiqua. Thanks for helpin' with the purse. Catcha later." Before I could say anything else, Hip-Hop Monique took her $3,000 BV hobo and split.

What happened after that was Retail Hell at its worst. Apparently Hip-Hop Monique had *another* $3,000 Bottega Veneta hobo that she more than likely stole from another store. She then went to two different Big Fancy Stores and returned them both on my employee number by splitting the receipt and the price tag. I got hit with two returns that The Big Fancy took back my commissions on—one of which I was never even paid for. It wasn't uncommon for the Store to allow customers to return with just one receipt, so Nasty-Ass Thieves doing multiple returns on one set of receipts would go crazy and make all kinds of instant cash—at the expense of us salespeople. (Thankfully, some brilliant computer geek finally figured out a way to track the Nasties' returning, and it's no longer a problem at most stores. Merchandise can only be returned once!)

Feeling as if Hip-Hop Monique had just mugged me and taken $140 right out of my wallet, I stormed up the escalator and into

Two-Tone Tammy's office. It was nothing new to her, and she couldn't have cared less. In her Sicky-Sweet voice, she said, "You'll have to fill out this form. We don't handle commission credits here in HR. It's something Security must do." I filled out the form and waited for someone from Security to get in touch with me. I waited and waited and waited and waited. Nothing happened. No one knew anything. It was like dealing with a government office. Like everyone at The Big Fancy who got screwed by Nasties doing multiple returns on them, I got tired of asking for my $140 credit and forgot about it.

Then, late one night, months after that horrible incident, I was working the closing shift alone, and at about 7:30, Nasty-Ass Thief Monique resurfaced.

This time she had disguised herself as what she thought the winner of *America's Next Top Model* would look like. Fashion-Model Monique had long, golden-amber, flowing hair (a wig I'm sure), light blue Dolce & Gabbana shades (fake, I'm sure), chunky gold Chanel hoops (also had to be fake), a V-neck, lace-trimmed, purple silk top (covering her mom jeans), and probably a pound of makeup (poorly applied).

Fashion-Model Monique also looked like she'd dropped at least forty pounds. Maybe all the stealing she'd done had paid for a lap band. Or she'd gone on the Meth Diet.

"Hi there," said Fashion-Model Monique, all sugary and sweet, flashing her split-teeth smile, "I want to return these purses."

Fuck me with a Bottega Veneta hobo. It's Monique Jonesworthy!

I looked inside her shopping bag and saw three black Cole Haan Shoulder Flap bags, all the same. Identical.

After taking them out and getting a closer look at the tags, I discovered the proof-of-purchase stickers were torn and looked as if they'd been peeled off other tags. Totally shady.

"I've been out of the country shootin' for *Elle* magazine," Fashion-Model Monique explained, "My photographer had me get 'em, but he nixed them at the last second, so I need to return them and get my cash back, cuz I paid cash."

In the past I would have had a good time playing a game with her by asking what country she was shootin' her *Elle* spread in and what did she wear, but all I could think about was the $140 in commission she stole from me.

But this time, I started to shake, and my face instantly looked sun-burned. I so wanted to hit her with a nearby handbag, which happened to be an Isabella Fiore with lots of hardware on it, but I had to keep my mouth shut. Any accusation made would have just bitten me on the ass. The Big Fancy would side with Monique Jonesworthy because, other than my memory, there was no proof that she was the *actual* customer who paid me $3,000 in cash on that fateful day.

Still, I felt like I had to say *something*. My fury over being robbed by Hip-Hop Monique was too deep. So I opted for one of my I-know-who-you-are-and-what-you-did approaches.

"Monique!" I said with a giant, shit-pleasing retail smile, "It's been a while. You look so different. I almost didn't recognize you."

"Excuse me, but do I know you?" said Fashion-Model Monique.

Nasties hate it when you call them by their first name. Especially ones like Monique who work so hard to cover up their identities. It's like they've just been outed.

"Oh, I've waited on you many times," I said to her calmly, "In fact, you once bought a three-thousand-dollar Bottega Veneta bag from me. I think you returned it—must not have worked out."

"Are you sure? I don't think that was me. I never had me one of those purses before."

That's because you returned TWO of them on me, you nasty fucking bitch.

Monique knew exactly who I was.

I stared her down.

"I do returns for you all the time, Monique. Surely you remember me."

Fashion-Model Monique did not like this at all.

"I ain't never seen you before in my life. Are you gonna help me, or what? I didn't come in here for you to get all up in my business and ask me questions about who the hell I am. You gotta problem? You best be calling your manager, cuz I know how this place operates."

Fashion-Model Monique was right. She did know. And that is why I caved without a fight and processed her bogus return. Later on some salesperson at a Big Fancy would be getting some bad news from me. They'd have to go fight their HR manager and Security. I hoped they'd have better luck than I did.

"Take this up to Customer Service. Your money is up there. You know the drill," I said dryly, handing her a refund slip so she could collect cash.

Fashion-Model Monique flashed a smile, showing off those wretched teeth, and said, "Thank you so much, pleasure doing business with y'all."

As Nasty Monique headed down the aisle toward the up escalator to go cash in her chips, I was about to start cleaning the glass countertop when a wonderful, serendipitous thing happened.

I saw something on the counter that wasn't a designer handbag.

It was a lump of keys attached to a large key ring with three dirty pink-and-green pompoms and a grime-covered troll doll with orange hair. Fashion-Model Monique had run off and left her nasty keys behind. I took a piece of tissue and, using it as a glove, I grabbed the pompom-troll-doll keys.

Payback's a bitch. The way I saw it, I was finally receiving goods worth $140. Sure, they were gross and dirty and useless, but nevertheless, I had paid a lot for them. $140 is expensive for keys you'll never use!

A smile more devious and nasty than anything Monique had ever produced with her split teeth crept across my face. I held up the pompom-troll-doll key ring full of keys and made them jingle for my own enjoyment.

"Now you see them . . . now you don't!"

I dropped the keys into the trashcan under the register and covered them up with the tissue.

Fifteen minutes later Fashion-Model Monique came racing into the Handbag Jungle, looking anything but ready for a photo shoot.

In fact, she looked quite distressed. "I can't find my keys. Have you seen them anywhere?"

"Keys?" I said, with great joy, "I haven't seen any keys. Are you sure you left them here?"

"I ain't been but a few other places," said Monique, "I looked all over. They must be in here somewhere."

I decided to have some fun.

"I'm not busy right now," I said, "I can help you look for your keys, Monique."

She looked at me funny when I said her name, but then quickly went back to searching and worrying. I took Monique all over the handbag department looking for her keys.

"You can't miss them," she said, "They got pink and green pom-poms and a little troll doll with orange hair."

You mean grimy, grody pompoms and a cootie-covered troll doll.

Monique searched every crack of the department (except the trash can under the register, of course). She dropped to her squishy knees and looked under tables, sat on the floor and pulled stuffing out of bags, and even rifled through the wallet bins hoping her keys fell behind a stack.

"Look under all the fixtures and be sure to check any handbag you were looking at," I said, chuckling under my breath as I stared at her fat ass sticking out from underneath the sale table as she scanned the floor on all fours.

After twenty minutes or so, a haggard-looking Fashion-Model Monique gave up.

"I don't know what I'm going to do," she whined, "I don't have my cell on me and my car keys are on the ring. I don't know what I'm going to do."

You have nine hundred fifty-three dollars in your pocket, you fucking Nasty-Ass Thief. I'm sure you'll be just fine.

"If you go to Mall Information, I think they can suggest a really good towing service," I offered, doing the happy dance inside my head.

Monique frowned at me, mumbled something about mall security, and shook her head.

Perhaps she'd burned her bridges with them as well.

"Sorry, Monique," I said, "If they show up, I'll take them to Cus-tomer Service right away."

Fashion-Model Monique wandered away in a daze.

Unfortunately, that wasn't the end of Monique. There were many other disguises that followed. But for once I felt I had really gotten my money's worth. The thrill of my overdue purchase lingered as my fantasizing screenwriter mind played out the story of how Monique Jonesworthy was dealing without her pompom-troll-doll key-ring loss.

It went just like a MasterCard commercial:

Towing her 1988 Honda Accord to her apartment . . .

$182.

Replacing a broken window she had to crawl through to get inside her apartment because the apartment-complex manager wasn't around to give her a spare key . . .

$328.

Having a locksmith replace all the locks because of her lost pompom-troll- doll key ring . . .

$583.

Smile on Queer-Eye Handbag Guy's face . . .

Priceless.

Is Deescount?

Perhaps the most annoying shoppers in all of Retail Hell are the people I call Discount Rats. Aggressive and usually underhanded, these sale-sniffing rodent-customers stop at nothing in their hunt for any kind of discount. They beg and haggle us to death, often becoming our worst nightmare and making us wish we could actually call a number like this: 1-888-Discount-Rat-Exterminators.

ACME DISCOUNT RAT REMOVAL—Stopping hagglers since 1910. You point out the stingy rats, and we'll make it so they can't afford anything! Relax and leave the bartering to us!

Big Fancy's worst Discount Rat was a woman named Patty.

I can't recall or even pronounce her last name. It had like fifty letters.

I have no idea where Patty or her name came from.

Somewhere on the Other Side of the World.

Every time I ran into her, I wished she'd just go back there.

I don't even think her real name was Patty. It probably had twenty letters and was even more unpronounceable than her last name. Like so many foreigners who take up residence in the good ole U.S. of A., Patty probably picked an easy American first name so people could remember her.

Unfortunately, I would have remembered her without an easy American first name.

Hunched over and disheveled, with clumpy hair the color of dirty hay, Patty scavenged the store like vermin in search of free garbage.

She drove us all crazy, asking for discounts on everything, trying to get more discounts on things that were already on sale, and wanting discount adjustments on items she had purchased months before. None of us knew what Patty did with all the discount bags she bought. Jules concluded she was returning them to other Big Fancy Stores, while Marsha believed her to be one of those out-of-control hoarders we've all seen on talk shows. Whatever the case, Patty was clearly a candidate for Shopaholics Anonymous.

Although I despised the actions of Discount Rats like Patty, I understood their persistence and desire to save money. We all love to get stuff on sale and often go to extremes trying to get discounts. I've had Cammie keep a pair of $200 jeans on hold for me past the allowed three-day limit so I could wait and see if they got marked down to a price just shy of free.

Okay, that was slightly underhanded, but, what the hell, I wasn't bothering anyone, just waiting for a markdown. It's a lot different from badgering a helpless salesperson.

"Excuse me, do you work here? Is this Kate Spade handbag on sale? If it's not on sale, can you give me a discount?"

Whenever a customer asked me for a discount, it always surprised me. How is it they thought I, a lowly Big Fancy salesperson, was authorized to hand out discounts at the whim of a request?

"Sure! No problem! You bet! How about 50% off! You look like a nice lady; why don't I go ahead and mark this new Ferragamo 75% off for you? Will that do?"

Every time I was asked for a discount, my response was the same.

"The Big Fancy does not give me authorization to discount anything."

But that rarely stopped a desperate Discount Rat from haggling.

"This bag should be discounted!" the Discount Rats whined, "It looks shopworn. There's a scratch on it. Isn't there anything you can do for me? I think I saw it on sale at another store."

I went into autopilot and repeated myself, "The Big Fancy does not give me authorization to discount anything."

The constant daily begging from Discount Rats on patrol at The Big Fancy was nothing compared to an encounter with Patty. She was the Queen of Discount Rats.

It was like playing a game of Department Store *Deal or No Deal*, but instead of a numbered briefcase, Patty would pick up a designer handbag and ask, "Is deescount?"

Every time she did this, I wanted to scream.

What do you think, Patty, you goddamn Discount Rat? No, there is no fucking deescount. No fucking Deal. The banker has left the building. You're not getting shit discounted today, Patty! GO AWAY!!!

"Is NOT deescount," I always replied.

Patty didn't notice my sarcastic mimicry. It was almost as if she didn't hear me at all.

"Is deescount?" she repeated, as if I'd suddenly change my mind.

"NO Patty, is NOT deescount," I said slower and more forcefully, like someone scolding their dog who wants to eat something gross off the sidewalk.

Patty would look up at me with her dark, Other Side of the World eyes, ignoring my command, and with a shady smile, she'd try again.

"Is deescount? Yes! You give me to! I pay it for you! We together it go to up."

It would have been so much easier if Patty had gone to night school and learned English. Then we could have at least argued about deescounts in a language I could understand.

Patty Whatever's sentences were either simple to understand or made no sense at all.

"Is for me beautifuls bag, yes. You see me to it."

When she rambled incoherently like this, I just stared at her.

"Is deescount? Give me to?" she asked.

"No Patty, NOT deescount," I said back.

"Pleeeeeez deescount for me. For Patty!"

"No deescount for Patty, sorry."

"Is scratched! Deescount scratch!"

"We don't give deescounts for scratches."

"You nice man, you gives to Patty percentages of twenty deescount?"

"Patty, I can't give you any percentages."

"Little percentages?"

"No."

"Is deescount twenty dollars?"

"No."

"Ten dollars?"

"No."

Then Patty Whatever would give up, drop the handbag she had been trying to get discounted, look around briefly, and pick up another bag.

"Is deescount?"

This was about the time I would start looking for another customer to wait on before I ended up strangling myself with the chain from a Chanel handbag.

Although I've never given Patty any kind of unauthorized discount, she never gave up and often resorted to desperate tactics.

She would wink at me. Smile at me. Bat her eyes. Pet my shoulder. Giggle. Ask how I am doing. Compliment me on my tie. Tell me how nice I am. Offer to buy me coffee.

"You drink? You want from place?" Patty would ask, pointing to the Coffee Bar.

All in the name of trying to crack my NO-deescount standing.

One day Patty showed up at the counter flashing a deceitful mousy smile. "Candies for you," she said, dropping a handful of what looked like saltwater taffies on the glass countertop. "You take. I like you."

I stared at her candies. They weren't saltwater taffies. They had weird colorful wrappings and foreign words written on them.

Candies from somewhere on the Other Side of the World.

Oh my god! I am not going to eat that! For all I know, they could be laced with some sort of drug that would overcome me instantly, making me so delirious I'd give Patty all the deescounts she wanted. Go for it, Patty! Deescounts away! How about 75% off everything! Or I could just stuff several shopping bags and give you everything free.

Patty eagerly waited for me to eat the candies.

I fingered them, trying to figure out what they were. Cyanide and Date-Rape Drug flashed through my mind. No. Not eating them.

I am not putting anything in my mouth that came from your hands. No. Fucking. Way.

I showed my appreciation with a shit-pleasing smile.

"Thank you, Patty. You're so thoughtful. I'll save them for later."

Patty's shifty eyes tried to read me, watching intently as I scooped up the brightly colored candies in one hand, opened a drawer under the register, and dropped them inside.

Patty was disappointed.

Why does she want me to eat the candies so badly? Maybe they ARE laced with something?

I considered calling mall authorities.

Patty's candies stayed in the drawer until she wandered off. Then they went directly into the trash under the register.

Besides wanting a discount on everything, one of the other reasons Discount Rat Patty was overly nice to me was because of all the shady returning and exchanging she did so often.

My impatience with her had come to such a breaking point, sometimes it was easier to just give her what she wanted if it was within Big Fancy's Customer Service Rules.

Like the yellow DKNY handbag she bought at 25% off a month ago. We had another one on our clearance table that had just been marked down to 50% off, and of course, the Discount Rat sniffed it out during her afternoon burrow.

"Is deescount more! You give deescount more to me, for Patty's."

She pulled her own yellow DKNY out of a tattered Big Fancy shopping bag.

"Is deescount more! Patty want!"

Technically, there is only a two-week turnaround for adjustments. Unless you're Patty Whatever.

"Sure Patty, I give you 25 percent more deescount on your DKNY."

Patty looked like she was going to kiss me. Thank God for the counter blocking the way. That would have been way worse than eating one of her candies.

It was a good thing I gave Patty her deescount on the DKNY, though.

If I had said no to Patty, she would have returned the one in her bag and bought the one on the sale table, causing me to do more work on the register.

Or she would have complained to Suzy Davis-Johnson, like she did when Judy wouldn't give her a price adjustment for a Juicy Couture bag she had bought six months earlier. Suzy admonished Judy, telling her that as a manager she should have accommodated Patty because she was a regular customer.

"There are times we have to bend the rules for our best customers," Suzy said.

Discount Rat Patty Whatever was in the store several times a week, but I really couldn't see how she fell into the "best customers" category.

Sneaky and conniving customers maybe, but certainly not best.

Aside from Suzy Davis-Satan's decree of letting Patty have price adjustments after the time limit had expired, there were other instances when she lost and did not get deescounts.

Like when the old Coach handbag she bought last fall never went on sale because it was popular and sold out. Patty thought that since so much time had passed, surely it was on sale by that time.

"No Patty, this is not deescount," I said, overjoyed because I was the one who had sold her the Coach bag last fall, and I sure as hell did not want to give my commission back to Big Fancy.

"You check for me," said Patty, grinning.

"I've scanned it twice, Patty. It's not on sale. No deescount."

"I later try," she responded, putting the receipt in her wallet.

Then there was the time she tried to get a second price adjustment.

"Patty, you have already received a discount on this bag."

"Is deescount more? You give me more deescount!"

"No Patty. You are only allowed *one* deescount."

And there was the time she wanted a Kenneth Cole handbag on sale, so she claimed she got it off the clearance table. She pointed to the sale sign on the table and then the Kenneth Cole.

"Is deescount! Is sale! You give Patty!"

"No Patty, it's not on sale. Someone dumped it on the table."

Again she pointed to the sale sign on the table and then the Kenneth Cole.

"Says deescount! Is sale!"

I took the bag from her hands, walked over to where the other Kenneth Coles were displayed, and pointed at them.

"IS NOT ON SALE! IS NOT DEESCOUNT!"

Forcefully, I plopped the bag down on the shelf with the others.

Patty didn't say a word after that.

But the slippery antics of Discount Rat Patty never stopped.

By far, the most underhanded thing Patty had ever tried on her quest for a deescount was when she asked me to buy a Burberry tote with my employee discount.

It was a quiet Monday morning, and she had signaled for me to assist her in the Burberry shop. When I reached her, she was petting the tote like it was a mink coat, proclaiming, "Is beautiful. Patty loves! Have a must!"

I sighed. Any second the "Is deescount?" was coming.

"I have offer," she said, "I give you money. You buy Burberry with, how you say, employee deescount. I meet you in parking arena. Pay you ten dollars. Is good for you? You do for Patty?"

Either someone had coached her or Patty had started night school. It was the only thing ever to come out of her mouth that made sense to me.

In a Nasty-Ass Thief sort of way.

Meet her in the parking structure? Use my employee discount for her? So Patty Whatever can get a deescount? And she'll pay me ten bucks? I wouldn't walk to the escalator for ten bucks. And certainly not for her! What is this loon's problem?

"Patty, I am not allowed to use my employee discount for you."

"Is okay. You do for Patty. Is good, yes?"

"No Patty, is not good. I can get into trouble."

"No trouble. We meet in parking arena."

"We are not meeting anywhere. I can't. The answer is N.O.! NO!"

"I take you lunch? You like? Where you want to go?"

"Patty, I can get fired for letting you use my discount."

"No one know. Only you and me."

"That doesn't matter."

"Pleeeez! You help Patty, I help you. Is secret. Yes?"

"No, Patty, not gonna happen. You can't use my deescount."

"Patty love Burberry. To want badly."

The department phone started to ring.

Thank you, Retail Gods!

It was one of those few times I looked forward to dealing with whatever problem would blast out of the phone line. Sometimes it was all about trading one nightmare for another in Retail Hell.

"I'm sorry," I said, "I have to get the phone, Patty."

I left her to salivate over the Burberry she was not getting my deescount on.

Apparently, I wasn't the only one Patty had hit up for an employee discount.

Cammie, Marsha, Jules, and Tiffany had all been courted.

If I ever chatted with Douche or Marci about Patty, which I didn't, I would imagine they'd also been approached as well. We all had to wait on her at one time or another.

When I asked Cammie about her experience with Patty's devious deescount request, she got pissed: "I told the fucking bitch to fuck off and get the fuck out of my face before I called security and had her fat ass thrown out of the store."

"Did you really say that to her?"

"Damn straight I did. I've fucking had it with that skanky little rat."

"What did she do?"

"She just stared at me because she's a fucking bitch."

Patty probably didn't know the word fuck.

Marsha said she'd laughed in Patty's face when prodded for use of her discount.

"Hon, I'd like to keep my job. I'm retiring soon. You know what retirement is?"

I doubt Patty knew that word either.

Tiffany told me she gave Patty the formal Big Fancy textbook response: "It is a violation of The Big Fancy employment expectations for employees to utilize their discount for anyone else but themselves. Noncompliance results in immediate termination."

A whole bunch of words Patty probably didn't know.

"Did she understand all that?" I said.

"I don't think so. She sort of just stared at me," replied Tiffany.

Jules was clever when handling Patty's desire to obtain an employee discount. She quickly brushed off the request, rushed to the clearance table, and showed Patty a similar handbag with a big reduction. "Our employee discount is only 19 percent. This bag is 50 percent off, and it's gorgeous!"

"Did she buy the bag?" I asked Jules.

"What do you think?" she replied, "Like a rat to cheese."

I had a quandary: Should I do what Cammie did and tell her to fuck off? Laugh at her like Marsha? Waste my time trying to talk her into another bag like Jules?

So many options for Discount Rat extermination. But would any of them work?

I was hoping that Patty would leave while I was handling the call, but when I finished, she was right there, gazing up at me with the plaid Burberry handbag in her hand.

"Is deescount for Patty now. You give to me your percentages," she said, flashing her ratty smile.

Since Patty didn't seem to understand anyone else's answer, I decided to speak in her own fucked up language.

"Is NO employee deescount for Patty. Is no good. Is no okay. Very, Very, BAD. Patty go to JAIL if use my deescount. Police. Crime. Prison. Big Fancy no like Patty percentages off with deescount. PATTY GO TO JAIL!"

Her face flushed with worry.

"JAIL! Patty not go jail! Ack! Oh my. No, no, no, no, NO!!!"

Patty handed me the Burberry bag and ran off.

Finally I had found a word she knew.

Jail.

The Two Virginias

Meet Virginia ... and Virginia. Both haunted The Big Fancy on a daily basis. No, they weren't ghosts. Unfortunately, they were customers. But I wish they *had* been ghosts! I'd have shooed them away with rice or garlic or burning sage.

Virginia Number One was Retired. Virginia Number Two was Crazy. Retired Virginia was in her late sixties. Widowed. A former bank teller. Crazy Virginia was in her early fifties. Single. Mentally insane. The Two Virginias were polar opposites.

Retired Virginia had bouffant hair the color of gray flannel topping an overly powdered face with too much bright makeup, reminding me of a manic Marie Antoinette. Her clothes were classic, moderately priced designer knit suits, sweater sets, gabardine slacks, and low-heeled dress shoes. And no matter what she wore, a glistening gold cross hung proudly from her neck.

Crazy Virginia had gray-brown frizzy hair the color of dried dog shit over a bloated, pockmarked face with black bean eyes. Her wardrobe consisted of a green-and-blue plaid flannel shirt with holes, light gray sweatpants, and dirty white tennis shoes. Like Retired Virginia, Crazy Virginia also had a cross hanging from her neck, though hers was much smaller and not as shiny.

Crazy Virginia wore the same outfit every single day. The only thing that made me not think of her as a homeless person was the fact that her ratty clothes were laundered, she didn't stink, and on occasion I'd see her wearing light makeup.

Retired Virginia carried brand-name handbags, and many of them had been purchased from me, usually during sales. Retired Virginia had sophisticated old-lady fashion flair.

Crazy Virginia didn't carry a handbag. Instead, she clutched a ragged, dirty, old teddy bear that looked as if it had barely survived her childhood. She never bought anything from me. Crazy Virginia had no fashion flair whatsoever. Everyone in the store had nicknamed Crazy Virginia Teddy Bear Lady.

Retired Virginia earned the title of Jabbermouth because of the way she would corner a salesperson, deluge them with her verbal diarrhea, and chatter for hours about inconsequential things in her life that none of us wanted to hear.

The bunions on her feet hurt. She ate a sandwich at The Big Fancy Restaurant that gave her indigestion. Her son was having an affair. She was tired but couldn't sleep. Jabbermouth Virginia ran one subject right into the next like a demolition derby.

Crazy Virginia, on the other hand, had liar-liar-navy-sweatpants-on-fire mouth and chattered for hours incoherently about her life as a corporate lawyer and about how the Good Lord told her things.

The clients she had were nagging her. She was late for court. Local law enforcement was harassing her. The Good Lord said not to eat any muffins that day. Crazy Virginia spurted out jumbled lies like she was running for office.

The Two Virginias came to The Big Fancy Department Store every day. During the course of their daily rituals, they passed each other constantly. They were like cars with tinted windows speeding down the freeway, ignoring each other. For hours on end they'd wander all over the store, sucking the life out of everyone. Whatever lives the Two Virginias used to live had been traded for marbled floors, mirrored columns, track lights, and the involuntary attention of Big Fancy salespeople.

Jabbermouth Virginia sauntered down the main aisle as if she was tipsy. Crazy Virginia steamrolled down it as if she was power-walking.

It wasn't until a week into my position that I actually conversed with one of the Virginias.

"You work in Handbags?" Jabbermouth Virginia asked one morning while looking at some new Isabella Fiore bags.

"So I'm told," I replied.

"Since when do they have men workin' in purses?"

"Since now, and they're called handbags."

"I know that," she replied, "I was testing you."

"Did I pass?"

"Suppose you did. How'd you end up in Hand-Bags?"

"It's where they put me."

"I guess it's as good a place as any. Don't try and sell me another handbag. I need another handbag like I need a hole in the head. Got a closet full of handbags. I can't wear them all. Why the hell did they change the powder in the mocha lattes at the Coffee Bar? It tastes like chalk. My feet are killing me today, I need a footbath. I have two bunions, one on each foot. Makes walking a bastard. I'm starving. I think I'll get a pizza from Mario's. They make the best pizza in town, but sometimes they put on too much sauce. Their sauce gives me the runs. Is there something wrong with the lighting in here? Seems darker than normal. They tryin' to cut back on electricity? It's so windy outside. I paid seventy-five dollars to have my hair done, and now the wind is gonna rip it to shreds. I don't even want to get out of my car. Wonder what's on TV tonight. Nothin' but all reruns. Maybe I'll just go read something at Borders."

Verbal diarrhea.

I just stared at her.

What the fuck is wrong with this lady? Does she have Alzheimer's? Should I call someone?

Luckily, the phone rang and saved me. Jabbermouth Virginia wandered off to bother some other person. Over time, I came to understand that she was simply chatty, a walking open book. Jabbermouth liked me because I'd stand there and let her gab my ears off.

Sometimes she'd chat about current events, but most of the time it was all about Virginia. Past and Present. I'd heard all the intimacies regarding her life. More detailed than a six-hour King Tut special on the History Channel.

Jabbermouth was born and raised on a farm in Wisconsin; had eight brothers and sisters scattered all over the U.S., some dead, some alive; and she loved babbling about them. "My oldest brother, Jerry, has been dead for ten years," she reminisced, "But when we were kids, he loved cheese. Used to eat blocks of the stuff. Even as an adult. He'd have nothin' but cheese and crackers for dinner. His favorite was cheddar. Suppose that could have been the thing that killed him. Too much cheese. I can't eat a lot of it. I get all bloated and gassy."

Okay, you can stop now, Virginia! That's way more than I want to know.

"My sister, June, lives in Utah. She's married to a jerk. I don't see her often, cause I can't stand him. I told her if she divorced the bastard, she could come live with me."

Jabbermouth had been married for forty-three years to a man named Larry, a produce manager at a grocery store. Oddly enough, she didn't talk much about him, but she did have a lot to say about her children, their spouses, and her grandchildren.

"They're all driving me nuts. David is cheating on his wife, I'm sure their two teenagers are on drugs, they're zoned out every time I see them, my daughter, Samantha, works way too many hours at her law firm. She'll never find a husband. She has no life. I told her to go out and live a little. My other daughter, Karen, is a baby machine. Her husband is a dealer at Toyota. They have six kids! She needs to have her tubes tied. That's a total of ten grandkids! Can you even imagine? Love 'em all to death, but I can't keep them straight!"

Jabbermouth resides a few miles from the store in a four-bedroom condo she shares with her divorced son, Rick, and his two small children, Jacob and Julie.

"I don't mind that they live with me, but geez! They're like pigs. Always eating. Bowls of leftover cereal everywhere. I'm constantly cleaning up after them in the kitchen, and I have a cleaning woman. Can you even imagine? She's good for nothing. Lupe is her name. I asked Lupe to wax the kitchen floor, and she tells me no 'cause she doesn't like my mop. There's nothing wrong with my mop! Lupe is lazy. Now I'm gonna have to do it myself."

Jabbermouth constantly updated me about her physical condition.

"Just came from the doctor's today. Got a clean bill of health. The gall bladder is fine. Thank God they don't have to remove it. They did some sort of ultrasound, like I was pregnant. Can you imagine? At my age? Still don't know why I'm having indigestion. Must be the food from the restaurant. I'm so sick of the food down there. Did I tell you that I have a bruise on my leg the size of Kansas? Have no idea where it came from. I think I'd remember if I fell."

Jabbermouth Virginia complained a lot.

"Nothin but crap on TV nowadays."

"They came to fix the air conditioning in my condo and got dirt on my carpet."

"Every time I go to the supermarket, the prices keep going up. Five dollars for cereal!"

"I don't like that new girl in Accessories. She's a spoiled little princess."

"I have so many aches and pains, I can't keep them straight."

"The girl at the salon did not do my hair right today. It's horrible."

But the thing Jabbermouth Virginia complained about the most was the parking.

"The parking is horrible. I drive around and around trying to get a spot up front. You'd think a mall this size would have better parking. The other day I had words with the parking attendant. I don't know why, but anyway, he made me mad, and he said where's your handicapped card after I got out of the car and found a spot up front. I said see, right there. I told ya I'd go around and around until I found a place to park up front. He thought he was being funny by asking where my handicapped card was."

"Virginia, why don't you just get a damn handicapped card," I said one day, after I'd tired of her parking gripes. "It would make things so much easier for you."

"That's what my daughter keeps telling me: 'Mom, why don't you get a handicapped card from the doctor?' I could get one from my doctor if I wanted. Well, I'd have to go and get a thing from the insurance companies, but yeah that's a good idea. I got a parking ticket once cause they were cleanin' the damn streets and I got Tuesday and Wednesday mixed up. Eighteen-dollar ticket. Sheeez. That taught me a lesson. Every time I'm parking on the street now, I read the sign as soon as I get out of the car."

Jabbermouth Virginia wouldn't even stop talking after you'd ended the conversation.

"Gotta get the phone, Virginia," I'd say while it was ringing, "I'll talk to you later."

"Okay, Freeman, I'm going home. Think I'll sit in the sun. Maybe read Janet Evanovich. I can't read her books fast enough. I'm only on *Hard Eight* and she's already up to twelve something. How can a person write so fast?"

I'd be halfway to the phone and Virginia would still be talking.

While she walked away.

"The grandkids are having a recital tomorrow. That will be exhausting, but my daughter won't be happy if I'm not there and I don't wanna upset the little ones, but all those kids everywhere, running around, screaming. I'm exhausted. My nerves can only handle so much. I need to water my plants when I get home. Lupe won't do it. How hard is it to water a few plants?"

I'd pick up the phone and she'd still be talking, halfway down the aisle, her back to me.

"I'm hungry. Maybe I'll get some dinner from Mario's. I hope they're not busy, the parking is horrible. Need to be home by 4:00 though. May not have time."

Even though Jabbermouth Virginia yapped me into a coma with her torrent of talk just about every time I saw her, sometimes my sympathetic social skills paid off.

She'd dig into her retirement money and pop for a handbag. The first handbag Jabbermouth ever bought from me was a $254 black Isabella Fiore satchel with a big red leather flower mounted on the front of it. Pretty pricy for a retired bank teller. I think she was excited to buy from Big Fancy's first male handbag salesman. But the sale did not come without a price. I had to listen to Virginia chatter for an hour, and she hemmed and hawed for days over whether or not to buy the Fiore bag.

"I want you to know this is it for me," Virginia said as I handed her the shopping bag, "I need another handbag like I need a hole in the head. I have a closet full of handbags."

The Fiore bag was the only handbag she ever bought at regular price, and she wore it proudly until sale time, when she bought a red Kenneth Cole satchel.

Although Jabbermouth did buy periodically, Judy couldn't stand her. She saw Jabbermouth talking to all of us for lengthy periods of time, taking us away from waiting on other customers and doing departmental duties.

"You need to not waste so much time with her," the General said.

"I can't help it. I have to give Big Fancy customer service."

"You better start helping it, because talking to Virginia is not going to save you from Misfiring."

Everyone else on the crew tolerated Jabbermouth like a pimple, rising up painfully, blistering to a whitehead, and then slowly disappearing. On any given day, I'd observe her from a distance talking to one of the Women's Shoes guys, then a short time later to Marion in Hosiery, then to Suzy Davis-Johnson, then to Robert in Men's Sportswear, and then to Marsha in my own department.

A lonely old woman. Bored with life and her family, Jabbermouth Virginia came into The Big Fancy every day to run her mouth, finding casual friendships with a handful of ears that were forced to listen. She made The Big Fancy her home away from home.

Getting to know Crazy Virginia wasn't as easy. It took a while to make a connection. At first I didn't even know her name was also Virginia. She was known by everyone as Teddy Bear Lady. I watched her for weeks marching down the aisle, wearing the same shabby clothes, carrying the same old decrepit bear.

Looking like Curious George, the monkey . . . if Curious George were a crazy fifty-year-old woman with frizzy gray-brown hair.

Getting to know Teddy Bear Lady took some time. She rarely stopped and looked at the merchandise; she was always on the move, always headed somewhere.

"Hon, you better stay away from that one," warned Marsha one day, when I told her I was captivated by Teddy Bear Lady.

"It's so bizarre," I said, "She goes in and out of the store like twenty times a day."

"You know what I heard?"

"Spill it, Marsha."

"Michael in Men's Furnishings talks to her sometimes and he said she goes over to the phone by the elevator and pretends to be talking on it for hours."

"No fuckin' way."

"All true. Brenda up in Customer Service said the same thing. Teddy Bear Lady pretends like she's arguing with someone from a company or something."

"How do they know she isn't really talking to someone?"

"Brenda saw her walk over to the pay phone, pick it up, and start talking without dialing."

"That's so insane. I wonder what her story is."

"You stay away from her, sweetie. She's already stalking Michael."

"I'm not afraid of her. She looks harmless."

"Harmless? Hon, are you kidding? If you don't stay clear of that nut job, I guarantee you, it will end in a restraining order."

I really didn't want Teddy Bear Lady stalking me, but she was so bizarre, I couldn't resist. I had to find out more. I decided to dive into the world of Crazy Virginia.

Barricaded safely behind the Corral, I yelled out a greeting to her one day as she stormed on by. "HELLO! HOW ARE YOU TODAY? HAVING A NICE AFTERNOON?"

Teddy Bear Lady stopped, turned, and squinted at me curiously, as if the sun was in her face. After a couple of seconds, she'd had enough and continued her stride toward the escalator.

I've spooked a wild animal at The Big Fancy! Too bad I don't have any treats to throw. Maybe that would soften her up.

A few minutes later on the return trip, Crazy Virginia's black eyes met mine.

I wanted to put my hand out and say, "C'mere girl, it's okay, I won't hurt you."

Instead, I shot her the biggest shit-pleasing retail smile ever and said, "HI THERE!"

Teddy Bear Lady stopped in her tracks.

"Hello?" She said the word as if she was learning it for the first time.

The fingers on her left hand were twitching. The other hand had a firm grip on the teddy bear. The worn-out stuffed teddy looked even worse up close. He had an eye missing.

Teddy Bear Lady's first words weren't like Jabbermouth Virginia's. No questions on why a man was working in Handbags. Nothing about her closet full of handbags. Her first words to me were about my hair.

"You sure do have spiky hair," she said.

I quickly glanced at myself in the mirror.

Damn, Teddy Bear Lady is right.

I could have won a jousting match against Ty Pennington. My hair was way sharper and pointier than his has ever been. "I use super-strength cement," I replied, teasing.

Teddy Bear Lady said nothing, squinting at my stiff hair. She may have been trying to figure out how I cement it. Then she was off again, back down the aisle without a word.

The next day Teddy Bear Lady sat at a table by the coffee bar, watching my every move. It was kinda creepy, and Marsha's words echoed in my head.

"It will end with a restraining order."

After she was done, Teddy Bear Lady came up to the counter and squinted at me while I looked at our sales figures from the previous day. "Your tie sure is bright," she said, gazing at my billiards tie with colorful pool balls all over it.

"I always wear fun ties," I replied.

From that moment on it was easy to talk with Teddy Bear Lady. Every day she'd want to see what kind of tie I wore. After commenting on my tie, I might ask her a question (which is how I found out her name was Virginia), or she'd just hit me with an avalanche of chitchat, just like the other Virginia.

But Crazy Virginia's ramblings made no sense at all most of the time, and I suspected there was a plethora of lies covering up her real life.

Like the one about her being a corporate lawyer.

"I have my own corporate law practice, you know," said Crazy Virginia, "and I'm semi-retired, but it's all about keeping busy and being on the move, and I says to one of my clients the other day, 'You gotta do what you gotta do, it's going to be fine, you know,' and he says, 'I don't think about that,' and I says, 'you better think about it, because you have to know it before you do it.' I'm not going to court so much, you know."

"I thought you went to court a lot," I said, egging on her craziness, completely fascinated.

"Oh please, Freeman, you know it amazes me. I'm a lot happier now than I was in July. I was told not to plow through all my work, like I normally do, and I don't have to go to court for my practice, you know, my clients all come to me, and I says, 'It's all fine, it all works out,' you know what I mean?"

"But, Virginia, how can you practice law from home?"

"The Good Lord says I can practice my law anywhere."

Yes, Teddy Bear Lady had her some spirituality, as the little gold cross around her neck suggested. The Good Lord guided her on everything. In fact, it often seemed she had the Good Lord on speed dial.

"The Good Lord says to me, 'Have faith, you'll win that trial.'"

"The Good Lord says to me, 'Have milk today, but don't drink it tomorrow.'"

"The Good Lord says to me, 'Don't go to the other side of the mall next week.'"

After many of her ramblings, she would finish up her chatter by ending it with a signature Good Lord phrase.

"The Good Lord works in wondrous ways."

"Don't you mean mysterious?" I asked, after hearing her say it for the first time.

"I've heard mysterious. But I don't believe that. That's not right, you know. But wondrous ways, I mean, that's the way it's supposed to be, you know."

"I think the phrase is mysterious ways, Virginia. The Good Lord works in mysterious ways."

"You know he says to me, he works in wondrous ways. Mysterious is wrong. The Good Lord is not mysterious, you know, he says that to me all the time. 'I work in wondrous ways, Virginia,' and he says, 'Don't forget that.'"

"Then he must be right," I replied, giving up.

Who am I to judge on how the Good Lord works? Wondrous is a perfectly good adjective. Like Jabbermouth Virginia, Crazy Virginia is always complaining about someone crossing her or something going wrong.

"The crosswalk sign does not give you enough time to cross the street, you know, over at Beverly and Main, so you know, now I have to file a complaint."

"I've been on the phone for two hours talking to a lady who knows nothing about what they did to me, and I says to her, 'You can't talk to me that way, I'm an attorney and I'll sue you, you know.'"

"I am not happy with the selection of breads at the grocery store, and I says to the manager, 'You need to do something,' but you know, the Good Lord works in wondrous ways."

One of the big dramas in Teddy Bear Lady's life was with the highway patrol.

She claimed they were harassing her. Why? No idea. If there was any truth to her CHP claim, it was locked up inside her jellybean mind. Every day she rambled on about it incoherently. "The California Highway Patrol is going to be sorry they harassed me. I was told they were going to process it, and it went all the way to Sacramento, and I thought about it and, you know, I'm not going to do it anymore, and I thought about it and, you know, maybe there's another way I can do it. That's why I'm calling Sacramento with the complaints, tell them, 'You do it! You do it! Cause if you do it, then you know how to do it.' You know that way won't be as tough as you thought it would be."

You bet, Crazy Virginia, whatever you say! Makes total sense to me! I'm so inspired.

Sometimes she'd involve another law enforcement agency in her madness.

"I got a message from Van Nuys police. I didn't call Van Nuys, they called me, and the captain says you know there's a report I'd like you to do. I knew the report was on somebody that worked there and it was back in April or March. And I said, 'You know, it's a miracle that you called me,' and he said, 'Why's that?' and I rattled off a couple of resources to him and he said, 'I think you were slipped,' and asked, 'How are you?' And I didn't know if I should tell him or not. 'If you're not able to talk to me about it, you know, why don't you talk to me about it,' and I thought about it, and I told him, and he says to me, he says, 'You know what, I support you, I care about you, I'll pray for you,' and he said all that and 'We're here for you.'"

I had no fucking idea what any of that meant and held back from asking if any of them were cute and single. "That's cool, Virginia," I'd reply.

Sometimes Teddy Bear Lady came up to the counter with nothing to say. On her third aisle rotation, having already commented on my hair and tie, she'd be at a loss for words, so she'd stand there. Squinting and twitching her hands, waiting for me to ask a question. If I wasn't busy and Judy wasn't around, I'd think of something to ask her.

Like the time I noticed she had on a gold ring with a giant blue stone. It looked all plastic and cheap, like a Cracker Jack prize, and I hadn't remembered seeing the ring before.

"I like your ring," I said, obviously lying, "It really sparkles."

"My boyfriend got it for me, you know it's not from here, he says it came from Universal Studios."

"Boyfriend?"

I was stunned.

Teddy Bear Lady has a freakin' boyfriend? How come she can have a boyfriend and not me?

This world is so cruel.

Then I thought for a moment about what her boyfriend must look like.

He's gotta be just as crazy looking as her. Wiry hair, squinty eyes, twitching fingers. Probably wearing a hunting jacket, navy sweats, and carrying a stuffed Barney doll. I'll stay single, thank you very much.

"Now it ain't no engagement ring, you know," said Crazy Virginia, "He says, 'I got it for you as a friendship ring,' but you know what it is with rings, and everyone thinks it's an engagement ring, but I don't want to get married. I says to him, 'I'm not going to be your wife, you can give me a hundred rings. I like my freedom and I've got too much going on to get married. Let's just keep things the way they are. The Good Lord will make it happen when it happens.'"

"It's a pretty ring," I said.

"Yeah, it's okay. I like it. I picked it out. It's pretty. Do you have a girlfriend?"

Oh shit!

When she asked me this, it threw me for a loop. Hadn't expected that one. Considering I'd been quizzing her for weeks like Larry King, it was only fair to indulge her.

But what do I tell her? "I'm a homo, Virginia. I like men." What does your Good Lord think about that?

Something told me her Good Lord wouldn't approve. I could just say, "No, I don't have a girlfriend," and leave it at that. But something told me that might not be good either. Teddy Bear Lady might break up with her boyfriend and come after me.

I opted for a lie.

"See that cute blond girl over there," I said pointing to Cammie helping a customer in the Marc Jacobs shop, "That's my girlfriend."

"She's beautiful," said Crazy Virginia, squinting away at Cammie.

Since we had divulged so much personal information to each other, after several weeks I felt confident enough to drop the big question. The question everyone in the store wanted to know.

"Why do you carry a teddy bear, Virginia?"

She brought the gross thing up to her cheeks and cuddled it.

"He's my Buggle Bear."

I wanted to puke.

"Buggle Bear?"

"That's his name. I don't go anywhere without him."

"Aren't you a little old to be carrying a teddy bear, Virginia?"

"HA! That's what you think! You don't know Buggle Bear!"

Then she plopped the filthy, matted thing on the counter. (I made a mental note to disinfect the counter after she left.) Crazy Virginia turned gnarly old Buggle Bear over. A zipper ran down his back. She unzipped it, revealing a large pocket. Inside was a conglomeration of handbag junk: Cell phone, wallet, keys, candy, discarded paper. Completely normal handbag junk.

Oh. My. God. Crazy Virginia's Buggle Bear is her fucking handbag!

The only response I could give her was one that would hopefully get me a sale.

"Virginia, you really need a new handbag! We just got in some new Juicy Couture bags that would look great on you."

"Oh NO," she replied, "I love Buggle Bear. He's a cutie and the Good Lord says I need to take care of him. He carries everything I need, he loves me. Looks out for me, you know."

I'm sure he does. With his good eye. You might want to get him a patch, though.

I decided not to tell anyone Teddy Bear Lady was actually carrying a handbag named Buggle. It was more fun to watch her shock people as she stormed down the aisles of Big Fancy dragging Buggle Bear by a paw.

Unlike Jabbermouth Virginia, who yammered away even after I'd ended a conversation, Crazy Virginia would leave quickly if I had to wait on someone or answer the phone. The only problem with her was that she'd reappear minutes later, when I was free. Squinting and twitching. Waiting to suck me into her nonsensical world. It was a Big Fancy handicap I'd accepted. After all, I was the one who had approached *her*. This is what I got for befriending wild crazies off the hard aisle.

One morning I saw Teddy Bear Lady eating her muffin and drinking coffee at a table by the Coffee Bar. After that she was talking to one of the guys in Women's Shoes, and then I saw her on the phone by the elevator, and then I saw her talking to a Cosmetics girl who was trying to get her to buy lipstick. As she bolted down the aisle like a busy woman on the run, her frizzy hair flopping all over, I realized Crazy Virginia was just lonely.

Bored with her life, she came into The Big Fancy every day to use it as a stage where she could pretend to be someone important to a few ears that were forced to listen.

Like Jabbermouth Virginia, Crazy Virginia had made The Big Fancy Department Store her home away from home.

On some days I talked to one Virginia right after the other.

I'd turn around and Crazy Virginia would be there, clutching her teddy.

"My boyfriend is going with me to meet the Van Nuys police chief, but I says to him, 'You know, I don't think it's such a good idea. I'm the lawyer. I do the talking. You keep quiet. The Good Lord says this to be true.'"

I'd leave her, and Jabbermouth Virginia would show up.

"My sister-in-law still wants me to come and visit her in Arizona, but I just don't want to get on the plane. Too much hassle. I told her to get her own butt on a plane."

Then I'd leave her, and Crazy Virginia would appear.

"Do you believe in Angels? I saw one in the ladies' lounge just now."

I'd leave her, and Jabbermouth Virginia would arrive.

"You wouldn't even believe the mess I just saw in the ladies' lounge just now!"

Day in and day out, The Two Virginias blanketed the store with their babble. Though most of the Retail Slaves were severely annoyed with their unremitting presence, I couldn't help but be fascinated. They were so similar yet so different.

What is up with these two?

Then one day fate played a card.

The Two Virginias arrived at the handbag counter simultaneously.

I couldn't believe my eyes! The Good Lord must have been involved. Teddy Bear Lady and Jabbermouth stood right next to one another. Marsha crept up behind them and put her right hand up to her right ear, making a phone call gesture and mouthing, "Do you want me to call you?"

Calling each other on the phone was a secret weapon the Angels and I used to save each other from Crazy Customers. We'd run in the back and call or sometimes just use the department extension out on the floor and stay on the line as long as necessary, until the bloodsucking customer left. Jabbermouth caused constant deployment of this weapon. Since I am the only one who talked to Teddy Bear Lady in our department, it wasn't used often on her, though Judy did call me once and say, "I'm not paying you to chat with homeless people who aren't going to buy anything. End it."

It was slow the day the Two Virginias stood side by side at the counter, and I was intrigued by their coincidental clash, so I gave Marsha a slight head sway to mean no. She rolled her eyes and walked on. Having both Virginias there at the same time was so bizarre I couldn't pass on the opportunity to see what would happen.

Crazy Virginia had arrived first with a lot to tell me.

Her harassment problems with the California Highway Patrol were escalating, as they always do, and she was being forced to take action against them, as she always does.

"The Good Lord said I will be vindicated. If it has to go to trial, so be it. The police captain is meeting me, and he said there is no excuse for their behavior. Today is not the day for it and I'm not putting up with it."

"You're absolutely right, Virginia," I said.

Jabbermouth Virginia completely ignored Crazy Virginia just a few feet away and instantly began telling me about how a gold button had just fallen off of her St. Joe knit suit. "I just bought this damn thing last week. I'm taking it back upstairs and Martha'd better get it fixed or I'm returning it. I'm hungry too. Haven't eaten all day. It's already three and I've missed lunch."

"You'd better eat something, Virginia," I said.

"I told the captain I wanted the CHP investigated or tomorrow I'm filing a lawsuit," said Crazy Virginia.

"Got the button right here. Seamstresses better be good," said Jabbermouth Virginia.

The Two Virginias were talking to me at once. Un-fucking-believable.

Then a silly idea occurred to me.

Introduce them! Maybe Jabbermouth Virginia could help Crazy Virginia find some new clothes. They could shop together! Have makeovers together. Come to the sales together. Drink coffee together. Go to the movies together. Maybe they'll become best girlfriends!

"Virginia, meet Virginia!" I said excitedly, motioning them to look at one another. "Isn't that great? You both have the same name! And you're both here at The Big Fancy every day."

They eyed each other disapprovingly.

Not exactly the love connection I'd hoped for.

"Maybe you two Virginias should have lunch in the restaurant or something? I'm sure I could get Suzy Davis-Johnson to comp you both."

Jabbermouth Virginia looked at me like I had suggested she jump off the Hollywood sign.

Crazy Virginia squinted and twitched her fingers.

Neither one of them said anything to each other.

"So anyway," said Jabbermouth Virginia, focusing back at me, "I got that jerk new manager in the restaurant to bring back the clam chowder. Guess I wasn't the only one complainin'. Of course it's not great clam chowder, kinda watery, but at least it's there when I want it. I can't believe the price of gasoline. I'm glad I'm not drivin' anywhere long-distance. I'd go broke!"

"Yeah, gas is really high," I said.

Crazy Virginia didn't even look at Jabbermouth Virginia.

"The Good Lord works in wondrous ways," she mumbled.

"He sure does," I said.

Jabbermouth Virginia ignored Crazy Virginia completely.

"I woke up this morning with a rash the size of Hawaii on my stomach," she said. "Don't know where it came from. Now I have to go to the damn dermatologist, and I don't like that guy. Somethin' not right about him."

Crazy Virginia could have cared less about Jabbermouth Virginia's rash.

She took off, power-walking down the aisle, probably headed to make a fake phone call.

Jabbermouth Virginia kept right on talking.

"I didn't sleep last night. Damn owl right outside my window, hoo-hooing all night!"

I don't know what I was thinking, attempting to pair up the Two Virginias. It was like trying to make a Republican and Democrat have a bake sale together. Not going to happen.

I had been caught up in the serendipitous moment of their synchronized arrival and the fantasy of being a matchmaker!

Teddy Bear Lady and Jabbermouth would never be BFFs.

But one thing was for sure. Come rain or shine, tomorrow the Two Virginias would be roaming the aisles of The Big Fancy.

They just wouldn't be doing it together.

This Little Piggy

Search and destroy. This is the motto of Piggy Shoppers everywhere. They stampede through stores like barbaric animals. Eating and drinking. Breaking and ruining. Tossing and dropping. When a Piggy hurricane crash-lands, Retail Slaves turn into maids, and not the merry kind.

Raelene Reynolds was one of my regular Piggy Shoppers.

In fact, she could be Miss Piggy's white-trash second cousin once removed. The one who doesn't wear makeup or take showers.

Besides *looking* like a pig, with her plump, porky body, and a snout-shaped nose, Raelene didn't give a shit about her image or hygiene, sweating so profusely you'd have thought she'd just spent two hours on the treadmill. Her grayish black hair was always pulled tight into a stubby ponytail that stuck out of her head like wild grass, and she usually wore frumpy, oversized colorful V-neck tees and black tights that were always covered in animal hair and stains. Raelene's number-one choice of shoes were flip-flops—for summer *and* winter. Whenever she got too close, the smell of stale corn chips assaulted my nose, and I'd have to hold back the urge to vomit.

Every time Piggy Raelene blew into Handbags like a wayward piece of garbage, I wished I'd had a fire hose full of Lysol so I could have blasted her scuzzy butt right back out into the mall.

She was a human wart hog if ever I saw one.

Although Raelene felt no need for a salon or decent clothes, for some reason she loved her designer handbags from The Big Fancy. And since all of the women in the department avoided her like the plague, she usually had to summon me for help. Which, unfortunately, put me on a first-name basis with the Fritos-fragrant Raelene Reynolds.

Although I was disgusted by helping Piggy Raelene, and I needed a bulldozer to clean up the mess she'd make after searching for—and destroying—a new bag, she almost always bought something.

It was a small consolation for the price my nose paid.

While helping Raelene replace any of her mutilated handbags, I had an up-close and personal view of what she had annihilated. Every one of her bags looked as if it had been mauled by a pack of hyenas, and the insides were even worse, resembling mini-landfills. Most of Raelene's handbag contents were trash and half-eaten food. I tried not to think about how it all got there. I just took a big customer-service breath and jumped into the septic world of Raelene.

I don't know what she did or where she went every day, but I know every handbag that left The Big Fancy with her was on a suicide mission.

Along with her lack of hygiene, Piggy Raelene seemed to be missing the ability to communicate.

When Raelene hunted for a new bag, she said very little while decimating the department like she was leveling a rain forest. Sometimes she would ask a question, but I was the one who usually did all the talking. To almost everything I said, Raelene would respond with a single word: "Yah." And she always said "Yah" like she was somewhere else and didn't care.

"You should look at the new LeSportsac print we just got in, they're indestructible," I'd say.

"Yah," she'd say, while molesting a white DKNY hobo made of buttery calfskin.

"Hey, Raelene, the Dooney & Bourke all-weather leather doesn't stain," I'd say.

"Yah," she'd reply, while mauling a pink suede Kooba shoulder satchel.

"How about a sturdy Italian backpack with brass hardware, it will really take a beating."

"Yah," she would say, tearing the stuffing out of it and flinging it aside like a cigarette butt.

Sometimes I would just ramble on nonsensically, bullshitting about one bag after another.

And Raelene would respond in her own nonsensical, bullshit way:

"Yah . . . yah . . . yah . . . yah."

The first time I was subjected to Raelene's "yahs," I thought perhaps it was her way of saying she didn't want a salesperson hovering over her and she wanted to be left alone. So I left her alone. Gladly. I tried to get as far away from the corn-chip aroma as possible. But within minutes, she called me over, "Yah, are you going to help me or not?"

Every time the Raelene tornado hit, she made messes so quickly in so many different places in the department that I couldn't keep up with her. Judy would bound out of the stockroom and suddenly be up in my ass, "Free-man, you just left five bags on the counter with stuffing all over the place. Suzy is doing a walk-through any second. You'd better get it cleaned up."

But Piggy Raelene took no responsibility for her messes. That was my job. Her job was to assault as many handbags as she could, and then toss them aside like spoiled tomatoes. Stuffing was yanked out and thrown everywhere, and bags she didn't like were left anywhere she pleased, which meant the floor most of the time. I actually witnessed Raelene drop a bag to the floor and then step over it on her way to grab another bag that had suddenly captured her attention. And when Raelene needed a wallet, look out. By the time she left, it was like playing a game of fifty-two card pickup—wallets everywhere! Until Raelene Reynolds settled on that special bag or wallet willing to sacrifice its life to her slovenly ways, this Piggy Shopper was a forced to be reckoned with.

More often than not, Piggy Raelene searched for her next handbag victim with food or a drink in her hand. I once watched breathlessly as she shopped haphazardly while drinking from a 7-Eleven Big Gulp cup and devouring chicken nuggets and fries right out of a McDonald's bag. But most every other time I waited on Raelene, she had an iced chocolate something-or-other from the Coffee Bar and some kind of snack in her hand: soft pretzels, raspberry crumb cake, nachos, or her favorites, Mrs. Fields cookies.

If you followed the cookie crumbs all over the floor, you'd find Raelene.

As her porky fingers become covered with whatever she was eating (something usually wet and sticky), they wanted to touch everything. Grease and condensation were the leading causes of death for many handbags and wallets that had just met Raelene.

That was the case for a new Kate Spade floral collection we had just received.

Three handbags were killed in the line of duty after Raelene's cookie grease bombing.

There were seven different shapes on the table, and Raelene rubbed her oily paws all over each one like she was trying to make a genie come out. By the time she had completed her violent, greasy groping, there was severe stain damage. Kate's flowers were hemorrhaging.

A half-hour later, after desecrating the sale table and half of the designer department, Raelene returned to the handbag crime scene and picked up a satchel she had damaged.

"I decided on this Kate Spade," she said while eating another cookie, "But it has a mark on it."

I was speechless.

It has a mark on it because you just about ate it, Raelene!

"Really?" I said, picking up the bag for examination. "It wasn't like that this morning. We just put them out. They're brand-new."

"Yah well, it's dirty, and I'm not buying that one."

"Umm . . . okay. I'll get you a new one from the back, Raelene."

What else could I do?

In a court of law, the security cameras would have busted Raelene Reynolds with the truth.

But at The Big Fancy, whatever this little Piggy wanted, this little Piggy got.

Weeeeeee!

One Picky Bitch

When she was in the heat of determining whether a handbag passed inspection, Constance Beaumont looked like she was trying to have the biggest bowel movement of her life. Odd grunting noises then accompanied her shiny, scrunched-up, constipated face.

"Humph . . . humph," she'd say, followed by triple-smacking her tongue to the roof of her mouth like it was full of sticky peanut butter. Smack-smack-smack.

Constance Beaumont was one Picky Bitch.

The face she made should be in Wikipedia as a visual reference.

"Humph. Humph." Smack-smack-smack.

I know firsthand about Picky Bitch psychosis. Although I'm not one of those anal freaks who run around terrorizing salespeople for hours with my Picky Bitchness, I am finicky about the condition of T-shirts, books, shoes, vegetables, and fruit before I buy. I'll dig through a bin of apples, searching for ones that are firm and shiny. I hate apples that are soft and dull. Can't eat them. Call me a Picky Apple Bitch.

I can't even imagine what Constance Beaumont is like at the grocery store.

She probably spends three hours in the produce section alone. Or maybe she doesn't eat produce.

Judging by her anorexic body, she doesn't eat much.

I found that odd because of who she claimed to be married to.

Not one to talk about her personal life, Mrs. Beaumont revealed this to me one day when she was looking for an evening bag to match her gold Prada shoes. The best match we had was an inexpensive $35 Big Fancy–brand silk clutch. She shot me her crinkled, constipated face.

"Humph. I can't wear that dreadful thing. I'm the wife of a surgeon."

Not doctor. Not physician. Surgeon.

Picky Bitch Beaumont was the wife of a surgeon.

What surgeon would marry her? Dr. Wither-Away?

Someone needs to read her the surgeon general's warning about not eating!

Aside from her anorexic, skeletal body, everything else about fifty-ish Constance Beaumont appeared to be the best a surgeon's salary could buy. Her wispy shoulder-length sandy hair was expertly high-lighted, and her makeup was flawless (even the lipstick on her fat lips). She dazzled in conservative designer clothing and accessories, dressing as if she was headed to a formal dinner party or luncheon. Everything looked like it was made to go together. Even her reading glasses were color-coordinated.

Mrs. Beaumont had Picky Bitched her way to looking picture-perfect. And it probably took forever.

The first time I waited on Constance Beaumont, I said, "Thank you for shopping with me, Constance. I hope you enjoy your new Cole Haan."

She shot me a look of indignation and said, "I prefer you address me in the formal, professional manner, as Mrs. Beaumont."

"Umm . . . sure . . . Mrs. Beaumont. No problem."

You bet, Connie, you fuckin' Picky Bitch. Whatever you want!

I *so* wanted to call her Connie. But it was better for me not to upset Picky Bitch Beaumont. Despite her persnickety affliction, she'd buy only from me.

I'll never forget the look on Douche's face the first and only time she tried to snake Mrs. Beaumont away from me when I left her alone to answer the phone.

"I'll be happy to help you with that Ferragamo bag," Douche said, slithering up to her.

Mrs. Beaumont lowered her reading glasses and stared at Douche.

"Freeman helps me. Please don't approach me again. It's annoying."

Douche never said another word to her. I wish that could have happened with all the customers Douche tried to steal from me.

Selecting a handbag or wallet could take Mrs. Beaumont as long as two hours. Whenever she appeared out of nowhere asking for my assistance, I knew I was in for a handbag root canal.

I asked Jules if real estate agents have this much trouble when they're selling ten-million-dollar homes. "They're ten-million-dollar homes," she said, "Not handbags and wallets. *Mrs.* Beaumont needs therapy and a good nutritionist."

When Mrs. Beaumont showed up, it wasn't just to window-shop. She was there on a mission to find the perfect handbag she needed for an outfit.

Like a museum tour guide, I waltzed her around the department, tediously showcasing every handbag and lecturing on their fashion benefits and useful features. After she had gathered no fewer than ten bags, cleared an area on the counter, and lined them up like criminal suspects, the reading glasses were slipped on, and Picky Bitch went into interrogation mode.

She would slowly scrutinize every handbag, one by one, all the while saying "Humph. Humph." Followed by a smack-smack-smack.

She tugged every strap, removed stuffing, examined the inside linings, and checked every seam, searching for any kind of fatal flaw that would deem the handbag unacceptable.

"Humph. Humph." Smack-smack-smack.

One day she was looking at a Coach signature satchel to bring on an upcoming cruise. While going through her obsessive-compulsive motions, she suddenly lifted the bag up to her nose and inhaled deeply.

"Humph. Humph." Smack-smack-smack.

"This bag smells like fish!" she announced.

I casually sniffed it. Nothing. Just leather and fabric.

"I don't smell anything."

Wrong thing to say to a delusional Picky Bitch.

"My nose is extremely sensitive," Mrs. Beaumont said. "This bag smells like it was in a fish market. Has it been returned?"

I checked The Big Fancy tag. No remnants of a purchase sticker.

"No. Never been sold," I told her.

"I highly doubt that. Something is wrong here."

I unzipped the Coach bag and held it up to my nose, practically sticking my head inside. Absolutely no fish smell. Only fabric and leather.

"I'm not smelling fish."

Mrs. Beaumont waved me off with a "Humph."

"Do you have others?"

I went to the stockroom and found four more of the very same design. They'd just come in, and some were still wrapped in plastic and tissue. The Picky Bitch sniffed every single one.

"Humph. Humph." Smack-smack-smack.

"They all smell like fish. Revolting!"

I sniffed right alongside her, like we were dogs looking for territory to mark.

"I still don't smell anything."

"All these bags have fish stink! I can't believe you don't smell it! They reek! I think I'm going to be sick. You really should call the buyer."

"Did you have fish for lunch?"

I didn't mean it to sound insulting. I thought it could be a legitimate reason for her sensitive nose, but Mrs. Beaumont lowered her reading glasses and shot me a look of repulsion.

"Excuse me?" she said.

I stammered. "Umm . . . maybe you ate something fishy, that's causing the . . . umm . . . smell . . . you are noticing."

"*No*, I did not have something fishy for lunch," she cried, indignant.

"I'm just trying to figure out where the smell is coming from," I said.

"Well it's *not* coming from me, Freeman. I don't appreciate your inquisition."

Oh shit. Big Fancy rule #1: Don't ever upset a super persnickety Picky Bitch! Especially if her name is Constance Beaumont, wife of a surgeon!

"I'm sorry, Mrs. Beaumont, I didn't mean to say you smelled like fish."

After that, Picky never claimed another bag smelled like fish.

Instead, her hound-dog nose picked up the scents of formaldehyde, rubber, peaches, licorice, sandalwood, and new-car smell from the handbags at Big Fancy. Though leather does have a rich scent, I've yet to notice any of it smelling of licorice.

Anything deemed an imperfection in the world of Beaumont was instantly pointed out to me. "Humph! You see that? Humph! You see that?!" Her French-manicured nails would follow, tapping the area in question.

"This is defective. It's no good." Smack-smack-smack.

Then she'd discard it like a dirty Kleenex.

Or I'd get the leather cleaner out and scrub at the flaw until my fingers ached, only to ultimately have it rejected because Picky Bitch would still see the scratch or smudge even after I had buffed it out. "It's still there. It will come back after the lotion dries."

After a while, I stopped trying to clean or repair an imperfection she had denounced. I just simply agreed in an exaggerated way, "Oh yes, the entire seam is crooked. I can see it a mile away. I don't know how they could have allowed this one out of the factory. It's tragic."

"It most certainly is," Mrs. Beaumont would say, wrinkling her nose, followed by a "Humph. Humph." Smack-smack-smack.

Once a bag was eliminated for not being perfect, if she was really interested in it, Mrs. Beaumont would say, "This handbag is defective. Get me one from the back."

She used this "Get me one from the back" line at least five times per shopping trip.

As with Lorraine Goldberg, Shoposaurus Carnotaurus, who definitely had Picky Bitch tendencies but was nowhere near as awful as Mrs. Beaumont, I'd learned not to wait to be asked.

My sanity was saved if I beat Picky to the punch.

The minute she spotted a flaw or said she was "very interested" in a bag, I'd say, "Let me go get one from the back."

On my way to the stockroom, I'd pray.

God, please let there be another one. And let it be in pristine condition. Wrapped up in plastic and tissue. Or at least not lopsided with a thread missing. I really need this Six-hundred-dollar sale.

Mrs. Beaumont didn't glow appreciatively the way Lorraine did when I returned from the stockroom with a brand-new, factory-wrapped handbag; instead, she just looked at me like, "What took you so long?" Then she'd yank it from my hands and begin scanning it.

If a handbag passed the Flaws and Defects portion of Picky's meticulous handbag interrogation, next up was the Try-On, where she'd stand in front of the floor-length mirror modeling each bag.

First the front.

Then the left side.

Then the right side.

This would be normal for any woman trying on a handbag, except that Picky Bitch Beaumont did it no less than twenty times, constantly rotating like a jewelry box doll and tilting her head while humph-humphing and smack-smack-smacking.

Calling Dr. Wither-Away! Is there a surgeon in the house? Your Picky Bitch wife has gone full-bore fanatically finicky, AKA crazy. I hope you have psychiatric credentials. She also needs to see a good neurologist about all the grunting and smacking.

More insanity would ensue when she started to complain about how the handbags weren't living up to her expectations.

"What was Kate Spade thinking? The inside zipper pocket is too small."

"I've never liked the way DKNY does their shoulder straps."

"The stitching on this Kenneth Cole is shoddy."

"Dooney & Bourke should have never put a multicolored rainbow zipper on this bag, it looks ridiculously absurd. I wouldn't be caught dead wearing this!"

When she went on a rampage, all I could do was pet her.

"You are absolutely right, Mrs. Beaumont. I couldn't agree more. I think the zipper ruined the look. They must have blind people with bad taste designing for them."

One time she called me to complain about the condition of her four-year-old Gucci shoulder tote when she picked it up at our store after we'd repaired a loose thread for free. I had been at lunch when she came in to pick up the repair. As soon as I returned, the phone rang.

"Hello Freeman, it's Mrs. Beaumont."

"Hi, Mrs. Beaumont."

"I picked up my Gucci bag today, and I must tell you, I am not pleased at all."

"Sorry to hear that, what's the problem?"

"There is no stuffing inside."

"I don't think it had stuffing when you brought it in, did it?"

"No, Freeman, it did not, BECAUSE I WAS USING IT. THAT'S WHEN I NOTICED THE LOOSE THREAD," she said, her voice agitated.

Tread lightly, dude. Mrs. Beaumont must have a zit today or something.

"The repair service doesn't put stuffing inside the bags when they send them back," I replied.

"Well, I don't know why NOT," she said, sounding miffed, "They should. My beautiful Gucci handbag looked absolutely atrocious! It was smashed and flattened and wrapped in plastic."

"The plastic is to protect it."

"I want stuffing."

"Umm . . . no problem, Mrs. Beaumont. Just come in, and we'll give you stuffing."

"What time are you working till?"

"Anyone can get you the stuffing. It doesn't matter if I'm here or not."

"I want you to get it, and I want Gucci stuffing."

"There is no such thing as Gucci stuffing."

"Humph."

Silence before the storm.

Here it comes. Picky Bitch Rampage.

"Freeman, you are completely incorrect. You of all people should know what's inside your handbags. Coach has a special stuffing! Juicy Couture has a special stuffing! Dooney & Bourke have a special stuffing! AND SO DOES GUCCI. I WANT GUCCI STUFFING!"

After her speech, I realized she was partially correct. Some of the handbag designers do have logo-printed tissue used as stuffing in their bags, notably Coach and Juicy Couture.

But for the life of me I could not remember what Gucci stuffing looked like.

However, the flaw in her petty request is that not *all* handbag designers make logo stuffing. Most of them use 100 percent Grade-A recycled tissue and paper.

"Sure, Mrs. Beaumont. No problem. When do you want to come in?"

"I need to take care of this right away. I'll be there in an hour."

Not a minute late, Mrs. Beaumont showed up with her flat, lifeless Gucci shoulder tote in its protective dust cover. Rather than have the stuffing waiting for her, I decided to empty out a brand-new Gucci bag right in front of her so she would know the stuffing was indeed Gucci brand, even though it appeared to be regular tissue.

"See! It's a different color!" she said with a "Humph," and a smack-smack-smack.

I don't know what the fuck she was talking about.

The stuffing was a mix of white tissue and grayish heavy-duty paper, the same shit inside half the bags in our department. I let the desire to prove I was right pass. Mrs. Beaumont would just find a way to discredit my findings. I bestowed her with a shit-pleasing retail smile.

"Now your Gucci bag will be well preserved."

I watched as she put the old, newly stuffed Gucci in its protective dust cover and then placed it back inside her shopping bag.

Then she put on bright green reading glasses, which matched her blouse.

"Since I've had to come back to your store I might as well start looking for a bag to match a St. John dress I'm wearing to the gala dinner for my husband's surgical conference in Miami. Show me everything you have in black."

My head started to pound.

I hoped it wouldn't be long before she demanded I get one from the back, because hidden in my box of business cards on my hold shelf in the stockroom was half of a Xanax in case of an emergency. A raving Picky Bitch certainly qualified as an emergency.

Humph-humph. Smack-smack-smack.

The Vampire Bavaro

For centuries, one of the most notoriously draining customers in Retail Hell has come to earn the title Bloodsucker. No matter what type of store you work at or shop in, you've probably encountered one of these coma-inducing freaks wreaking havoc on everyone around them.

Bloodsuckers have no need for fangs.

One look, movement, or word out of their mouth, and the energy vacuum revs into full blast. The poor Retail Slave waiting on them goes pale, then limp, completely bled dry, falling into a helpless heap of exhaustion in need of B-12 shots and a keg of beer.

The Big Fancy was teeming with Bloodsuckers.

The Two Virginias were considered Bloodsuckers with their non-stop lobotomizing chatter.

Sometimes Shoposaurus Carnotaurus Lorraine Goldberg could turn into a terrible Bloodsucker as she stopped at nothing to obtain three extra pairs of Ferragamo shoes in orange. And more often than not, I'd have absolutely no blood left after waiting on Mrs. Beamount.

But the most feared Bloodsucker in all of The Big Fancy was Marguerite Bavaro.

The Count Dracula of customers.

Lestat's ugly sister.

The love child of Vampira and Barlow.

The Vampire Bavaro looked so frightening, she could raise the dead and make them run away. She had gnarly black-widow hair, usually

crammed under a baseball cap or visor (red or blue), and bulging, buglike
eyes with dilated black pupils sticking out from a gaunt face that had
seen numerous skin diseases. Sometimes it was patchy and sickly, sometimes it was speckled with tiny reddish black bumps. Bavaro moved her
bony body in slow, mummified motion, and when those bulbous black
eyes caught you, it felt like they were hypnotizing you into a trance
that would make you do whatever evil bidding she commanded.

Every time the Vampire Bavaro appeared out of thin air, I wanted
to scream.

But screaming on the sales floor at Big Fancy was frowned upon.

Seeing Bavaro's horrific face wasn't the only thing that made me
want to scream; it was knowing she was about to open her mouth and
start speaking.

"JEFFERSON!" she would say, sounding like Gloria Swanson
from *Sunset Boulevard*, "You must help me! Everything is a God-awful
mess. It needs to be taken care of right away. I'm not at all pleased
with what's going on here, Jefferson."

The Vampire Bavaro never got my name right. It was always Jefferson, no matter how many times I corrected her.

"Jefferson, I don't understand how this bag works."

"Jefferson, you wouldn't lie to me about this, would you?"

"Jefferson, everything is a God-awful mess, I need you to correct
it."

Marguerite Bavaro also refused to acknowledge the correct names
of everyone else in the Handbag Jungle. She called Marsha Margo, Tiffany Brittany, and Jules Debbie (WTF? Doesn't even rhyme). Cammie
was known as, "That blond girl I dislike immensely"; Douche was,
"That foreign woman"; Marci, "That chatty girl"; and Judy was simply "The Manager."

I couldn't help but think she played games with our names on
purpose.

If I wasn't so scared of her, I'd have changed her name and called
her Bloodsucking Bitch.

The Vampire Bavaro was an equal-opportunity Bloodsucker.
Exclusive to no one, she roped us all into her brain-twisting, energy-
draining dramas. The unlucky person who answered the phone or
was standing in her path when she appeared was the victim du jour.

"Jefferson! Everything is a God-awful mess," she'd whine to me over the phone, "This needs to be taken care of immediately! The last person I spoke to—that blond girl I dislike immensely—did not call me back. Debbie has a Marc Jacobs on hold that Margo was supposed to get me but never did because the one I bought from that foreign woman has a scratch, and the one Brittney has on hold is not the right color, but I may be interested in it, and that chatty girl was supposed to get me one from another store but I haven't heard from her either. Your manager also said I could have a discount on the scratched one, so I want the one that Debbie has, but I also want another one, and there are two other handbags I want to ask you about."

I almost collapsed from exhaustion just listening to her on the phone.

Given the way the Vampire Bavaro looked, I'd much rather deal with her over the phone rather than in person. When she'd appear out of nowhere like a B-movie ghoul, it totally creeped me out.

"Jefferson, I'm glad you are here," she'd moan as I accidentally ran into her on my way out of the stockroom, "Everything is a God-awful mess. I don't want that foreign woman helping me. I wish to converse with someone who can clearly speak English. I've had a horrible day. I'm having an allergic reaction to my medication and I'm in no mood."

Neither am I. The blood bank is dry. Maybe you should just leave now and spare us all.

Besides "everything being a God-awful mess" with whatever ongoing handbag situation she had created, there was always a black cloud of tragedy hanging over Marguerite's head.

"Please extend my hold," she'd say, "I can't come in right now; the plumbing in my house is being repaired, and I can't leave the workmen alone. It's going to be a three-day job and then I'm having the roof repaired from the tree that fell on it last week during the storm. I don't know when I'll be in."

Or, "I need to return this bag. My sister just fell and broke both her legs. I want to take care of the return now because I won't be home for a while. I'll need to be a nurse for my sister."

Or, "I was in a car accident three days ago with a cable TV van and my body hasn't been the same. It was their fault, of course, and if I suffer any further medical problems they *will* be paying for it."

The Vampire Bavaro wasn't kidding when she mentioned any kind of further medical problems.

There was always something wrong with her, and she had no qualms in letting us know all about it: "The Manager said I could have the discount today even though the sale is over. I couldn't come in yesterday because I was ill. I'm on ten medications. I've got lupus, diabetes, osteoporosis, carpal tunnel, arthritis, clinical depression, high blood pressure, psoriasis, hay fever, and dry mouth."

Shouldn't she be dead with all that?

Besides being one of the worst Bloodsuckers ever, Marguerite Bavaro was also shady.

Nasty-Ass Thief shady.

She was always exchanging and returning with no receipts or with torn receipts and trying to get deep price adjustments on things by telling lies about when she bought them, claiming they were damaged, or producing coupons from other stores that were either expired or not the right coupon.

One time Judy denied her a return on a Kenneth Cole hobo because the price ticket she had with it wasn't even from our store. It was the correct price and had Cole's name on it, but another store's logo was stamped across the top.

"I know I bought it here," The Vampire Bavaro said, "and I'm not leaving until you give me the refund on this bag. What are you saying? That I stole it? My husband is a police officer and he's not going to be happy when I tell him that you accused me of stealing."

We all knew her husband was a police officer because she constantly reminded us, as if it was some kind of name-dropping power tool she had to use. None of us could understand why anyone would be married to her in the first place, let alone a cop. We all thought it was a lie.

"No one has accused you of stealing," said Judy, becoming frustrated, "I'm only saying that the ticket to the bag is not from our store."

"Then I'll take the ticket," said Bavaro, snatching it from Judy's hand. "Now you can credit it to my account without a ticket. Unless, of course, you'd like me to go upstairs and talk to Suzy Davis-Johnson about it?"

Judy wouldn't like that at all. Satan disliked the Vampire Bavaro almost as much as we did because she was always putting out numerous Bavaro fires all over the store and giving her thousands of dollars back in questionable returns. Because Marguerite bought as much as she returned, Suzy commanded that we give her whatever she wanted in the name of customer service.

"I know she doesn't have a receipt for this Fendi satchel," Suzy Davis-Johnson once told Cammie, the blond girl Marguerite disliked immensely, "but we can't afford to lose her as a customer. Mr. Michael's philosophy behind this is proven. She often spends more in this store than she returns."

I wouldn't be so sure about that, Satan.

The Vampire Bavaro had purchased and returned so many handbags at so many different Big Fancy stores, I was convinced she didn't keep anything and more than likely made quite a nice profit from her underhanded Nasty-Ass Thief ways.

Like most Bloodsuckers, Marguerite's favorite time to come feeding was at night, right before the store closed. She rarely made an appearance during the day because those hours were reserved for hellacommunications, when she'd call and stir the shit up with mass confusion and unreasonable demands.

I also think the Vampire Bavaro swooped in at night so often because Suzy Davis-Johnson was off, and so were half the managers. This gave her full access to wield the maximum amount of terror on Big Fancy salespeople and get away with whatever she could.

Ten minutes before closing one night when I was working by myself, the Vampire Bavaro materialized at the counter.

Looking scarier than normal, her pulsating, bloodshot buggy eyes seared into me, and her face was an absolute horror show, a chemical peel gone wrong.

"JEFFERSON!" the Vampire Bavaro moaned, "thank God you are here! I require your assistance. Everything is a God-awful mess!"

Your fuckin' face is a God-awful mess. I think you better look into that first, Marguerite.

I felt her fangs sinking into the back of my head as she dumped several tattered shopping bags on the counter. The contents were a closing Retail Slave's worst nightmare. She had a DKNY backpack I'd never seen before that she wanted to return, with no receipts; a Coach cross-body bag she also wanted to return, with no tag and a torn receipt; a season-old Cole Haan hobo she wanted a price adjustment on, with no receipt and only a price tag; and a Kate Spade satchel she wanted another adjustment on, with an expired 25% off coupon from a competitor.

While I removed the handbags from the shopping bags, she blurted out:

"The foreign woman and Debbie are holding three identical Burberry bags for me. The chatty girl was supposed to order one from another store, but she never called me back. Typical. She talks too much, probably not doing her job."

As usual, the Vampire Bavaro had dropped a bloodsucking bomb in my face. I wanted to fall to the floor and cry like a baby or run out of The Big Fancy screaming, but I knew none of that would happen.

I had to help the Bloodsucker.

Giving it my best shot, I charged in and tried to organize, in hopes of speeding up her messy transaction.

"Okay, let's see what we got here," I said, sounding like the deadline-driven host of a home-improvement show. "We'll put all the bags you're returning over here, the one you want a price adjustment on next, then the competitive coupon one." As I moved them into an order I could cope with, the Vampire Bavaro's craggy face turned to molten lava.

"NOT SO FAST!" she wailed, "You're rushing. I don't like it when people rush me. I get confused, and you make mistakes that cause me problems later on."

"I'm only lining them up so I can see what's what," I said.

"I'll tell you what's what. We are going to take this slowly. My way. One handbag at a time. First I want you to go get the Burberry bags I have on hold."

NOOOOO! GOD NO! WE WILL NEVER GET OUT OF HERE! I'LL BE SPENDING THE NIGHT AT THE BIG FANCY! BAVARO WILL KILL ME!

Marguerite's red marble eyes stared at me like she had just heard every word my mind had shrieked.

Then she opened her old Gucci satchel and pulled out a white plastic stick, which she began sucking on. I watched, trying to figure out why she was sucking on a plastic stick.

"Aren't you missing the candy with the chewy center, Marguerite?" I said.

"It's not candy, Jefferson, it's medicine. This place is making my whole body ache."

I wish I could make it disintegrate.

"We're all just trying to help you Marguerite," I said, glancing at my watch.

Ten minutes till closing.

"You can help me by paying attention to me instead of looking at your watch. Are you in a hurry to go somewhere Jefferson?"

"Umm . . . it's just that . . . it's almost closing time, that's all."

"To my understanding, The Big Fancy stays open until I'm finished shopping."

"Yes, Marguerite, it does."

"Before you get those Burberry bags I have on hold and I do any exchanging or buying, I want to look at the new Betsey Johnson collection," bellowed the plastic-chewing Vampire Bavaro.

And the bloodletting began.

Big Nightmare #2

In the world of retail, having two days off in a row is unheard of. Three days is like a vacation. So when the General accidentally gave me a Saturday, Sunday, and Monday off because the schedule overlapped into the next week and she wasn't paying attention, I took it and ran like I'd been awarded a Get Out of Jail Free card.

The screenplay I wanted to finish was not the World War I monster movie. After becoming bored with explosions and dragon-barbecued soldiers, I decided to change course. A Million-Dollar Screenplay had to be provocative! My new script would be critically acclaimed and win me that Oscar.

It was titled *Love in a Fitting Room*. An intensely dark, romantic thriller, the story took place in an upscale department store where two Men's Sportswear salesmen fall in love. At first they hate each other and fight over sales, but then all that rage turns to lust.

I saw studs Colin Farrell and Orlando Bloom as the salesmen.

Things become complicated for lovebirds Colin and Orlando when they both get cruised by a handsome executive customer, to be played by none other than Hugh Jackman.

In the wake of *Brokeback's* success, my script would be a sure-fire hit. In *Love in a Fitting Room*, Colin, Orlando, and Hugh fight over each other, and everything ends up all stalker-like. Someone would die. It wouldn't be Hugh, I could guarantee you that much. Maybe Orlando.

Before I could decide on who died, I had to start writing. . . .

My three-day weekend was all planned out. Ten pages a day. By the time it ended I would have half my script! If only.

If only I had been given three days off to prepare for my three days off. You see, in order for me to end up with three days off in a row, I had to work eight days in a row. During those eight days of opening, then closing, opening, then closing, and opening, then closing, without a day off, all the normal living shit that needed to be done didn't get done. I'm talking about laundry, cleaning, grocery shopping, haircut and color, tanning, and exercising. Oh and sex, lots of sex.

After taking care of all those things and then going to a movie, shopping, and drinks with Cammie, I had to have the brakes fixed on my car, which cost $700 (on my credit card, of course). Then it was e-mail, surfing the net, and returning phone calls to family and friends who were wondering why they hadn't heard from me in eight days.

By the end of the second day, I was exhausted.

On the third day I slept in.

It was around 4:00, after brunch with some gay buddies, when I freaked.

Where did my weekend go? I haven't done any writing! Shit! I still have thirty pages to write!

I knew that wasn't going to happen.

The best I could hope for was to keep the television off and park my ass in front of the computer.

Maybe I can do ten. Ten pages is better than no pages.

The first five pages were a snap.

I breezed through them so fast, by 6:00 P.M. I thought maybe I'd make my aggressive goal. Everything was going along just fine until I got to the dump scene.

No, I'm not talking about the action related to a bodily function.

In clothing departments with fitting rooms, "dump" is the term for tried-on clothes left behind by customers. Salespeople assigned "dump" duty have to gather up the piles of clothes, and refold, and rehang them. It's a hideous retail task, loathed by all.

In my scene Colin and Orlando are assigned joint dump duty in Men's Sportswear. But even though I've experienced massive amounts of dump, I just couldn't seem to make the piles of clothes jump off the page. I wrote:

```
INT. FITTING ROOM—DAY

COLIN and ORLANDO stand in front of a pile of pants and
shirts that need to be hung. The tension is intense.
Orlando is struggling with folding the pants correctly
on the hanger.

                    COLIN
          You're doing it all wrong. You fold like
          this. . . .

                    ORLANDO
          I know how to fold.

                    COLIN
          Dude, it's like this.

He moves in closer and places his hand over Orlando's
to show him the right way. Their eyes meet. A moment
happens. They . . .
```

They . . . ? I don't fucking know! Kiss? Rip each other's clothes off? Do it in the handicapped stall? After all, this is LOVE in a fitting room. Maybe they get into a huge fight? Beat each other up with hangers? Maybe Orlando isn't out of the closet and Colin is? Should Hugh walk in, needing to try on workout clothes? Maybe Colin and Orlando fight over who is going to wait on Hugh?

It needed a plot twist.

For the next five hours I rewrote the scene twenty times.

Before I knew it, my computer clock displayed 2:00 A.M.

I was more confused than ever.

And exhausted.

So many possibilities swirled around my head.

Then the mind wandering started.

I don't think I like the way my haircut turned out, and the color reminds me of Big Bird. I hope that sexy-hot guy from the gym calls me. I can't believe it cost seven hundred dollars to *fix* brakes on a car. And what's going to happen when I go back to work tomorrow? I probably had thousands returned. FUCK! It's the end of the pay period and there are only two days left. Cammie told me it wasn't busy today. Maybe all the sales will happen tomorrow. I hope so. I sure could use the money. A new Linkin Park CD just came out and there's this cool *Affliction* tee I want, oh and my car brakes! How the *fuck* am I going to pay that bill next month?

Too many thoughts. Too many words and images. All blurring together.

My eyelids became droopy.

Everything went black.

Then white.

A blank white page.

Black Courier font words magically typed across it.

A script!

Cammie the Vampire Slayer

An original screenplay by Queer-Eye Handbag Guy

Down at the bottom on the left corner it said:

Revised final draft
July 18, 2020
Rewritten 302 times
Represented by NRA
Produced by SPCA
Authenticated by FBI

Then those famous screenplay words appeared.

FADE IN

Followed by a screenplay writing itself.

EXT. BIG FANCY HANDBAG DEPARTMENT—ESTABLISH

FREEMAN is lost in a fog amongst tangles of leather handbags hanging from metal fixtures. He hears SCREAMS and begins to run, weaving in and out of the handbag trees. As he comes out of the bag forest, his eyes grow wide with TERROR. In a clearing near the Corral, he witnesses THE VAMPIRE BAVARO holding DOUCHE by the neck.

> DOUCHE
> I don't have another Marc Jacobs in Petal Pink! That's the last one. I swear!

> VAMPIRE BAVARO
> Listen to me, Foreign Woman. It's scratched. I want *another one! At discount!*

BAVARO suddenly spots Freeman.

> VAMPIRE BAVARO
> *Jefferson!* So nice of you to join us.

She drops Douche to the floor like a rag doll. Douche isn't moving. She's been sucked dry. Freeman's glad, but joy turns to worry upon seeing a terrified MARSHA and JULES cowering in a corner by the Coach Shop.

> VAMPIRE BAVARO
> Jefferson, I require your assistance! *Come to me . . . now!!!*

> FREEMAN
> *No way,* you bloodsucking psycho! *Not this time!*

Freeman bolts for the Corral. The Vampire Bavaro is right on his tail.

> VAMPIRE BAVARO
> Don't you dare run from me, Jefferson. Things are an awful mess, and I need you to fix them. You have to give me the discount I deserve. I want 100% off!

Freeman reaches the register and pushes a black key on the keyboard. All of a sudden a spotlight shoots into the air and hits the ceiling. The image is just like *Batman's* signal, only instead of displaying a bat silhouette, Cammie's Signal is two letter C's crossing each other—like the Coco Chanel logo.

                    MARSHA
          You did it! The Cammie Signal! Save us,
          Cammie!

Bavaro has Freeman pinned on the glass counter. He tries to fend her off using an Isabella Fiore tote that has a rhinestone-studded crucifix on it. Bavaro SCREAMS momentarily at the sight of the jewel-encrusted cross on the handbag, but is not stopped. She opens her mouth to reveal her razor-sharp teeth soaked in Douche's blood. She's about to bite Freeman's face off when out of the fog a shadow appears on the ledge high above the Corral.

CAMMIE THE VAMPIRE SLAYER!

CAMMIE has on a Chanel cheerleading outfit in black and white, complete with Chanel utility belt. The CC logo is bold and powerful on her chest. On her feet are black Converse Chuck Taylors. On her shoulder is a quilted Chanel tote. Cammie quickly puts on some Chanel lip gloss. She drops the tote and pulls out a Chanel Flail—a quilted leather stick with a gold ball hanging from it.

                    CAMMIE
          Let him go, Bavaro. Your bloodsucking days
          are over!

                    VAMPIRE BAVARO
          You! The girl I dislike *immensely!*

                    CAMMIE
          That's right, *bitch*, and you're going to
          dislike me even more once I kick your
          motherfuckin' ass to next Tuesday!

                 VAMPIRE BAVARO
          We'll just see about that! No one speaks to me
          like that at this store and gets away with it.

Cammie and Bavaro lunge at each other like two rabid
dogs.

Cammie SMACKS Bavaro in the face with her Chanel
Flail. There's a BURNING SOUND as the ball momentarily
sticks to Bavaro's cheek. The CC emblem is now branded
permanently on Bravaro's seared jowl.

                 VAMPIRE BAVARO
          You will pay for that!

She grabs the Chanel Flail, tears the ball from it, and
smacks Cammie in the head. Then the two roll around
the floor, screaming and pulling each other's hair.
Supernatural cat fight!

Bavaro hurdles Cammie into a display case full of
evening bags.

Cammie stomach-kicks Bavaro into a wall of glass
shelves holding Allure bags.

Bavaro pushes a handbag tree on top of Cammie.

Cammie body-slams Bavaro into the clearance table.

They go back and forth in a salesperson-customer death
match and destroy the department. THE GENERAL stands
nearby and SCREAMS when she sees the mess.

Cammie attempts to choke Bavaro with the cheap
LeSportsac shoulder satchel.

Bavaro tries to stuff old receipts in Cammie's mouth.

Cammie pulls a scan-gun from her Chanel utility belt
and fires a laser blast into Bavaro's eyes, momentarily
blinding her, but Bavaro reaches for a microfiber Hobo
International messenger bag with a really long strap.
She gets the strap around Cammie's neck and begins
choking her. Cammie falls to her knees. Bavaro is on
top of her.

                    VAMPIRE BAVARO
          How do you like that, blondie? Not so full of
          yourself anymore, are you? You are the worst
          salesperson in this store, and I'm going to
          drain you till there's nothing left.

Cammie struggles. It looks like this might be it.
Bavaro appears to have control.

But Cammie grabs a nearby Isabella Fiore hobo covered
in silver studs and whacks the Vampire Bavaro, knocking
her into a table of Juicy Couture cosmetic bags.

                    CAMMIE
          We are not taking any more shit from you
          Bavaro!

Bavaro appears momentarily disoriented. Cammie yanks
her by the hair and throws her to the floor. Straddling
her bloodsucking prey, she holds the broken Chanel
Flail to Bavaro's neck.

                    CAMMIE
          Free, get the wooden hanger out of my tote.

Freeman digs in the Chanel bag. Finds it. Throws it.
Cammie catches the hanger with one hand.

                    CAMMIE
          YOUR BLOODSUCKING BITCH ASS IS DONE
          TERRORIZING US!

Cammie drives the wooden hanger into Bavaro's heart.
She lets out a piercing SCREAM.

                    CAMMIE
          Free, toss me that Marc Jacobs Venetia in
          metallic silver.

Freeman hurls the satchel like a football. Cammie
catches it by the handles.

Using it as a HAMMER, she drives the wooden hanger deep
into Bavaro.

                    VAMPIRE BAVARO
          NOOOOO!!! I WILL NOT LEAVE! NOOOOOO!!

                    CAMMIE
          And by the way, bitch, MY NAME IS CAMMIE!

With one last pound, the hanger plunges as far as it
can go into Barvaro's chest. The top snaps off.

The Vampire Bavaro stops moving.

Cammie jumps off the former Bloodsucker and straightens
her Chanel skirt.

Bavaro's body shrivels up and turns into cotton candy.

Freeman, Jules, and Marsha crowd around Cammie,
cheering. But she is serious. Ready for the next
monstrous battle at The Big Fancy.

                    CAMMIE
          I must go now. A rabid Discount Rat is loose
          in Lingerie. But know this, the war is
          not over. Wherever there is a Bloodsucker
          terrorizing a Retail Slave, I will be there.

Cammie bolts for the aisle sprinting toward the
escalator.

```
INT. HANDBAG DEPARTMENT—LATER

Freeman, Marsha, and Jules are cleaning up the
catastrophic mess of handbags the Vampire Bavaro left
behind. Suddenly, there's a loud HOWL. They all look
at each other scared. Out of the fog steps TEDDY BEAR
LADY. She is 7 feet tall and hairy as hell, looking
like a possessed grizzly bear with yellow eyes and
jagged teeth.

                    TEDDY BEAR LADY
          The Good Lord sent me . . . RAAAAAAAWRRRRR!

Everyone SCREAMS.

Teddy Bear Lady lumbers toward them, SCREAMING . . .

SCREAMING . . .

"AAAAAAAAAAAAAGH!"
```

I jerked up from my keyboard pillow like it was on fire.

My skull alarm clock displayed 10:00 A.M.

For a moment I panicked, but then I remembered I was working the closing shift.

Close call.

What a long-ass, hideous nightmare.

Bavaro's bloodsucking face was left burning my mind's eye.

I stumbled to the kitchen, trying to shake it off.

Must wake up. Need coffee. Must make coffee.

I spilled water and coffee grounds, and knocked over mugs, blinded by flashes of Cammie's Chanel logo. What a way to end my three days off from The Big Fancy. Practically no writing done.

Total disaster.

Hundreds of dream experts contend that images occurring during sleep should be viewed symbolically, rather than literally.

They don't know shit.

Some seven hours after waking from this Big Nightmare, I rounded a fixture in the Marc Jacobs Shop and ran smack into the real Vampire Bavaro.

Her pockmarked face was pale, her black-widow hair pinned up on her head in a bun, and she had on a white oversized T-shirt, black leggings, and Keds. She looked too comfortable for my own good.

"JEFFERSON! There you are. I require your assistance," Marguerite proclaimed in her most dramatic voice. "I have a coupon from another store for a Marc Jacobs; Debbie has one on hold, but it's scratched, and the blond girl I dislike immensely never called me back. Everything is a God-awful mess."

I almost passed out.

No garlic or crosses at my immediate disposal. The Bloodsucking bitch had me right where she wanted me.

ACT 3

Misfire and Brimstone at The Big Fancy

Ready your pitchforks.
You are now entering the third floor of hell.

Sale Smack-Down

"No, everything is not on sale," I said through grated teeth. "Only the things with sale signs are on sale. All of the tables are on sale and those fixtures. That's it. Nothing else!"

The customer looked around, then pointed to the Marc Jacobs shop and asked, "What about those? Are those on sale over there?"

I wanted to hit her.

Instead I turned around and walked away.

We were under Discount Rat attack.

It was The Big Fancy's biggest sale of the year: the Once a Year Sale. The Ultimate Retail Hell.

We had replaced our regular fixtures and glass tables with big wooden bins and filled them with a combination of new handbags on sale for a limited time and permanent markdowns. Hordes of hungry sale shoppers surrounded the tables, pawing and pilfering, throwing bags everywhere. When the tables got completely surrounded, I couldn't help but compare the menagerie to a bunch of pigs at their troughs. From open to close, the place was trashed, looking like a nuclear handbag explosion. Bags on the floor. Bags missing stuffing and crumpled up on the counter. Bags hanging off shelves by their straps. At one point, a woman bumped into me and said, "It's a zoo in here!"

I looked over at the sale troughs, and replied, "I could not agree with you more."

Besides General Judy, there were ten of us staffed for the Once a Year Sale. The Big Fancy was all about overstaffing—believing it created a "survival of the fittest" environment and got the store more sales. However, by noon, we all thought ten was too many, as we constantly bumped into each other and approached customers who had already been approached. My Handbag Angels looked out for me, and I for them; we handed off customers to each other and protected the ones we had. We made sure the Demon Squad stayed in check, but it was impossible to stop Douche and Tiffany. They were like great white sale sharks, gobbling up customers in packs. The extra salespeople hired for the event never stood a chance. They sold nothing. Using their amazing fashion prowess, Jules and Cammie raked in the sales, beating Tiffany, but not Douche. Marsha held her own because she'd been there so long and had a lot of regulars, while Marci pretty much drowned because her talking slowed down each transaction.

As for me? I survived. Almost.

Despite The Big Fancy's overstaffing, I had done really well with sales during the morning hours. But it wasn't long before the parade of Big Fancy Serpents and Bloodsuckers had taken their toll on me. Patty harangued me for at least a half-hour, wanting deescounts on everything. I finally snapped and said, "Patty, I'm cutting you off. No more deescounts for you. You've reached your deescount limit and you don't have a designated driver." She had no clue what I meant, just as I had no clue what the fuck Teddy Bear Lady was doing charging down the main aisle wearing dirty Lion King slippers. Did they have secret pockets? And there was her nemesis, the other Virginia, whom I tried to avoid, but she cornered me by the DKNY sale bags and gave me details about her gall bladder attack the night before. Of course, my Shoposaurus Carnotaurus came in and devoured half the store. It was fun parading Lorraine around as always, but also stressful and tiring—as always. She did drop ten grand though, so I was one Retail Slave who had nothing to complain about. That is, until the Vampire Bavaro and Mrs. Beaumont showed up within minutes of each other. After waiting on them, my head got a little fuzzier, my clothes a little sweatier, and my vision blurrier.

What's my name? Where am I? I sell handbags at The Big Fancy? You got to be fuckin' kidding me!

As lunchtime arrived, the department resembled a retail Vietnam War. All the chaotic shit that happens during sales happened. The registers went offline at least twice, making us wait ten minutes for an approval. The phone rang every ten seconds. Judy screamed at us because our sales were down from last year and we were missing the department goal. Cammie and Marci fought over sales. Tiffany and Jules fought over sales. Douche and everyone fought over sales.

Every time I turned around, something was missing a ticket.

"There's no price on this wallet?" a customer said.

I bent down and picked up a tag from its spot on the floor next to her feet.

"Well what about these five others?" she demanded.

"They're missing because people are eating them," I said.

For a minute she looked like she believed me.

By late afternoon, The Big Fancy was in the throes of Once a Year Sale mania.

I had to tell a lady there were no overnight holds on sale bags. She snapped at me and said, "Listen here, young man. I am the customer. You put no conditions on me. I do as I wish. If I want you to hold these bags till my funeral, you'll hold them. Got it?" I took the bags, thinking *if only*.

I then spent ten minutes explaining to a woman that 25% off an original price does not mean an additional 25% off. The woman kept arguing saying "But that would mean it's an additional 25% off!" Finally I went all Sale Hell Bitch on her: "Does it say 'additional' on the sign? NO! They are NOT an additional percentage off. THEY ARE 25 PERCENT OFF ORIGINAL! THAT'S IT!"

Then, for the millionth time, a woman came up to me and asked, "Why isn't everything on sale?"

I bitched back at her, "Because life isn't fair."

The sale questions continued to pummel me:

"I found it on the sale table; shouldn't it be on sale even if the price is not marked?"

"It's not my fault someone dropped it on the sale table even though it's not on sale. Shouldn't I get it on sale anyway!"

"Can't you just put it on sale?"

"Will you give me an extra discount?"

"How much is it with tax?"

"There's a mark on the bottom of this bag, can you clean it off?"

"Is this the right sale price?"

"Can you call another store and get me one in black?"

"Is that the final sale price?"

"Is there an additional amount off?"

"Is this all you have on sale?"

"Why isn't everything on sale? I thought the whole store was on sale!"

I couldn't take any more. Queer-Eye Handbag Guy was going to kill a Discount Rat!

Let me just squeeze these leather handbag straps tighter around your neck and you can go to a place where everything is on sale and get an additional 20% no matter what!

I ran for the stockroom as if my life depended on it.

I needed to energize myself, so I hid there for twenty minutes talking to Judy, who looked like she had laid down in front of a lawnmower. She drank Coke and ate Funyuns while I downed Diet Rockstar and devoured chocolate and potato chips. It was the most relaxed I'd ever seen the General. I wasn't the only one the sale had beaten down. Unfortunately, my temporary reprieve and refueling didn't help much.

I'd become a sales zombie.

My movements were slow. Eyes glazed over. I reached out toward potential spenders only for them to give me the cold shoulder. They'd look at me funny and say Douche was helping them.

Queer-Eye Handbag Guy couldn't have sold porno to a gay man.

At that point the only thing I could do without exerting too many brain cells was to straighten. The handbag sale tables reminded me of my closet after I hadn't done laundry for a month. Piles of bags lay in mounds that looked like tangled kelp. Paper stuffing was everywhere. Handbag zippers were left open. Handbag flaps were left open. Handbag straps twisted with other straps. The wallets were even worse, dumped in heaps like old magazines. Bags and wallets were scattered haphazardly all over the floor. The place was a fucking mess.

My ability to service and sell had died and I felt like *I'd* been marked down to 75% off. All I could handle was entering my employee number into the register and putting things in shopping bags. Retail Droid mode took over. I prayed a circuit in my broken-down body wouldn't overheat.

Finally, around 7:00, the General realized she was getting nothing else out of me and said I could go home. I was too dazed to even feel excited.

As I attempted to run for my gay life, I ran smack into Fashion Disaster.

I'm calling her Fashion Disaster because when I first met her by the sale tables earlier in the day and saw how she was dressed, I thought she had to be either blind or on drugs. This girl had on a white fedora with multicolored feathers sticking out from it, gaudy pink plastic dangly earrings, and an atrocious halter dress that had blue checkerboard print around her boobs with abstract palm trees in white, yellow, and purple for the lower half. On her feet were short purple boots with fringe. Heidi Klum would have screamed and reached for her shotgun!

After choking down laughter, I spent a good half-hour trying to help Fashion Disaster. She either hated everything, had everything, or couldn't afford anything. The only item she showed any interest in was a cheap, $50 green suede hobo we had gotten in for the sale. She wanted it in black, but the bag had been hot and was gone within several hours of opening.

"You told me there weren't any more of those suede bags in black!" Fashion Disaster yelled into my discount-worn face.

It had been such a long, hideous Big Fancy sale day. I had to think back for a minute. Black suede? What the fuck was she talking about? Then like any bloodsucking nightmare it all came screaming back.

"There aren't any left! I told you the truth," I replied, agitated she was throwing this at me now.

"How come that woman has one?"

I looked over to see Douche helping a girl with huge gold hoop earrings and a leopard print scarf wrapped around her head. She wore a camouflage army jacket with jeans rolled up like pedal pushers, and orange pumps. On her arm was a huge raffia straw satchel with a blue flower.

She was Fashion Disaster's alter ego, Fashion Meltdown.

Sure enough, Fashion Meltdown was playing with the black hobo while Douche talked, probably telling her not to buy because it was cheap.

"I just saw her pick it up off the sale table," said Disaster, "I was going over there, but I couldn't get there fast enough."

"I don't know," I said with a big, exhausted, I've-had-it sigh, "Maybe it was on hold or something."

Fashion Disaster went ballistic: "I'm really pissed! I WANT THAT SUEDE BAG. You have to get it for me. NOW! Or I'm going to the store manager to complain and tell her how you lied to me and completely ruined my day *and* the outfit I was trying to put together."

Give me a fuckin' break. I'm going to barf all over your fringe boots.

Fashion Disaster's soap opera tirade was the last thing I wanted to deal with. My feet felt like bloody stumps, my eyes were watering, and I was starting to limp.

"I WANT THAT BAG AND I'M NOT LEAVING UNTIL I GET IT!"

"Okay," I sighed, "I'll see if she's going to buy it."

I maneuvered closer to Douche and Fashion Meltdown, pretending to straighten sale bags, all the while feeling Disaster's hungry-for-suede eyes boring into the back of my head.

After eavesdropping, I discovered that Meltdown wanted Douche to help her decide between several bags—DKNY, Coach, Kenneth Cole, and the Allure hobo suede bag. All were on sale except for the Coach. Of course Douche could have cared less about what Meltdown wanted and she was pushing her into the Coach, which wasn't on sale and cost nearly $500. After what seemed like a month to me, Meltdown finally said, "You are right! The Coach is a better investment, and I'm sure they will be sold out next week!"

What a gullible idiot Fashion Meltdown was. I wished she'd been my customer. With the decision made, I moved in for the extraction. Fashion Disaster was right on my heels.

"Are you done with this?" I said, reaching for the suede bag. "My customer would like to see it."

As the words came out of my mouth, I knew I'd made a critical mistake.

I felt like a zombie, so I wasn't thinking clearly. What can I say?

From experience, I knew what was going to happen next. You see, whenever there is only one left of something on sale, and two women suddenly start eyeing it for whatever reason, the one that picks it up first wins. And even though the winner may not really want it, if she's a bitch, she'll buy it out of spite, just to keep the other one from having it. It's a common occurrence in the Handbag Jungle.

And that's exactly what went down here.

"Someone else wants to buy it?" yelped Fashion Meltdown. "Is it the last one?"

Of course, Douche opened her greedy fuckin' Jaws trap and said, "Yes, they've been very popular today."

I wanted to scream when Douche said that. A sharky move if ever I saw one. If that wasn't bad enough, then the sharky bitch continued, "Maybe you should get it along with the Coach? It's so inexpensive."

Douche's sale sword just cut my head off.

Before I could say anything, Jules yelled from the Corral. Douche had a call. As Douche left, Fashion Meltdown gripped the suede hobo.

"I've changed my mind," she said, coddling it like a Fred Leighton diamond.

"You only want it because I want it," said Fashion Disaster.

"I was looking at it first, but now I'm going to buy it!" replied Fashion Meltdown.

"I can't believe you're being such a bitch about this. You don't even want it."

"How do you know that?" said Meltdown, "I have an awesome pair of Steve Madden shoes this would look kick-ass with."

"You said you wanted that other bag. Now all of a sudden you want *this* one?" A showdown between Meltdown and Disaster was about to take place. As much as I would have enjoyed seeing these hipsters charge each other, rip their fugly clothes to shreds, and hopefully climax to hair pulling and nail scratching, all I could think about was getting the fuck out. I'd had enough of The Big Fancy's Once a Year Sale.

That's once a year too much for me. Time to start drinking.

I don't know where the energy or creative power came from, but the words that saved me from major sale drama popped into my head. I wasted no time in delivering them:

"Don't worry about it. I'll get you one from the stockroom of another store if you really want one, but I wouldn't advise it."

Disaster and Meltdown broke their suede-bag-war stare with one another and turned their attention to me.

"Why not?!" demanded Disaster.

"Because all of these bags were removed from the floor. We received an e-mail from the buyer telling us to pull them immediately."

"Why were you supposed to pull them off the floor?" asked Meltdown, now alarmed.

"Apparently the black suede is bleeding. It's rubbing off and ruining clothing."

Meltdown gasped in horror.

Disaster looked unfazed. Maybe she was thinking of wearing it with all black and the bleeding suede wouldn't matter. Maybe she wanted it to bleed. Who knew what Disaster was thinking?

At that moment, overcome with Big Fancy Sale exhaustion, I held my breath, hoping against hope that my sudden spur-of-the-moment tactic to lie my ass off would save me from these bloodsucking bitches.

Maybe I should add something about how the suede bag is cursed and the woman who carries it will be subject to a life of bad skin and bad taste in clothes. No, probably too much.

"Well I don't want it then," said Disaster, walking away.

"I don't either," said Meltdown, throwing it where it didn't belong on top of the sale wallets.

Seconds later, Douche came back, "Where's my customer?"

"Oh, she left," I said, "She decided against the Coach and the suede bag. I don't think she liked the quality."

Take that, you sharky bitch!

"Aagh," Douche said, waving me off and torpedoing toward a woman looking at sale backpacks.

Just then a customer tapped me and asked, "Is everything on sale?"

I stared at her, my eyeballs aching and feet throbbing.

"You bet it is," I replied, "and that woman named Douche over there will be glad to help you."

Then I took my sale-ravaged body home.

Babysitting the Devil's Spawn

I love kids. I really do. But like most Retail Slaves in the entire world and universe, I *don't* love kids who invade our stores with (or without) their parents and turn into pint-sized demons, shrieking and crying at the top of their lungs while annihilating everything in sight and leaving a path of merchandise devastation that we have to clean up.

Devil Spawn indeed. Behind every one of those little devils is a parent with her head totally up her ass.

The Corral at The Big Fancy was positioned along the main aisle right next to the mall doors, and while this was great for handbag exposure, people watching, and date hunting, it was a bitch when it came to Devil Spawn attacks. Just about every ten seconds a stroller or gang of children would pass by, leaving the odds highly in favor of kids fighting, having temper tantrums, and roughhousing, and, the absolute worst—a baby wailing. It was not easy to talk on the phone or try to sell handbags with that kind of hellacious background racket.

"I want to hear that brat scream like I want to drink leather lotion," Cammie once said to me after a woman let her baby cry like a banshee for fifteen minutes while she shopped. "What the fuck! Shut your fuckin' kid up, lady!" Cammie never did so well with kids and always kept her distance.

How we each handled children ranged from devilish to angelic. Like Cammie, my other coworkers with child phobias included Judy, Tiffany, Marci, and Douche. For whatever reasons, they had no maternal instincts and stayed clear of anyone under the age of fourteen.

Jules, on the other hand, let her motherly skills and passion flow out all the time. Once I spotted her in the Marc Jacobs shop holding a baby while playing with a three-year-old girl and five-year-old boy. The mother was nowhere in sight. Luckily for Jules, these children were being Perfect Little Angels, instead of Devil Spawn, but I asked her, "What the hell? Are you charging for babysitting?" She winked, leaned in, and whispered, "Mom's in the shoe department taking a few minutes rest for herself. She just bought a $2,000 Marc Jacobs. It's the least I could do."

While I wouldn't have gone as far as Jules, Marsha and I both tolerated children. If they were Perfect Little Angels, then it was fun times, but if they were Devil Spawn, we ran for the stockroom, although Marsha had no qualms about scolding unruly guttersnipes. She'd get right in their tiny faces and put on her scariest Disney Witch face, and say, "You stand there and behave. No screaming or running! I'm not messin' around here! You are at The Big Fancy, not a playground! Do you understand me?" Some of them cried, but most stood paralyzed by fear. If parents bitched, she told them all to get the hell out.

Golden Girl Marsha could get away with that, but Queer-Eye Handbag Guy couldn't. I once reprimanded a destructive little female Devil Spawn for pulling at the glass shelves in the wall. Her mother was too busying looking at a Kate Spade in the mirror and not paying attention. When the Spawn didn't listen and kept pulling on the glass, which could have fallen on her and killed her, I shouted, "DID YOU HEAR ME? I SAID, STOP PULLING ON THE GLASS! YOU'RE GOING TO HURT YOURSELF!" The little girl then started crying at my raised voice, and her uptight mother ran over and smacked me on the back of the head (lightly, or else I would have had her and her Devil Spawn arrested). "DON'T YOU PARENT MY CHILD!" she yelled at me before storming out.

No problem, ma'am, next time I'll just let the glass shelves fall and cut her fuckin' head off, and you won't hear one little peep from me.

Although I have many hellacious stories involving Devil Spawn running amok at The Big Fancy, one of my most horrific happened on a quiet Thursday, late in the afternoon.

In hindsight, I should have known something wicked was coming my way. Things were just too calm and peaceful in the Handbag Jungle. No phone ringing. No crazy customers. No Returners. No Nasty-Ass Thieves. No Suzy Davis-Johnson checking up on us. No General ordering us around. No Douche stealing sales.

Just Cammie and me manning the fort, without customers, standing in the middle of the department hiding among a cluster of fixtures, and chitchatting about who we felt should win a Best Actor Academy Award.

"Johnny Depp is long overdue," I said.

"The man is a god," Cammie agreed, "I'd be his wench on the high seas any day."

Suddenly, out of nowhere, a nauseating scent stole into our noses.

"Do you fucking smell that?" she said, making a face. "It's like rotting tomato juice."

"I think I'm gonna vomit," I responded.

Then the handbag fixtures rustled.

Six children stepped out, surrounding us.

Ages three to fifteen. Four boys. Two girls. Unkempt clothes. Bristly reddish hair. Freckled faces. Missing teeth. Pudgy bodies. Mean looking. They weren't the kind of kids you wanted to buy candy for or give airplane rides to.

They were the kind of kids who looked extremely angry for being dragged into a store not named Toys "R" Us, GameStop, or Build-A-Bear.

The kind of kids who looked possessed by demons.

I almost screamed as my horror-obsessed mind compared their stepping out of the handbag fixtures to Stephen King's "Children of the Corn."

If you've never read King's scary story or seen the classic horror film, let me give it to you in a nutshell: Led by the evil-looking kids Isaac and Malachi, all the children in a small town are hypnotized by a monster in the corn forcing them to kill all the adults. In the cheesy but memorable '80s movie, the opening scene finds a bunch of seniors at a diner getting poisoned and slaughtered by the Children of the Corn.

Of course, my overactive imagination ran wild with the prospect of the cult still existing.

They've moved to the big city and upgraded to a Big Fancy Department Store. I'm dead!

The Children of the *Retail* Corn were staring at us like we were their own personal playthings.

You belong to us. There's no escape.

A round, disheveled woman with ratty dirty-blond hair appeared. Obviously Mother of Spawn. She pushed a covered stroller, which I'm sure had Rosemary's Baby slumbering inside.

"I need a new backpack," said the Children of the Retail Corn's Mother, "I've been looking everywhere. No one has a good selection anymore. It's just so hard to find a backpack."

"We have lots of backpacks," I said, nervous, the Devil Spawn watching my every move.

"NO!" one of them suddenly shouted, "NO, YOU DON'T!"

Okay, now I know who Malachi is, and I'm about to wet myself.

Cammie ran for the stockroom. "I'm fuckin' out of here," she said under her breath.

Before I could protest, she had vanished, and the Mother of Spawn was all over me. "I need a backpack! Why is it so hard to find one these days? Stores used to carry thousands of them!"

"Umm . . . Perlina makes really nice backpacks," I stammered.

The Spawn Mom ignored my offering, preferring to chat with herself. She continued rambling on about her backpack drought while pawing at handbags and not looking at me.

Or her kids.

If there was some kind of tribal warning sound with a conch shell, I sure as fuck did not hear it. If I had, I would have joined Cammie in the Devil Spawn Shelter.

All at once the Children of the Retail Corn went berserk.

The three boys began running around me in circles and shouting old-style Indian war cries, possibly preparing me to be tied up and have my head shrunken.

The teen girl mauled a Juicy Couture bowler bag like a pit bull discovering a new chew toy. She tore out the wads of paper stuffing and threw it on the floor. One of the boys snatched up the discarded stuffing, ripped it into tiny shreds, and tossed it in the air, claiming it was snowing.

The other, younger girl began yanking bags off shelves and kicking them across the floor to make a pile, which I assumed she was going to light on fire.

All the while, Spawn Mom completely ignored the devilish behavior and said to me:

"My backpack needs to have lots of pockets. And I want something in leather. . . ."

I was about to answer her when suddenly one of the little redheaded monsters, who must have been three or four, started screaming savagely, ran up to my right leg, and wrapped his arms and legs around me like he was going to shimmy up a pole.

Mortified and shocked, I looked down at the Devil Spawn attached to my leg.

It totally freaked the shit out of me.

But not before getting a million times worse.

While continuing to wail, the little beast squeezed as tight as he could and began humping my leg like a possessed poodle in heat.

I was standing in a suit in the middle of The Big Fancy Department Store trying to sell a woman some shitty-ass backpack, and her beastly little brat had decided to use my leg as a hobbyhorse.

I had reached a new low in Retail Hell.

Total damnation.

At the hands of Devil Spawn.

As the kid continued to undulate and ride my leg like it was a bull, I couldn't move or speak. I looked to his mother for help. Nothing. No sign of shock or concern. It probably happens all day long. "I want a bigger backpack with more pockets," was all she said, staying focused on the handbags, "Something with gold hardware."

Even though I was stunned beyond belief by this spawn's actions, I figured there was something medically wrong with this kid. Still, why was Spawn Mom allowing this to happen?

I tried to end the embarrassing scene by attempting to pull him off, but Thumper Humper locked his hands tighter, yelled louder, and used my foot as a chair.

Speechless, I stood there.

Continuing to turn a blind eye, Spawn Mom darted around a fixture and wandered away to another part of the jungle, leaving me alone with the clinging freak and his two demonic siblings, who were now playing catch over my head with a $3,000 Gucci satchel.

I tried to kick and shake the humper, but he only screamed louder, clutched harder, and humped my leg faster.

Where the hell is Super Nanny when you need her?

I'd had enough of Devil Spawn babysitting. Something needed to be done fast, before I grabbed a nearby can of leather protector and sprayed the little wretch until he let go. So I limped after Spawn Mom, dragging her shrieking, humping brat with me, as if I had a broken leg.

I caught up to her and the fifteen-year old brutalizing a $900 Fendi backpack. Their looks of nonchalance at seeing the boy ride my leg freaked me out even more.

I had reached my limit and was about to kick the kid to kingdom come when, oddly enough, it was the teen who saw the mix of terror and anger in my eyes. She took pity and removed her evil, bouncing sibling from my leg.

As I smoothed out my now-wrinkled pants and tried to deal with what had happened, the Mother only looked at me and said, "I need a larger backpack and one that has lots of pockets. This Fendi is too expensive. Do you have anything cheaper?"

I stared at her, stunned, and contemplated calling Child Services.

Later I berated Cammie for leaving me, and all she could say was how pissed she was that her cell-phone camera shot of Humpy and me didn't come out.

When I got home, I took off my pants and threw them away. No dry cleaning would wash out that Devil Spawn nightmare. Besides, they were kinda worn out anyway, and it gave me a perfectly good reason to go buy some new Ben Sherman slacks I'd been eyeing.

That night I drank heavily.

Hot Stuff on Mount Fancy

As I walked down the street, even before I got to the Employee Entrance door, I could hear the pulsating beat. Ten feet away.

That's how loud it was.

And then when I pulled open the door, the musical blast hit me in the face.

"HOT, HOT, HOT ... STUUUUUFF. HOT, HOT, HOT ... STUUUUUFF."

Donna Summer's "Hot Stuff."

"HOT, HOT, HOT ... STUUUUUFF. HOT, HOT, HOT ... STUUUUUFF." Hot stuff in hell. How apropos.

A new kind of theme had taken over Mount Fancy.

They called it Disco Nights.

What was it with the dumb-ass stairwell themes?

"We do it because it's festive and fun," Suzy Davis-Johnson replied when asked why the stairwell had been transformed into the Barnum & Bailey Circus.

You're so right, Satan! Climbing eight flights of stairs is absolutely festive and fun! Might as well throw in a circus. Maybe you should hire elephants to carry us to the top!

The whole decorate-the-stairwell thing was aimed at inspiring us salespeople before we hit the selling floor of The Big Fancy, and Marsha told me the ones responsible for dreaming this shit up were Satan herself, Two-Tone Tammy, and Marcella, the Display Art manager—a fashionless, frumpy girl in her twenties who looked about as artistic as a tax auditor. Together the three of them concocted one nauseating theme after another, spending thousands of dollars a year on colorful paint and cheesy props hijacked from the nearby party store.

With all the money they flushed trying to lift our stair-climbing spirits with lame decorations, they could have made a down payment on an elevator or sky tram.

Or maybe built a complimentary juice bar and tropical fish tank.

Instead we were bombarded by one imbecilic theme after another. And while I had simply ignored the nauseating, cutesy propaganda of the other themes, Disco Nights sent my irritation to a whole new level.

The walls of Mount Fancy were painted yellow with rainbow swirls all over them, and the railings were doused in hot pink. Large decals of flowers and weird-looking creatures floated across the rainbow walls, making me feel as if I was trapped inside a psychedelic version of Alice's rabbit hole. Shiny silver strips dangled everywhere.

Many Mount Fancy climbers had tried to use the strips as safety ropes while they plodded up the staircases, only to end up yanking them down onto the staircases, increasing the chances of slippery-strip accidents.

The pièce de résistance of Disco Nights was a rotating disco ball hanging under dimmed fluorescent lights a few feet from the entrance door. Little white spots swarmed around the darkened room, bringing back God-awful '70s memories of roller-skating and proms.

Try coming down a sixteen-step staircase with disco ball spots blinding your eyes. It ain't easy.

But it wasn't the weird creature decals, spinning disco ball, or shiny silver strips that caused me to go mental on Big Fancy Disco Mountain. It was the goddamn motherfucking music.

Just inside the entrance doors, a few feet from the mirror ball, was a mini boom box sitting high up on a small shelf in the opposite corner. Blaring from its speakers were three dance songs on looped rotation: Donna Summer's "Hot Stuff," the Village People's "YMCA," and Kool and the Gang's "Celebration." Three fucking songs. That's it. There are thousands of disco songs and hundreds of CD compilations, but no, for some stupid reason Satan and her minions decided to use only those three songs.

Over and over and over and over they played.

"Hot Stuff," "YMCA," and "Celebrate" reverberated in my ears.

Twice a day. Five fucking days a week. Maybe more if I worked overtime.

And for some reason I'd always arrive at Mount Fancy's disco right on cue: "HOT, HOT, HOT ... STUUUUUFF. HOT, HOT, HOT ... STUUUUUFF."

I endured the Mount Fancy three-song disco for almost a month before I snapped. I just couldn't take any more celebrating YMCA hot stuff. Disco Death Star had to be destroyed. I tried to reach the player, but the bastards had thought of everything. The shelf was just high enough so the volume slider and off-button couldn't be reached.

Was that done on purpose? Did they know we would get irritated by this? I became even more irritated by the thought of their preparing for our irritation.

There had to be a way to stop this three-song disco—without bringing in a shotgun. After staring at the bellowing player for several moments, I saw a weakness in their system: The player's power cord. Apparently, Display Manager Marcella had not covered all security aspects surrounding her automatic disco DJ.

Several inches of cord were sticking out from the player, snaking its way up to the nearby outlet. Just enough excess to grab hold of.

Feeling like Michael Jordan, I jumped up and yanked the cord from the wall socket.

Sweet silence prevailed. No more "HOT, HOT, HOT ... STUUUUUFF."

Unfortunately, my silent happiness was short-lived.

No matter how many times I unplugged the player, the next day I'd walk in to "HOT, HOT, HOT ... STUUUUFF."

The fight was on. To the Death, "Hot Stuff"!

Having no idea who my Cord-Plugging Opponent was, for days I continued to unplug the cord every chance I got, hoping the message would be delivered.

NO MORE "HOT STUFF!!"

My crusade to kill the Mount Fancy Disco was met with the wild approval of my fellow climbers. They cheered and clapped as I vaulted to unplug and snuff out Donna.

After several weeks of plug-pulling wars, I entered Mount Fancy early one morning around 8:00 and was instantly pummeled even more loudly than usual by "HOT, HOT, HOT . . . STUUUUUFF."

What the hell?

I had unplugged the player when I'd left after my closing shift the night before. There should have been no disco music playing that early in the morning.

I quickly catapulted myself up and yanked the fucking cord out, stopping Donna from telling me what she needed once again. Silence commanded the stairwell.

Take that, you fucker, whoever you are.

As I reached the second flight of stairs and rounded the corner on platform three, I came face to face with my worst Big Fancy nightmare.

The Stephanator.

The pissed-off look on Store Secretary Stephanie's plasticized face said it all. She'd obviously been lying in wait to ambush the person that turned out to be me.

"YOOOOU!" she wailed like she was the daughter of Darth Vader. "ALL THIS TIME IT WAS YOOOOU!!! YOU'RE THE ONE UNPLUGGING THE MUSIC!"

I stared at her.

Shit. It's too early in the morning to face the Stephanator. What did she want from me? A fucking confession? Yes, I did it! So what? Take away my dance card. Call the Disco Police.

"WHAT ARE YOU DOING?" she shouted, her mechanical green eyes practically popping out of her head, "YOU ARE WAY OUT OF LINE, MISTER."

Should I admit it? Should I fight? Should I spin a clever lie like Cammie would? It was just too fucking early. I hadn't slept the night before, I'd had no coffee, and I felt like a raving bitch. So I did what any other raving, coffee-less bitch would do at 7:45 A.M.

I attacked back.

"IF I HAVE TO HEAR FUCKING 'HOT STUFF' ONE MORE FUCKING TIME, I'M GOING TO FUCKING KILL SOMEONE!"

In retrospect, spouting off the f-word like that probably wasn't the smartest move to make in dealing with this half-woman, half-machine. I've seen enough sci-fi movies to know she could tear me apart with her manicured steel hands.

"I WILL NOT TOLERATE BEING SPOKEN TO LIKE THAT!!!" The Stephanator roared.

If I'm going to take out the Stephanator, we're looking at a red alert. All hands on deck!

I shouted right back at her: "WELL, I WILL NOT TOLER-ATE HEARING 'HOT STUFF' A MILLION FUCKING TIMES! I CAN'T FUCKING TAKE IT ANYMORE!"

We stared each other down on platform three with all the intensity of two UFC fighters ready to engage in a no-rules iron-cage match. I knew my moves. If she took one lunge at me, the bitch was getting a choke slam right down flight two.

"I'm reporting this to Suzy the minute she comes in," the Stephanator said sharply. She then did an about-face, dramatically whipped her hair around, and began marching up the third flight of stairs.

"Whatever," I mumbled, following the stomping Stephanator.

Step after grueling step up Mount Fancy, our mouths tore at each other.

"I can't believe you've been doing this," Stephanie spat with labored breath.

"Someone had to do it," I spat back with my own labored breath.

"I don't know who you think you are."

"I'm a human being sick to death of hearing loud, repetitive songs."

"You obviously have team-player issues."

"The only issues I have are with 'YMCA,' 'Hot Stuff,' and 'Celebration.'"

The Stephanator halted on the middle of the fourth flight, and I nearly crashed into her.

"Do you have any idea what inconvenience you've put poor Marcella through?"

"Do you have any idea what kind of torment my psyche has been put through by poor Marcella? She deserves whatever she got. I can only hope it involved tar and feathers."

Stephanie glowered at me, her circuits smoldering. "FREEMAN! I cannot believe you just said that. Very uncalled-for and mean-spirited.

Every time you unplug the player, she has to haul a stepladder up and down these stairs. She has to climb up that ladder and plug the player back in. She's had to do it almost EVERY DAY. ALL BECAUSE OF YOU!"

The thought of Marcella dragging a ladder up and down the mountain was music to my worn-out ears.

Thank the Retail Gods! At last, retribution.

"Is that supposed to make me feel bad?" I hammered back, trying not to laugh. "It serves her right. She was the one who decided to put the shelf up so high. Let her listen to 'Hot Stuff' nine hundred fucking times and see how she likes it. Everyone hates it. I've actually been applauded by other employees for unplugging it."

"OH MY GOD! PEOPLE ACTUALLY SAW YOU DO THIS?"

Uh-oh. An Employee Entrance blacklist is about to be born.

"YES! And that's because 'Hot Stuff,' 'YMCA,' and 'Celebrate' are pissing us all off!"

"You are completely incorrect. I happen to know several managers who have complained to me when the music wasn't on. They said it pepped them up. THEY LIKED THE MUSIC!"

"MANAGERS don't have to use this entrance," I railed back defiantly. "YOU don't even have to use this entrance. The only reason you're here right now is to bust me."

"Yes I am! What you did was horrible. You are wrong; everyone loves the music."

"They don't."

"They do."

"They don't."

"They do."

I gave up arguing with her. It was hard enough breathing while climbing.

We clomped up the remaining flights in silence.

At the summit of Mount Fancy, she turned to me and said calmly, "Well, Mr. Smartypants, since you seem to think that everyone dislikes the music so much, I need you to get me three hundred signatures agreeing."

Did she actually think I couldn't handle that challenge? Think again, Stephanator. I was the editor of my high school newspaper and launched a total rebellion over the crappy food in our school's cafeteria. I instantly saw myself going from department to department with a clipboard.

"Hate the repetitive, loud disco music in the employee entrance? Vote No! On Disco Music. Sign this petition and it's GONE!" Three hundred names? Easy.

"Not a problem, Stephanie. Uprising is my specialty."

The Stephanator's laserlike eyes tried to melt me. "I'll be having a discussion with Suzy and Tammy to see what kind of disciplinary action will be taken regarding this incident. They will not be pleased with what you've been doing."

At that moment I wanted to push her down the stairs.

But I held back on my cinematic fantasy of watching her tumble down, and I went into Retail Droid Team-Player Mode instead. Don't ask me why, but I pulled open the heavy door leading into the store and held it for her. Stephanie walked through my kind gesture without a word. Talk about being mean-spirited.

"Have a nice day," I said sarcastically to the back of her head as she silently stormed down the hallway toward her office and the plotting of my demise.

Hours later, I found myself seated in HR surrounded by Suzy Davis-Johnson, Stephanie, and Tammy, looking at me as if I had clubbed thousands of baby seals.

A serious tribal counsel.

In my hand was a long receipt roll from the register—the only paper I could find quickly to gather No!-on-Disco-Music names. I had managed to obtain twenty-five names of people who did not need any more Hot Stuff. Cammie's name topped the list, followed by Marci, Glenda, Jules, and Marsha (I called everyone at home, waking them up for permission). I also got a few girls from Hosiery, a few dudes from Ladies' Shoes, and a bunch of people from Cosmetics.

"That's just from a few minutes of campaigning," I calmly told Suzy, handing her the list.

Satan looked at me blankly. Was she really pissed off? Or was I off the hook?

"Dude, there's no need for you to continue with your petition. I find it heartbreaking that many of you disliked what we did in the stairwell. We wanted to create something festive and fun that would be inspirational as you came in to work."

Donna Summer singing "Hot Stuff" 900 times is not festive and fun. It's suicidal.

"I just don't think the repetitive music was the right inspiration," I said, trying not to add words I'd regret, like lame-ass or moronic. "The problem is the same three songs play over and over, and the blasting volume could be a potential health hazard."

Suzy Satan shot a knowing look at Tammy and then said, "We thought the music would help wake up the employees so they would hold on to the handrail going up and down the stairs. The medical claims in the stairwell have been high. Employees are not being careful."

No shit Sherlock! Mount Fancy is a deathtrap. You build eight flights of stairs and have tired people in dress shoes and heels climb up and down them every day, and there's bound to be trouble.

"I don't see why the company doesn't just build an elevator," I said, offering up my dream solution, "or move the Employee Entrance and close the stairwell down."

"Close the stairwell down?" Suzy Davis-Johnson repeated, followed by a guttural chuckle. "That will never happen. There is absolutely no budget for a new employee entrance."

But there's one for yellow paint, silver streamers, a disco ball, and Donna Summer?

At the end of my Mount Fancy Disco Disaster, I did sort of get off the hook with the whole unplugging thing. I wasn't written up and nothing derogatory went into my performance file (which meant I could still use my discount to buy the $60 Ed Hardy cap Cammie had stuffed in a handbag on the hold shelf). However, I did get a twenty-minute lecture from Satan about my language and being a team player. She "encouraged" me to make amends with Stephanie, which I completely hated but executed with a nice shit-pleasing smile. The Stephanator responded with one of her I'd-love-to-rip-your-head-off smiles.

I also had to apologize to Marcella, the display manager. She glared at me, said, "I hate you," and then walked away. It was a good thing

Marcella didn't turn around because she'd have seen the giant evil grin I had from imagining her fat ass hauling a stepladder up and down eight flights of stairs.

That's what you get for building such a noisy monster. Think before you annoy.

The image made all my efforts worthwhile.

A short time later, Disco Nights came down. No more dizzying disco ball spots. No more dangerous silver strips. No more earsplitting Donna. The Great Stairwell was once again silent.

The multicolored railings and walls were the only thing left as they awaited their next *festive* transformation, whatever that would be. Climbing the fucking stairs still sucked ass, but at least I wasn't forced to shake my booty, look for hot stuff, and see it's fun to stay at the YMCA.

The Shitting Room

Like most Retail Slaves, most of the time the Handbag Angels and Demons fought over getting morning shifts. But on one fateful Big Fancy day, I regretted begging Jules to switch shifts with me so Cammie and I could go see our friend's band play.

By the time noon hit, I wished I'd told Cammie to forget it; I'd catch their next gig. Then I would have gotten to sleep in and avoid the following hellacious events.

The night before, the General told me the store was having a special cosmetic-makeover-trendy-fashion-whatever show. Half of what she said did not even register.

I was too busy focusing on the fact she told me to come in at 7:00 A.M.

"Seven!" I cried—I wanted the early shift, but not *that* early!

"The store is opening at 9:00, right after the show," said Judy.

I was dumbfounded. Women actually get up at 7:00 A.M. to attend some makeover-trendy-cosmetic-fashion-whatever show at The Big Fancy at 8:00 A.M.? Ludicrous.

But as I thought about it, I realized why ludicrous made sense.

Free makeovers and goodie bags.

There are women who will get up at 3:00 A.M. for a free lipstick. And Lorraine was one of them. (I made a mental note to get her a few goodie bags.)

When I got to the store, at least thirty boxes of stock were waiting. Within minutes I was sweaty, my pants were covered in dirt, and I had torn my favorite skull tie with the pair of broken scissors we used for opening boxes.

Great start. Nothing like zooming down the highway to Retail Hell at 100 mph.

Working alongside Mega-Mouth Marci and Judy wasn't exactly inspiring either. They bitched about everything from the store to the economy to the weather, and I momentarily thought about stabbing myself with the scissors.

We had barely finished putting everything out when Suzy Davis-Johnson's voice screeched across the PA. She was pissed about business and had decided to unload.

"Whyyyyyyyyyyyy??? Oh Whyyyyyyyyyy???" bellowed Satan, sounding like a hyena in heat. "This is tragic! How could it happen? What is wrong with us? Tell me what I am doing wrong. How can I help you? Are we not a team? Do we not love each other to death? Can't we do well together? I love our store. It's the best ever. We should be number one. I'm so sad, you guys!"

By the time the store opened I was irritated beyond belief. Marci had talked so incessantly about nothing, my ears were bleeding. Judy turned bitchy because Satan had called us out over the PA as one of the departments with unacceptable decreases. Teddy Bear Lady sat down in Ladies' Shoes and stared at me. Jabbermouth sauntered up to the counter and started talking about her attack of food poisoning. Then a customer from the cosmetic-trendy-makeover-whatever-fashion show got all pissy with me because I didn't have any goody bags and I didn't know where she could get any . . . the hell went on and on.

All before 9:30.

On a normal day the store wouldn't even have been open yet.

I took a deep breath.

What was I going to do? Tell Judy I had decided to go back home and go to bed?

You have chosen this path of retail damnation! Suck it up and get your ass to work. You've got bills to pay and Coach handbags to sell!

As my morning wakeup cocktail of coffee, Rockstar, and 5-hour Energy swirled around in my empty stomach, I was suddenly overcome with that tingly feeling that says it's time to pee!

I told Marci I'd be right back.

As I walked into the men's room, the smell of shit assaulted my nose.

Whoa, somebody must have taken a big dump in here!

I had no idea.

Public restrooms are often stinky, especially if there's a lot of traffic, and The Big Fancy's men's room often smelled bad because it was so small, but this stench was different.

It permeated the room like an air freshener gone wrong. Terribly wrong. Shitty wrong.

I headed over to the area where the urinals were. The stink got stronger.

As I wondered why it reeked *so* badly, I looked over and saw one of the urinals holding a mountain of poo.

I say mountain because it was no Lincoln Log or Baby Ruth bar. It was a pile so massive it could have been a model scale of Mount Everest.

Some guy must have dropped his pants, backed his ass up to the urinal and shit it all out.

The really strange thing about his urinal dump was that it was in perfect ice-cream-machine shape. No spills or splatters. Perfect form. It also looked like it came out of a large dog.

How in the hell was the poor Housekeeping Slave going to clean that up? They would probably have to go to the store restaurant and borrow a service spoon. Or a ladle. Or maybe they would call Maintenance for a fucking shovel.

Satan Suzy's voice echoed in my head.

"Whyyyyyyyyyyyy??? Oh Whyyyyyyyyyy??? This is tragic. How could this happen! I'm so sad, you guys!"

Satan and I finally agreed on something. Why is it people have to do such disgusting things with their poo in public places? I'm not safe even in the men's room!

The smell was so awful I couldn't even stand there for thirty seconds and do my pissing. Grossed out and sickened, I bolted for the down escalator. At least the private employee restroom downstairs in Receiving wouldn't smell like shit. I hoped not, anyway.

The escalator was packed with fashion-show-cosmetic-trendy-makeover-whatever attendees, all clutching their Gifts-with-Purchase and talking excitedly.

Way too much happiness this early in the morning. Did someone lace the free lipstick with Ecstasy?

I had to pee so badly, I nearly let it loose right there. What the hell! Everyone else was acting like animals at The Big Fancy; maybe I should have as well, just relieve my tension and let it all flow out of my dress pants, making an escalator waterfall.

When I got to the single-stall employee restroom, the door was locked. Fuck. Someone was using it. I stood by waiting, cross-legged.

Finally, the door opened. A salesman from Sportswear came out and said, "Whew. Had to come down from upstairs, someone took a giant crap in the men's room urinal. It smelled awful."

Rushing past him, I said, "I think it was a St. Bernard."

When I returned from my fifteen-minute piss, the first thing Marci said to me was:

"You look sick. Have you eaten anything yet? I have some brownie left."

Judy was standing next to her and followed it up with: "Maybe you need some coffee."

Then a nearby customer jumped in: "You need some chocolate. That always works for me!"

What I needed was to stop being reminded of the stinking pile of poo that had forever blowtorched its image into my brain.

What I need is to find a bar and start drinking. I don't care if it's 9:00 A.M.

Just then a customer walked up and said: "I'm looking for something big in deep, dark, chocolaty brown? Can you help me?"

It took everything in me not to direct her to the men's room urinal. Instead I began showing her brown bags while trying not to throw up.

As gross as it was to see a human dookie bigger than my foot at 9:00 in the morning, it paled in comparison to another incident that has left me with such a revolting memory of The Big Fancy that I should have made them pay for therapy.

One summer afternoon during a lull, I was having a chuckle listening to Marsha tell me how she had trained her cat Mr. Butters to turn off her bedside alarm clock (was I ever impressed), when Two-

Tone Tammy called. She informed us that one of us needed to go keep an eye on the Swim department. Neither one of us wanted to help girls find swimsuits, so we declined instantly, but Tammy turned on her Dragon voice and informed us that we weren't being asked. Someone was out sick and the girl working over there needed to go on her lunch break.

Okay, Two-Tone! Since you so kindly put it like that. Whatever you need! We're here for you!

Lucky for me, I didn't have to become Queer-Eye Swimsuit Guy. Marsha agreed to watch Swim for an hour. The other lucky thing was that the Swim department was only a short distance away—across the aisle. Because swimsuit business had been so bad, Suzy Davis-Johnson had decided to move Hosiery temporarily into Lingerie and give Swim some exposure on the busy floor of the store.

Within minutes, I was bored. I drifted over to Marsha and joined her at the Swim counter. I didn't totally abandon the Handbag Jungle; I kept an eye out for customers and an ear open for the phone. We were able to continue chatting about Marsha's talented cats.

After just a few short minutes, this skinny woman in her thirties with long brown hair wearing a light blue dress and red patent high heels came out of the fitting room. Empty-handed.

"None of the suits worked for you, hon?"

The swimsuit lady looked at us both, cocked her head, and said, "Umm . . ."

"Hon, you took in six swimsuits. I asked you to bring them out when you were finished," said Marsha, who I could tell was slightly annoyed that the lady had left them back in the room, probably all over the floor.

The lady didn't say anything. She just walked by us.

Marsha and I exchanged "what-a-weirdo" looks with each other, and then we watched her leave.

That's when we noticed the wet brownish liquid on the backside bottom of her light blue dress.

Our eyes could not help but continue traveling down to the back of her legs and shoes, which also had smears of something brown and wet on them . . . something that was leaving a trail across the carpet leading back to the fitting room.

"Oh my God," I said, as we both ran toward the fitting rooms.

As soon as we entered the fitting room hallway, a septic smell strangled the air.

The worst coming from the room she'd been using. Last one on the right.

"This is like a fuckin' horror movie, Marsha," I said as we neared it.

Marsha opened the fitting room door like she was in a haunted house and this was the portal to hell. Little did we know, it *was* a portal.

A portal to a potty.

As the door swung open, our eyes burned and our noses almost closed up.

The weird woman in the light blue dress had shit all over the place.

Total assplosion.

The room was covered in her runny defecation like floodwaters from the Hershey highway. It was everywhere. Across the floor. Across the bench. Across the mirror. Swimsuits were strewn all over the shit-covered floor and soaked in a mucky brown crud as if she had used them as toilet paper. Hangers were equally coated. This was beyond Montezuma's revenge—it was Montezuma's volcano! I kid you not, it looked like the chick had bent over, raised her ass in the air like a canon, and spray-painted the walls with her shitty diarrhea.

We're talking Jackson Pollock painting.

Dexter crime scene.

Brutal paintball attack.

Somehow a bit of the excrement had splattered onto the ceiling.

How the fuck does shit end up on a ceiling???

It was bad enough the Shit Lady had unloaded (accidentally or not) in our fitting room, but to ruin six bathing suits and squirt it all over the walls and ceiling like she was a rotating shit-sprinkler was just beyond any thought process we could understand. This was not the sign of a person who had a medical potty accident. It was what monkeys do.

She could have at least said, "Umm . . . by the way, I just shit all over your fitting room. You might want to call someone."

We would have called someone all right. The fuckin' Hazmat team.

"Hon, I am *not* cleaning this shit up!" announced Marsha.

"You got that shit right," I replied.

Marsha was aghast: "I'll have you know my cats have never shit this bad. Even when little Shania Twain ate all that tomato sauce and got the runs."

"This is some bad shit," I said.

The entire fitting room area had to be closed for the rest of the day due to the shitty stench. In fact, the smell was so intense, it wafted out into the department, where browsing customers made faces and asked questions.

"What's that smell?" a customer said.

"Oh they're just doing some construction," Marsha replied, "You know, welding some iron."

Once the gross shock of what the Shit Lady had done wore off, the jokes started. I dared Marsha to approach the customer and ask her if she'd like to get a shitting room started. There are three good ones left! Marsha chimed in with, "It certainly gives new meaning to the retail version of the word dump! For dump duty you won't need hangers—just take this can of scrubbing bubbles."

We both cried with laughter.

Soon after the Shit Lady left her ass mark all over The Big Fancy, the Swim department salesgirl returned from lunch into what would be her Retail Hell. Marsha and I bolted. The girl was not happy about having to work the rest of her shift smelling shit, but the person I really felt sorry for was the petite Latino woman working in House-keeping that day. I'm sure she'd see more shit-storms than anyone. She actually seemed quite unfazed at the mess until she looked up and saw the brown splatter on the ceiling, to which she exclaimed, "Aiyiyiyi!!!"

And she was right. When you see something like that, it never leaves you. The Shit Lady's mess has left me slightly poop-phobic. The vision of her ass-work has burned itself clearly into my mind's unde-letable photo album, and to this day, whenever I go into any fitting room to try on clothes, I can't help but see shitty bathing suits and walls. When I look up to check the ceiling my mind goes wild.

How much shit was unleashed in this room? Did someone piss on the walls? I'm not touching anything and I'm so not sitting down. Maybe I'll just take the clothes home and try them on.

Unfortunately, fitting rooms are not the only place customers have bodily function accidents.

One day there was an old man and his wife walking down the main store aisle. Apparently he'd forgotten to put on his underwear, because when he accidentally lost control of his poop while he was walking, a little log slid right down his pant leg and landed on the marbled floor. The oblivious couple kept on walking. At least it was just one turd and not a river of butt mud.

On another day a crazy customer tinkled on the Cosmetics carpet right in front of the MAC counter. She was not old. No excuses there.

And a friend of mine told me there was a woman wearing a housedress who liked to show up at the lawn and garden center of his store, stand over a drain in the ground, point a toe over the drain, and quietly let the urine drip down her leg, along her foot and toe, into the drain. *Creepy.* Maybe my next screenplay should be called *Tales from the Sewer.*

I guess the best way to deal with my shit phobia was to understand that what comes out of people's asses is just a basic function of the human body. One that we all deal with.

It's like that children's book says: "Everyone Poops."

I just wish they wouldn't do it in front of me.

Merry Strep Throat
and a Happy New Flu

Like any retail store, The Big Fancy plans for the holidays like it's going to war, and when your department manager is a general, no detail is left unattended.

But on December 18 at 3:02 P.M., the General had no plan ready for what happened.

She had gone to lunch, leaving Cammie, Marci, Jules, a temp named Venezuela (all the temps had weird names), and me on the floor. There were way too many salespeople, considering there were hardly any holiday shoppers. Since we were in the middle of a late-afternoon lull, we kicked out the new girl, sending Venezuela on an extended break.

Cammie and I were on box duty. The Big Fancy offered free gift boxes to customers for all their purchases. A nice courtesy, but it was a bitch for us because Suzy Davis-Satan required not only that we *make* boxes, but that we tissue-swaddle each item inside before handing the package over to the customer.

"I don't want to see one customer leaving this store without a made box," she said one morning at a rally, while wearing a Santa hat, "And don't forget to say 'Happy Holidays!' We need to think of ourselves as elves! We are Santa's cute little elves making life easier for all our customers." After that *adorable* analogy, as expected, someone in the crowd pointed out that they were Jewish. Suzy didn't miss a beat, "I would never forget my Jewish friends—why you are all just little candles of light burning brightly in the menorah."

I wanted to puke for all my Jewish friends and light her Santa hat on fire.

But I digress . . . back to that fateful afternoon where Cammie and I constructed boxes in the back of the department. Having finished our chat about our personal lives, it wasn't long before the monotony of folding five different size boxes crept in, box after box after box after box. As heinous Christmas music echoed over our heads, we decided to play our favorite Big Fancy holiday game: Fuck Up the Christmas Songs. The way it worked was that we'd start singing along (just loudly enough for us to hear) and change the lyrics. A little yuletide rewrite to warm our hearts.

Some of Cammie and Freeman's Fucked-Up Christmas Song transformations:

"Let It Snow" to "What a Ho!"

"Most Wonderful Time of the Year" to "It's the Most Fucked-Up Time of the Year."

"Silver Bells" to "Satan's Balls . . . It's Time to Drink in the City" (dedicated to Suzy).

"Winter Wonderland" to "Slaving in a Winter Horrorland."

"Have Yourself a Merry Little Christmas" to "Have Yourself a Shitty Fucking Christmas."

So while we were popping out wallet boxes, Bing Crosby's "White Christmas" began warbling over our heads for the gazillionth annoying time. Cammie came up with the best lyrics ever, singing, "I'm dreaming . . . of a black penis . . . just like the big ones I used to know. . . ."

I almost hit the floor with laughter. We then got silly singing our new words, and as the song came to an end, we telepathically finished it off together like we were Big Fancy's Sonny and Cher: ". . . and may all your penises be black!"

Suddenly, our retailicious holiday game was brought to a halt.

"CAN I GET SOME HELP AROUND HERE?" a voice screamed behind me, followed by a loud sneeze.

I turned around and came face to face with a craggy old white-haired woman who looked like the Burgermeister in *Santa Claus Is Comin' to Town*. She wore thick brown glasses and some sort of a peach-colored crocheted shawl, and she was carrying a cane and a poinsettia-covered box of Kleenex.

My eyes couldn't help but go straight to the poinsettia-covered box of Kleenex.

What in Christmas hell was this lady doing wandering around a department store with a box of tissues under her arm? We didn't sell Kleenex, so I knew she wasn't going to ask me to ring them up.

Unfortunately, the troubling mystery revealed itself all too quickly. I observed a gallon of snot dripping from her nostrils. Only it wasn't just dripping—it was pouring out. Like a nosebleed. Like molten lava flowing out of a volcano. As fast as she wiped, the clear liquid poured.

I couldn't help but stare in astonishment.

Then she sneezed and coughed, forcing me to back up.

This lady shouldn't be shopping, she should be in bed! Or in a damn hospital! Or quarantined underground. On an island. Far, far away from me!

My next shock came seconds later, watching this disgusting creature reach out with her wet, snot-covered fingers and fondle a black Perlina shoulder bag hanging on a nearby fixture.

"I need to find a new black bag," said the sickly woman.

I actually heard Cammie gasp the minute her phlegmy hands touched it. My mind was going a hundred miles a minute.

Run, Freeman! Run like Jamie Lee Curtis did in Halloween! *Don't look back. Cammie is a strong girl. She can save herself.*

But before I could even consider running, the Snot Monster screamed at me while coughing, "I NEED YOU TO HELP ME!"

NO WAY! FUCK NO! I'd rather be forced to make Big Fancy gift boxes for the rest of my life!

I considered calling someone. But who? The police? The Centers for Disease Control? An exterminator? I briefly thought about paging Security and telling them there was a problematic customer who needed to be removed from the store. The handbag team had deemed her a public-health threat. But then I remembered what Suzy Davis-Satan had said about Polly.

"We are all about giving the best customer service possible. Sometimes you have to give to the community without expecting anything back. Just go with the flow."

Snot Monster's flow was going to kill us all.

"I need a new black handbag," she said bringing a tissue to her runny nose, "And I'm not leaving until I find one!"

"Umm . . . okay . . ." I responded, "if you want to just look around, there are many nice bags over there." I pointed to the other side of the department, where Marci was circling for sales.

Snot Monster sneezed, spraying splatters of influenza everywhere. That's when Cammie tried to leave. "I need to go in the back and . . . uh . . . unpack stock . . ."

"NOT SO FAST!" yelled Snot Monster. "I need your help too. I am a handicapped senior citizen and I require extra service. When I come to The Big Fancy, I often have two people help me. You will hold my cane while I look."

I slowly took the contaminated stick from the base, thinking that would be the safest place to hold it, but protecting myself from her cooties didn't matter anyway because Snot Monster fired several sneeze-cough rockets right at me.

I was completely mortified. Even if none of it had landed on me, I was still breathing in her germs.

Oh my God, I'm going to get sick. No! I don't want to get sick!

Then she turned to Cammie and said, "YOU—gather all the black handbags you can find. I need lots of pockets and zippers and it has to be roomy inside. I also want a new wallet!"

For the next twenty-five minutes Snot Monster ravaged our inventory like she was Godzilla taking New York. She sneezed and coughed nonstop while barking orders at us to show her one bag and wallet after another. Snot Monster left a path of vile slime all over everything, her fingers—wet with clear nostril fluid—touching counters and bags. She pulled tissues from the box, blew her nose, and then stuffed them in the pocket of her housedress, but it was overflowing and many of them fell to the floor. She simply left other snot-soaked tissues on the counter.

No one was spared Snot Monster's nasal napalm, not even the girls not helping her. Jules walked by and got hit with a sneeze that could only be described as atomic.

Marci was helping a lady with a Burberry and had no idea the Snot Monster had crept up behind her until she heard the loud, wet sneeze launched at the back of her head. When Marci turned around, she looked like she was meeting Freddy Krueger for the first time.

I tried to keep my distance, as the carrier of her death stick, but when Snot Monster needed to see a price tag or the insides of a bag, I had no choice but to touch what she had touched. Finally, Snot Monster's reign of influenza destruction came to an end as she decided on a black Monsac tote. I let Cammie have the sale because she'd endured the worst in germ warfare, having to interact with her and try on different bags. We could not get the flu freak out of there fast enough. And of course she wanted her fucking bag put in a damn box! (I did that part.)

After Snot Monster left, it was like a scene from the movie *Outbreak*. Everyone freaked out. We couldn't find the antibacterial lotion that's usually on hand, so Cammie announced she was going to the ladies' lounge and left. Jules followed seconds later. I was about to bail for the men's room and take a long hot sink bath, but a customer walked up to the Corral to buy a Coach bag and wallet. A sale is a sale, and I took it, even though I felt like I was about to become an influenza poster child.

Marci had a rag and the glass cleaner, attempting to disinfect the place. "I have to clean! I know her germs are everywhere!" she said in her usual yappy annoying way, "We're all going to get sick. What did you touch, Freeman? Did you touch anything of hers? Were you on the phone? She was all over you. I can't afford to get sick. Don't get too close to me."

I wanted to spray glass cleaner in her face and wipe until she shut the hell up.

The Snot Monster was not my fault. We were all victims!

So, I turned to her and said, "Well at least she didn't sneeze all over the back of my head."

"Oh my God! She got some on me, didn't she? Ewwwww!" Marci yelped.

She dropped the cleaner and ran for the ladies' lounge, leaving me completely alone.

It doesn't matter what time of day it is from December 17 to December 27; if you're a Retail Slave left alone at a counter, hell will come.

And mine did.

Within seconds there were five customers needing help, and of course, the phone started ringing.

That's when the General walked up and had a hissy fit.

"FREE-MAN! WHERE IS EVERYBODY!?"

"They went to the ladies' lounge," I replied, handing a customer a shopping bag.

"ALL FOUR OF THEM?"

I was about to explain, but Judy got involved with one of the waiting customers, at which point she saw several of the Snot Monster's tissues on the floor.

"And what are all these tissues doing all over the place?" she demanded, running to pick them up. "Suzy is on her way down and this place is a mess. I can't even go to lunch without everything falling apart."

Judy scrunched the tissues in her hand and held them while talking to the customer. I knew I should have warned her, but all I could do was cringe and stare. I'd had to touch Snot Monster's cane of Black Death. Judy might as well have the tissues.

Just then Venezuela came back from her break. Seconds didn't pass before she came up to me rubbing her fingers and saying, "Did someone spill water over by the Perlina? It's all wet."

Two days later, everyone was sick.

Even the people who didn't work that day. They got it from the rest of us.

And as the holidays wore on, we probably gave the Snot Monster plague back to half the customers.

The Snot Monster's gift is a gift that keeps on giving. Whether you want to receive it or not!

People were calling in sick, while others, like myself, were living on flu remedies. I made Theraflu–Jack Daniels cocktails after every shift and pretty much canceled Christmas, spending every moment I was outside The Big Fancy lying comatose in bed.

Three weeks after the Snot Monster had attacked the Handbag Jungle, I still felt like shit. With Inventory right around the corner, General Judy made it clear to us that if any one of us called in sick on Inventory, we should start calling around for a new job.

So I broke down and went to see the doctor.

My influenza had turned into bronchitis.

Thanks so much, Snot Monster! I guess you gave me the best gift of all!

The doc gave me meds so I didn't miss Inventory.

But my cough stuck around till March.

Cock in a Box

After-Christmas returns suck no matter which department or store you work in. At The Big Fancy, our biggest problem with post-holiday returns was women attempting to get refunds on bags and wallets that weren't from our store but were packaged in Big Fancy boxes. It wasn't a pretty scene telling a woman that the ugly green vinyl handbag her husband got her came from the Dollar Store.

One afternoon Piggy Shopper Raelene Reynolds flip-flopped her way up to the counter, wanting to return a Kenneth Cole handbag inside a Big Fancy gift box. She had bought it as a gift for her mother. "Yah, bought this in San Diego. It's too nice for her," Piggy Raelene said, followed by a sip from her Big Gulp. "She'll just ruin it. Besides, I'm pissed at her right now. If she behaves herself, maybe I'll come back and pick something else out."

I decided not to ask any further questions. I was not interested in Raelene's bitch-fest about her mother.

She placed a shopping bag containing the gift box on the counter.

As I took the gift box out, the seemingly empty shopping bag tipped over.

A cockroach the size of my big toe crawled out.

I jolted back.

Raelene acted like she didn't see it, turning her attention to a tray of Juicy Couture cosmetic bags on the opposite side of the counter. "Yah, do these come in purple?"

Don't try and act like you didn't see that. You've just unleashed a giant bug in The Big Fancy!

Raelene was obviously trying to distract me from watching the insect.

"Umm ... I don't think ... they make ... blue," I said, feeling a shiver run up my spine.

This was definitely not the cute variety you'd find in *A Bug's Life.* This cockroach had two-inch tentacles, frog-like legs, and wings big enough to take flight. It was the most athletic-looking roach I've ever seen.

Coming from Raelene's house, it must have been well fed.

Oreo cookies, Cheetos, and raspberry crumb cake for life!

Athletic Roach darted across the glass counter at breakneck speed.

My first thought was to scream, "ROACH!!! THERE'S A ROACH!" Being surrounded by women on both sides of the Corral, I quickly realized it wasn't a good idea.

But then it didn't matter anyway.

Cammie was just a few feet away showing a customer an orange Isabella Fiore hobo. The cockroach crawled up the side of a Plexiglas museum case housing a drawstring feed bag that, oddly, looked like something a bug would crawl all over. Once it reached the top of the case it halted and almost appeared to be watching Cammie while she talked to her customer about the Fiore bag.

That's when Cammie turned and saw Athletic Roach.

She screamed like she was auditioning for a remake of *Psycho.*

Then her customer saw it and joined in, creating a double-murder scream. They both leaped away from the counter. Athletic Roach freaked, scurrying down the side of the encasement and right over the top of the Isabella Fiore handbag.

Jules came running over.

"OH, MAMA! That is one *huge* roach!"

It scaled up a large pink and green striped Kate Spade tote hanging from a metal hook fixture.

Jules joined in the scream-fest.

Together the women huddled and did the willies dance.

Now Marsha was on the scene. Fearless, she moved in closer than anyone and studied Athletic Roach, who clung to the strap of the striped Kate Spade tote.

"It looks like an oriental cockroach because of the red coloring. Must be a male. It has wings."

Cammie screamed when she heard the word *wings*.

"If it flies, I will seriously freak the fuck out."

"They rarely fly," Marsha said.

"How do you know all that?" asked Jules.

"When you have cats who like to hunt, you learn the names of many critters."

The bug must have sensed Marsha studying it. Living up to its healthy look, Athletic Roach sort of hopped across the top of the Kate Spade tote and went right up the other side of the strap.

Marsha bucked backward and all the girls screamed.

The General suddenly charged out of the back stockroom.

"What is going on out here . . . ?"

When she reached the Corral and saw Athletic Roach, she didn't scream or do the willies dance, but her face said she wasn't going anywhere near it.

"Freeman, you need to kill it!"

"Can't you just call Maintenance?" I asked, backing away.

A small crowd had now gathered as the cockroach frantically sprinted along the counter, weaving in and out of bags and fixtures.

"It's behind the Petal Pink Marc Jacobs Venetia!" yelled Jules.

"Oh my God, I fucking hate ROACHES!" Cammie cried.

A passing Soccer Mom customer yelped when she saw it, and her teenage daughter screamed like Athletic Roach was a fifty-foot tarantula.

"FREE-MAN! DO SOMETHING! IT'S SCARING EVERY-ONE!" Judy shouted.

Why me? Just because I'm not standing on a chair and shrieking doesn't mean I want to play exterminator.

"What am I supposed to do?"

"You men are supposed to be good at killing things."

Not us Queer-Eye Guy men. Sorry, Judy. I only kill bugs with a super-size can of Raid, and even then I hold the nozzle down for ten minutes and drown the nasty little creatures.

Judy grabbed a roll of paper towels we use to clean glass with. "Here. Use this."

"Are you serious?" I said, "That thing will take my hand off!"

More screaming.

More people crowding around the Corral.

The Big Fancy Handbag Sideshow was in full swing. I looked around for something to smash the scary bug with.

The stapler?

Not big enough.

The register procedure book?

It's only a tiny book! Still not big enough.

The Marc Jacobs Venetia?

Judy would kill me.

Then I eyed the gift box holding the Kenneth Cole bag Rae-lene wanted to return. Piggy did not look the least bit concerned or frightened. She was trying not to look involved.

Or maybe she's used to oriental cockroaches. Maybe she breeds them. God, she's gross.

I grabbed the box and followed the roach down the counter.

I waited for it to crawl out into open counter space.

"It's so disgusting!" said Jules.

After a moment, Athletic Roach decided he'd had enough of the Kate and crawled back down it, pranced to the glass counter's center, and stopped. Perhaps he sensed I was stalking him.

Please God, I hope Athletic Roach doesn't have flying powers.

I took the closed box with the Kenneth Cole bag still inside and slammed it down. The girls screamed collectively. Then silence. Less the store's speakers echoing "Dancing Queen."

"Is it dead?" asked Cammie.

I shrugged and lifted up the box. The big bug didn't move. Every-one gazed upon it.

Was it dead? Or just paralyzed?

Athletic Roach answered our observation by springing to life and bolting toward a purple suede Coach. A choir of screaming girls once again filled the air.

Jules grabbed the Coach before Athletic Roach could use it for shelter. Judy quickly moved a rack of wallets and scooped up three more Coach bags that also lay directly in its path. Marsha snatched up three Burberry bags.

There was now nothing but wide-open glass counter space. Athletic Roach ran for his life.

"YOU'RE CLEAR!" yelled Jules, "KILL IT!"

"DIE, YOU MOTHERFUCKER!" I shouted, bringing the box down hard.

Again silence. The girls ended their over-the-top screaming.

"It's not dead. I know it's not dead," said Cammie, reminding me of a hundred horror movies.

If it's not, it will be. Sorry, Athletic Roach. The monster always dies in my movies.

I removed the lid of the gift box and took out the Kenneth Cole bag. Using the palm of my hand, I pressed hard on the box's bottom.

There was an awful popping, crunch sound.

"It is now," I said, "My work here is done."

Everyone breathed a sigh of relief.

Athletic Roach had been destroyed.

"I'm glad that's over," said Jules.

"My hero!" Cammie said, her hand on her heaving chest.

"Great job, hon," Marsha said.

I turned to Judy and said, "I killed it, but I sure as hell am not cleaning it up."

"I'll get Housekeeping," she replied, jumping toward the phone.

I took the Kenneth Cole bag back to the register area, where Raelene was still standing.

She feigned ignorance during the entire drama, acting like she had nothing to do with Athletic Roach's reign of terror.

"Yah, looks like you all have a roach problem in this store," Raelene said with a smile.

"Looks like we do," I replied, staring her down.

Don't try and get out of this one Raelene, you're the biggest roach of them all!

"Before I open this bag, Raelene, is there anything you want to tell me?"

If another Athletic Roach popped out I was going to fling it right at her.

Raelene ignored me like she usually does, took a sip from her Big Gulp nonchalantly, and said, "Yah, I think I'll get one of these Juicy cosmetic bags. You can credit the difference of the Kenneth Cole on my card."

You bet, little piggy. Happy to be of service.

From that point on, whenever any of us saw Piggy Shopper, Rae-lene Reynolds, rolling into our department, we always made sure there was plenty of glass cleaner and antibacterial soap handy.

A can of floral scented Raid was also on standby.

Purchased by yours truly.

♈

Full Moon Fancy

I knew something was amiss when I walked in at 1:00 P.M. to start my closing shift and Jules didn't even say, "Hi gorgeous," like she usually does. On this day it was: "Full-moon freaks all morning! Judy's been in a meeting since 10:00. It's total hell, I hope you brought drugs," and then she ran off to lunch, leaving me with the phone ringing and a woman at the counter wanting to know if we had a wallet that had thirteen credit-card slots.

Full moon? I didn't know it was a full moon. Should I be concerned about its being a full moon?

I quickly found out, I should be very concerned about a full moon.

There's a whole army of lab-coated geeks out there in scientific-study land who say that full moons have no effect on human beings whatsoever. All I have to say to them is, "Come work at The Big Fancy under a full moon and you will be rewriting your findings—while you're running for the street."

After I dealt with the woman who wanted exactly thirteen credit-card slots by counting every wallet's slot, only to find out none of them had thirteen, I was hit by a wave of full-moon craziness.

A woman on the phone wanting to know if I'd give her 50% off all the Gucci bags because there's a website that does it. "Go online and check it out for yourself," she said.

This tween girl wanted to return her Juicy Couture bowler because her girlfriend had spilled Coke all over it and she seemed to think that it would be no problem for us to give her a new one—and the bag was two seasons old!

An absolute nut-job Picky Bitch of a customer claimed that all three red Monsac totes we had in stock were lopsided. I had no idea what the fuck she was talking about, but she kept crouching down in front of the counter, eyeballing them like a human carpenter's level, and saying, "They are all off just slightly. Lopsided. I'm really surprised you can't see it."

Then I saw Judy get off the escalator and march toward the department. I could tell by her reddened face she was on the retail warpath.

I wanted to jump inside of the Marc Jacobs Venetia Satchel, zip myself up, and hide.

But there was no hiding from the General in the Handbag Jungle.

"FREE-MAN!" she yelled the minute she got to the Corral, ignoring the lurking customers, "I need a word with you."

Oh shit. Here it comes. I think I knew what this was all about.

My sales were way down for the previous several months. It was a slow time. February and March always suck in retail. There's little merchandise, everyone is freaked out about their taxes, and people aren't quite ready for that $400 Coach raffia straw satchel yet.

So, I had broken The Big Fancy's cardinal rule (which is *not* mentioned in the Employee Handbook) and had done the unthinkable—I misfired.

Misfiring was when a sales associate didn't sell enough to make their imposed goal and The Big Fancy reimbursed them by paying an hourly rate instead of commission. When I was hired, Two-Tone made it sound like they were the nicest company ever, having a cushion plan and watching my back to make sure I had a decent guaranteed hourly should I hit some slow cycles during the year.

Total fucking bullshit.

Turns out, anyone who misfired three times in a row was subject to being terminated. The Big Fancy felt that if you'd had a month and a half of poor sales (even in February and March), you were not the magical sales associate (SHARK) they were looking to have in their "family" (OF SHARKS), and you were then told perhaps it's time to seek out other options for yourself. Basically, your ass was fired.

"You need to have a meeting with Suzy, right now," said the General, "She is having one-on-one chats with everyone in the store who misfired during this last cycle. Yours is *right now*."

"But Jules is at lunch," I protested, trying to stave off the inevitable confrontation with Satan.

"I will work on the floor, and Marci should be here within the hour. *Go!*"

The General had spoken. I went to meet my fate.

Suzy Davis-Johnson's spacious office with massive windows overlooked the Hollywood Hills. When I entered she was seated in an elevated throne-like antique chair made from cherry wood and purple velvet behind an imposing wooden desk the size of a Cadillac.

"HANDBAG DUDE!! HOW ARE YA TODAY?"

God, please kill me now. Lightning bolt. Exploding fluorescent light bulb. Sniper. Anything! Just take me out!

"Hi, Suzy. Doing good, thanks," I said.

Except the moon is full and there are freaks everywhere.

"Well, have a seat and join the party!"

WTF? My misfire admonishing is a party? In that case, I'd like a beer and some Cheetos.

I sat down in one of the shrunken chairs in front of her monumental desk. Suzy Satan looked like she was about to swoop down on me. I felt small and insignificant. Like a worm. She had on a blinding black and white zebra-print jacket over a floral pink beaded camisole, and a silk scarf loosely rolled around her neck, attached with a gold flower pin. Her face was painted with deep bronze eye shadow, hollowed-looking cheeks, and orangey lipstick that made her look like a scarecrow.

I immediately noticed we weren't alone.

The Stephanator and Two-Tone were seated behind me in the back corner of the room. Her head bent, in deep concentration, Stephanie took notes like a court stenographer while Two-Tone Tammy sat with a stack of reports, ready to judge my Big Fancy performance.

Yay! Two of my favorite people. Maybe I should ask the Stephanator if she wants to dance?

"SOOOOO," said Satan, "Do you know why you're meeting with me today?"

"Umm . . . because I misfired?" I said.

"You got it, dude! For the last month, misfire in this store has been out of control, and I'm aiming to get a handle on it. This meeting is to see how I can help and how we can stop it from happening."

"Freeman has misfired two times consecutively in Handbags," Tammy announced coldly, as if I was not in the room.

Satan was not happy; her clown makeup looked like it was starting to crack.

"Oh nooooo. We can't let that happen. I have such great expectations of you always."

Suzy Davis-Johnson then winked at me wickedly and grabbed her calculator.

For the next several minutes she rattled off a bunch of numbers, tapped away on the calculator, added this number to that number, then subtracted another number from some other number, then divided a different number by one of the other numbers.

I went into a complete numerical coma.

My glossed-over eyes focused on her calculator and scratch pad as she wrote a bunch of numbers down. I nodded my head in agreement every time she asked me if I understood what she was doing.

"You see that, Freeman! If you had only sold five dollars more per hour, you would have made your goal!"

"I did make my goal, but I had 10,000 dollars in returns. That's what killed me."

"Returns are no excuse for not selling enough, Freeman. You need to sell more to compensate for your returns. Five dollars is a pair of socks."

"But Suzy, I sell handbags."

"And you are twenty feet away from the sock department. If you had suggested a pair of socks to your customers, you'd have made your goal. We have a whole store full of merchandise, and socks are included in that."

Are you kidding me right now? Sell socks with handbags? How about I shove a pair of socks down your throat and beat you with the fucking calculator?

"Umm . . . okay. Yes. I'll try to sell some socks."

"It's all about rockin' your multiple sales, Freeman! That's how you make your goals!"

"Yes, Suzy. I'm going to give it 100% to make sure I don't misfire any more."

"I am so pleased to hear that, Freeman," she said softly, then becoming serious, "because I have to tell ya, this meeting is about making it perfectly clear misfire is completely unacceptable. It is grounds for termination. Three strikes, you're out. Freeman, you are on your second strike. Corporate is not happy with the performance of salespeople in this store. Everyone has to pull their weight. I am counting on you not to misfire during the next pay cycle. If you do not make it, I'm afraid we will be having a very, very serious discussion. I don't want to lose you. You are a tremendous asset to this store."

What the fuck? Is she for real? I'm a tremendous asset to the store, yet I could be fired?

"I really do mean that, dude," crooned Suzy Davis-Satan, "I need you to put your game face on and make some touchdowns by getting those sales up!"

Oh God, now the lame sports metaphors. I wish I had a football to shove up her ass.

"Yes, Suzy, I'm going to get those sales up!"

"Do you feel all the information I have given you today will help you not misfire in the future?"

I could feel the heat from Stephanator's eyes searing into me as she prepared to write down my response for documentation.

I told them all yes and left.

I returned from Suzy's scary powwow feeling like I might as well start packing my Big Fancy bags. Jules and Marci were nowhere in sight, and the General was still manning the registers.

"This day is going to kill me," she said, as pissed off as I'd ever seen her. "Jules had to leave, one of her girls is sick. Marci's car broke down when she was coming back from San Diego. I can't get a hold of anyone else, so it's just you tonight."

I was already not liking the sound of that, but before I could protest too loudly, Judy handed a customer a shopping bag, turned to me and said, "I'm out of here, deal with it."

Then she was gone.

And I was all by myself under a Big Fancy full moon.

Eccentricity filled the air.

What followed was a parade of Crazies, Psychos, Nasties, and Bloodsuckers.

A Nasty switched prices and tried to buy a Juicy Couture handbag with a wallet ticket for $65. *How stupid did she take me for?*

Discount Rat Patty waddled in and drove me "Is deescount?" insane! She wanted more percentages on just about everything on the sale table.

A baby screamed for ten minutes while her big brother decided to lick all the cases and then play football with a $400 Cole Haan satchel.

Another Nasty-Ass Thief wanted to return a $1,000 Fendi with torn tickets and receipts.

A woman got angry and accused The Big Fancy of selling fake Coach bags because she thought the lining and stamp inside looked off.

A customer wanted a discount on a $75 sale bag because it had a tiny little scratch on the bottom. I'm like, "The bag was $200! You're already getting a huge discount!"

A woman brought in four handbags she wanted fixed and refurbished, so I had to fill out repair tickets and write notes on each one because she wasn't willing to spend past a certain amount to have them fixed.

Then this man wanted me to look up all 100 stores in the country and give him a register print-out. I told him I couldn't and he argued that they do it in customer service all the time . . . then a lady butted in, wanting me to take her credit-card payment. When I told her I had someone on the phone and a customer waiting to return, she got pissed and started screaming about how horrible the customer service was. "THIS IS NOT THE BIG FANCY WAY!"

Returns rolled in by the minute. One after the other. I just started hurling them into a pile behind the counter. Judy would be pissed, but whatever. I might be getting terminated.

Let someone else put them all away!

One of the returning customers said, "Why did you just throw it like that?" after I violently hurled her used Dooney & Bourke hobo into the pile. I looked her dead in the eye, and said, "Because I can and that's where it belongs—you used it and now we have to throw it away."

The woman was pissed. She didn't like it one bit that I wasn't happy with her irresponsible behavior, so she went up and complained to the night manager, saying I was rude doing her return. The night manager then called and said I'd better not get any more complaints or she'd be telling Satan about me tomorrow.

Satan is already twenty seconds away from firing me—go ahead!

I hung up the phone and turned around, and a woman wanted to return a Kate Spade she had used for six months because it wasn't wearing well. "I paid good money for this! Look at it?"

I gave her a huge fake-ass shit-eating retail grin and took it back.

Then, five minutes to closing, a plain-looking Asian woman appeared at the Corral.

As I approached her reluctantly, I managed to get out a civil, "Hello. . . ."

"Show me Coach," she said.

And then I saw the hair.

She had a five-inch hair that had to be as thick as a blade of grass growing out of a mole in the center of her chin.

I stared at the hair like it was a rare, newly discovered species.

Long Hair turned out to be a total Bloodsucker. She kept saying, "Show me" over and over. Who was she? The Vampire Bavaro's sister?

I finally stopped showing her anything. She clearly was not going to buy. I had to save myself.

So I went in the stockroom and called the department. Came back out of the stockroom with the phone ringing and Long Hair saying, "Your phone is ringing."

I smiled at her nicely, answered the phone, and pretended to have a customer conversation.

She was lucky I didn't reach for the scissors.

Long Hair finally wandered out the mall doors at 9:20.

By the time I finished cleaning duties and closing the registers, it was 10:00 and I was the last sales associate to leave The Big Fancy.

My trip down the stairs was unbearable. I was too tired to think about anything. My brain had melted. Nothing there. Blank. I could barely concentrate on not falling down the flights.

But as I opened the employee door leading out of Mount Fancy, I saw the big, bright, full moon, shining down on me in all its alluring brilliance.

How can something that beautiful cause so many people to go psycho inside a store?

Big Nightmare #3

It was a bad idea to think I could come home after barely surviving a full-moon shift at The Big Fancy and then actually do some writing.

But the chaotic events of the day had fueled my passion. If Suzy Davis-Satan planned on firing me, let her! I'd have a screenplay to start shopping around in no time.

I had decided a while back that *Love in a Fitting Room* was too much of a hard sell. Even though *Brokeback Mountain* was a huge success, was the public really ready for A-list male stars doing one another in fitting rooms at a Big Fancy Department Store? Probably not.

Thus a new script idea was born: *Escape from The Big Fancy.*

I'll pitch it as *Die Hard* in a department store, starring Brad Pitt and his badass woman, Angelina Jolie! They were amazing in *Mr. and Mrs. Smith*. I just knew that if they read my script (once it was written) they'd want to work together again—plus, they could even have their kids in it if they wanted! I'd write roles for everyone!

Before turning on the computer and diving into *Escape from The Big Fancy*, I decided to wind down a bit. I popped open a beer and watched a *South Park* repeat—the one where all the old people in town are running everyone over. It reminded me of half the customers at The Big Fancy.

During a commercial my mind started wandering.

I can't believe that woman tonight with that long hair dangling from her chin. So gross. Suzy Satan is such a bitch. I work my ass off for that store. I don't want to go look for another job, but if I have to, maybe I'll go apply

at a movie studio. Maybe they have a gift store I can work in. Wait a minute.
No! No more stores. I'm supposed to write screenplays.

My eyelids became droopy.

Before I knew it, everything went black.

Then white.

A blank white page.

Black Courier font words magically typed across it.

A script!

Night of the Shopping Dead

An original screenplay by Queer-Eye Handbag Guy

Down at the bottom, in the left corner, it said:

Revised final draft
July 18, 2020
Rewritten a trillion times
Represented by Big Fancy
Produced by Hell
Authenticated by Satan

Then those famous screenplay words appeared.

FADE IN

Followed by a screenplay writing itself.

EXT. MALL PARKING STRUCTURE ROOF—ESTABLISH

Late afternoon. Stormy and dark. Cammie and Freeman get
out of their convertible sports car. They look just
like Barbara and her brother Johnnie in *Night of the
Living Dead.*

                    FREEMAN
          It won't be so bad. It's only a full moon.

CAMMIE spots something and SCREAMS.

Standing next to a Range Rover covered in Coach
signature-print fabric is LONG HAIR.

                    CAMMIE
          Holy fuck! Look at her chin hair!

Long Hair ignores Cammie and looks straight into
Freeman's eyes.

                    LONG HAIR
          They're coming to get you, Freeman!

Long Hair explodes into a thousand black birds and
disappears.

Cammie and Freeman SCREAM and start running.

CUT TO:

INT. MOUNT FANCY

Freeman and Cammie have just entered the stairwell. A
strobe light is flashing. It's similar to the ending
of *Alien*. Very dangerous conditions for climbing Mount
Fancy, but Freeman and Cammie trudge up the stairs
with terrified faces, covered in sweat, looking like
Sigourney Weaver.

The rails and floors are covered with slime. They slip
and slide. It's nearly impossible.

CAMMIE SCREAMS

The Snot Monster is in front of them. Her nose is HUGE
and green goo is flowing out of it like a waterfall.
She COUGHS AND SNEEZES, hosing them.

                    SNOT MONSTER
          YOU TWO ARE GOING TO HELP ME!!

They take off their dress shoes and throw them at
her. The last shoe hits her in the nose, and she falls
down the stairs in a blob of SCREAMING goo.

They resume climbing. Flight after flight. It's
never-ending.

SCREAMS!

THEN A ROAR from behind them; it's THE STEPHANATOR.

> STEPHANATOR
> YOOOOOOU! YOU'RE THE ONE! YOU ARE SO BUSTED.
> I'M GONNA GET YOU FIRED! WOOOOOOOHOOOOO!
> I WANT YOU TO CLAP!!!!

> FREEMAN
> RUN!

Cammie and Freeman hightail it up the flight of stairs
with the Stephanator right on their asses.

Suddenly LORRAINE/SHOPOSAURUS CARNOTAURUS is in front
of them. And she is PISSED.

> LORRAINE
> YOU MOTHERFUCKING COCKSUCKING WHORE! YOU
> LEAVE MY FRAYMAN ALONE! I'M GOING TO RIP YOUR
> UGLY FUCKING ASS IN TWO!

The Shoposaurus attacks the Stephanator. The two
creatures go at it. It looks like an action scene in
a Michael Bay movie as they tumble around, smashing
concrete and twisting metal.

Freeman and Cammie continue up the stairs, not looking
back. They don't want to be around, no matter who wins
this battle of the monsters.

CUT TO:

INT. BIG FANCY THIRD FLOOR

They are running through the store, being chased by
Shoppers and Salespeople Zombies.

INT. BIG FANCY HANDBAG DEPARTMENT

The stockroom doors are open, and MARSHA waves them in.

> MARSHA
> HURRY! THE SHOPPING DEAD ARE EVERYWHERE!

Freeman and Cammie barely make it to the stockroom.
DOUCHE rips part of Freeman's dress shirt.

INT. BIG FANCY STOCKROOM

In the stockroom it's Freeman, Cammie, Marsha, JULES,
and MARCI.

The Shopping Dead are pounding on the doors. Freeman
and Cammie are barricading them with designer handbags
and wallets.

SCREAMS!

They turn and see Marsha dead on the floor. Marci has
turned into a Zombie and is now killing Jules. Cammie
runs to help her by attacking Marci with a Gucci
hobo. The stockroom door SLAMS open and the Stephanator
stumbles through, SCREECHING. Lorraine must have lost.

Stephanator attacks Cammie and kills her.

The room floods with the Shopping Dead—Douche, Tiffany,
Judy, the Vampire Bavaro, Virginia . . . so many of
them . . . but it's the scariest one of all who goes
after Freeman . . .

SUZY SATAN ZOMBIE

```
She jumps on Freeman, her mouth open, full of sharp
fangs covered in blood.

He grabs a nearby Marc Jacobs Venetia in black and
smacks Suzy Satan in the mouth. The hardware is so
strong, it shatters her teeth. But now they are sharper
and more jagged than ever. She leans in . . .

                    SUZY SATAN ZOMBIE
               YOU ARE MINE NOW!

She takes him . . . It's over . . .

                         FREEMAN
               NOOOOOOOOOOOOOOOOO!
```

I screamed myself awake.

Another damn Big Fancy nightmare.

Zombies! Everyone always dies at the end of zombie movies.

At The Big Fancy it's no different.

Coming out of the bad dream, I was still in front of the TV. The clock flashed 2:00 A.M. On the screen was an infomercial with some guying saying, "With my plan you can be a millionaire in two months and quit your job! Be your own boss!"

I turned it off and went to bed.

But I never slept this time.

I was too busy thinking about The Big Fancy.

And the shopping dead.

CONCLUSION:
SATAN'S SUPERSTAR

George Clooney opens the envelope and announces, "And the Oscar for Best Original Screenplay goes to . . . Freeman Hall—Escape From The Big Fancy." Applause thunders across the Kodak Theatre. As I reach center stage and the golden statuette is handed to me, George gives me a friendly guy-to-guy hug and says, "Well done on your escape!" My speech kicks ass. I thank director Steven Spielberg for not getting angry when I slipped my script into his shopping bag. I also give a shout-out to God, my mom, my sister, my acupuncturist, my fifth-grade teacher, my beta fish, Sid Vicious . . .

"FREEMAN!"

What? Who is that? I am not finished with my acceptance speech. Whoever it is will have to wait.

"FREEMAN, IT'S YOU!"

There it is again. Sounds like a woman. Whatever. Some jealous screenwriter in the audience. I'm at the Vanity Fair party. Everyone is there: Oprah, Johnny Depp, Madonna, Will Smith, Queen Latifah, Amy Poehler, Tina Fey—a virtual who's who of Who's Who. Robert Downey Jr. has a character he wants to talk to me about. Ellen DeGeneres comes up to me and tells me she wants me on her show. I can't wait. Love her! Megan Fox bumps into me. She's smoking hot! Gerard Butler bumps into me. He's smoking hot! Steven approaches me and says he wants to have a meeting with me about writing . . .

"Freeman, she just called your name, you better go up there!"

Crap.

I really want to hear what Steven had to say.

Suddenly, it's gone. The stage. The audience. Steven. All of it. Gone.

But the applause is real and I am sitting in an audience.

Just not the Academy Awards at the Kodak Theatre surrounded by Hollywood royalty. I'm at The Big Fancy department store sitting in a fold-out chair in the Kitchen Access department, surrounded by 400 managers, buyers, and salespeople.

A Big Fancy Rally.

A super-size Big Fancy Rally, with a mini stage, chairs—they're even serving coffee. Wow!

The irony is that it's just one month after my Come to Jesus talk with Satan, and I'm winning The Big Fancy's most prestigious customer-service award, Service Superstar. It is only given out four times a year, and I was chosen for spring.

Lucky me, just a little blossoming Queer-Eye Handbag flower.

Judy, who is sitting next me, is in my face, screaming, "FREE-MAN! YOU HAVE TO GO UP THERE! They just called your name. Remember, I told you?"

That's right. The General *did* tell me. I remember her saying that Suzy wanted to make me the Spring Service Superstar because I had so many customer letters and that I had better show up to the early morning meeting and I had better act surprised.

"Got it?" she asked. "Got it," I'd replied.

I must be in a deep Oscar trance, because for a minute, I think Judy is Dame Judy Dench. But she isn't. She's the Handbag General. (Incidentally, it's a role Dame Judy Dench could actually play. And quite masterfully, I might add.)

I snap out of my daydream and make my way to the stage. Satan hugs me like I'm her BFF. I returned the embrace, grossed out but not caring; I hug everyone.

After the clapping stops, Suzy pulls me close to her.

"I'm just so darn proud of you, dude!" she says, all maternal and shit. Then she turns to the crowd and starts reading from her notes, "The first man we've ever had selling handbags! Freeman Hall! Free-man is one of the most unique individuals I've ever met. His free spirit and fun personality. . . ."

I wince. *Stop with the fuckin' free-spirit-personality crap already! I'm not free, my spirit is trapped here in The Big Fancy, and my personality is the droid you see before you.*

"... his ability to find the perfect handbag for every customer he approaches is amazing. He sets a wonderful example to his team. He gives the kind of personal service our company is legendary for, and he is by far one of our best. I truly believe he sets a standard of service in this store that we should all take notice of."

All this from someone who said she'd fire my ass if I didn't sell five dollars more per hour.

"In the past six months," Suzy Satan continues, "Freeman has gotten more letters than anyone in the store. Here are just a few of the customers whom he has gone above and beyond the call of duty for and provided outstanding customer service to. Lorraine Goldberg writes: 'Freeman is my Big Fancy point man. He has the most impeccable taste and knows what I like. I've made him my personal shopper. I could not live without him. You need to give him a raise!'"

You heard the woman. I'd also like a bonus and a trip to Hawaii.

"Virginia Maplethorpe said, 'Freeman is always there and I love talking to him. I buy all my handbags from Freeman.'"

"And from a Mrs. Constance Beaumont: 'Being the wife of a surgeon, I lead a very busy social life, and Freeman has shown time and again that he has the BEST eye for accessories of any salesperson I have ever met.'"

Satan holds up the next letter for show-and-tell. "And we have a customer named Summer Sterling who wrote on the most beautiful pink leopard stationery. She says, 'I needed a new evening bag that fit my needs and Freeman found me the best one. It makes me feel like a movie star when I wear it. Here at the Wild Horse ranch, we girls always need to look our fashion best and ...'" Several chuckles and catcalls erupt from Retail Slaves who recognized Wild Horse ranch as a place other than a four-star resort. Suzy pauses for a moment. "Oh ... my ... uh ... Stephanie? I think this one wasn't supposed to ..."

Stephanie quickly grabs it while rolling her eyes and shaking her head in disgust.

Why are they embarrassed by a prostitute? Aren't we all prostitutes selling something? I'm selling handbags, and Summer is selling ... well, Summer is selling what she sells best.

"Anyhow," continues Suzy Satan, "Your customers love you, and I hope you know that."

What? No comments from the Vampire Bavaro and Monique? I'm so sad. They love me to death.

"Without further adieu, I hereby honor you with The Big Fancy's most prestigious customer service award, SERVICE SUPERSTAR! YOU ROCK, DUDE! CONGRATULATIONS!"

Everyone claps. I am sweating and maybe even starting to shake.

"It's not a raise," says Satan, "But I am pleased to give you this 31% discount to use for six months on anything in the store and this stunning silver bowl with your name beautifully etched into it! You also get your photo on the wall in Customer Service. WAY TO GO!!!"

Suzy Davis-Johnson hands me the bowl with tears in her eyes. I want to cry too, but for different reasons, mainly because I'm worried now. If customers are going to see my name and picture in Customer Service, how many more freaks will I attract? I glance briefly at my new bowl. It looks like something from the Dollar Store.

Not so stunning, sorry Satan.

"Are you excited, Freeman?" she asks.

No, I want to kill myself. Maybe with this bowl.

"Umm . . . yes . . . thank you, Suzy. It's a great honor," I reply.

"So what words of wisdom can you share with everyone about customer service?" she asks, shoving the microphone in my face.

Oh please, Satan. Stop with the Larry King interview. I can tell you I think this whole thing is bullshit, except for the discount. I really kinda like that, though I don't have any money most of the time.

I *so* do not want to talk about customer-service wisdom in front of 400 people at 7:00 A.M.

"Umm . . . I just try to be nice to customers . . . treat them like I am just hanging out and shopping with them . . . umm . . . find them what they want . . . be nice . . . you know."

My response is not something that would have Donald Trump rising for a standing ovation.

For two seconds, Suzy stares at me like I've just fallen out of a spaceship, and then she is ready to move on.

"LET'S HEAR IT FOR OUR NEW SPRING SERVICE SUPERSTAR!"

Everyone claps as I make my way down the makeshift stage to my chair. When I sit down, I feel nauseous and jittery, as if I'm going to pass out. Perhaps it was the Sugar Free Rockstar and two cups of coffee I had before the early-morning rally call.

Cammie, Judy, Marsha, and Marci, who are all sitting next to me, pat me and say things like, "Awesome job." Was it awesome? I believe I've just sold my soul to Satan for a lame silver bowl.

What the fuck am I going to do with this?

The rally rages on like a migraine that wouldn't go away. There's a lame skit about opening new accounts, with the customer-service manager dressed in drag, and then Satan screams out the names of the departments that made it happen yesterday, and we all answer her call by clapping and woohooing.

My nerves are being electrocuted.

Despite The Big Fancy shock and awe blazing away around me, my mind is far away.

What does this mean? That I'm a slave to The Big Fancy?

Forever condemned to burn in its Retail Hell?

Now we're clapping for the top ten salespeople in the store.

I can't let this happen. I don't want to spend my life at The Big Fancy clapping and being sucked dry by customers. Marsha and Jules love it here, they love working retail, and that's okay. But not me. Like Cammie, I have my own dreams that are outside this store. I'm here because those dreams haven't happened yet. I can't ever give up on my writing. I have to keep on keepin' on. Writing in the face of all my nightmares. If I stop and do nothing, my soul will be lost forever. The Big Fancy will keep me forever. I'll end up with a closet full of these bowls and . . . who knows, even worse, I'll be going to the movies with Satan.

After two hours, the Super-Size Big Fancy Rally finally comes to a close, with the Stephanator screeching, "EVERYONE NEEDS TO PICK UP THEIR OWN CHAIRS! MAKE SURE YOU GRAB YOUR CHAIR! STACK THEM BY THE ESCALATOR! COME ON, YOU GUYS! WE'RE LATE. THE STORE IS OPENING IN TWO MINUTES!"

I pick up my chair and collapse it. Like a good Service Superstar, I carry it toward the escalator with the bowl under my arm. Everyone is coming up to me and congratulating me.

Back in the Handbag Jungle we have like thirty seconds before the store opens, and everyone is cheerful and celebratory from my accomplishment, even the Demon Squad members. Marci brought in her world-famous cupcakes, Tiffany gives me a hug, and even Douche is civil, telling me, "You deserve it."

Cammie's ecstatic. "I'm taking you out tonight. There's this amazing new place called Rock Sugar and they have pear martinis that taste like fuckin' candy crack."

"Have you ever been Service Superstar?" I ask Cammie.

"Are you kidding? Fuck NO! I have my favorite Custy bitches, but Suzy would never give it to me. The only reason I'd want it is for the discount."

I didn't know it, but Marsha has been Service Superstar three times in her lengthy Big Fancy career, and Jules twice.

"Did you win bowls too?" I ask Marsha.

"You bet I did," she replies. "They're sitting on my kitchen floor right now holding cat food for Mr. Butters, Shania Twain, and Putz."

"My husband uses mine out in the garage for his nuts and bolts and whatever," adds Jules.

I look down at my silver bowl with FREEMAN HALL engraved on it next to the words Service Superstar. Not exactly an Oscar. Wrong color, and it's fat and hollow.

What should I do with this? Put it on my desk? Build a museum case for it?

Maybe I should just vomit into it.

Or not.

Actually, I know exactly what I'm going to do with it.

When I get home, I'm going to fill my Service Superstar bowl to the brim with Frosted Flakes and Jack Daniels. Then I'll eat until the room spins.

And maybe after that, I'll do a little writing. I have a new idea for a script.

But first I need to go break in my limited-time bigger discount.

There's a Marc Ecko jacket I can't live without.

Branded by Numbers

It was bad enough that I had to recall my social security number, phone number, bank account number, a shitload of pin and password numbers, and a two-part zip code, but like so many others working in retail, I had to remember an employee identification number.

The mark of The Big Fancy beast: 441064.

Like a prison ID, sales associates had to use 441064 on everything.

441064 documented every sale: **The Total Sales for 441064 = $15,984.**

441064 deducted every return: **The Total Returns for 441064 = $15,984.**

441064 opened every new credit account: **It is unacceptable that 441064 has only opened one new account this week; 441064 will be required to attend a training class.**

441064 verified time worked: **441064 failed to clock back in from lunch properly.**

441064 also appeared on all official Big Fancy paperwork: **Please sign your employee number stating you understand the company's sexual harassment policy.**

To the store's computerized systems, Freeman did not exist. Only 441064. Like the half-man, half-machine beings on *Star Trek*, I had been assimilated by 441064.

Having to remember 441064 melted at least 50 percent of my brain cells. It's the reason I can't recall birthdays or how much I have left in my checking account. I fully expect medical research to one day identify this dreaded retail disease. They will no doubt call it END—Employee Number Disease. Millions of sales associates will be diagnosed with this horrifying numerical memory-loss condition. Because of END, we won't be able to recall what year it is, our age, our shoe size, or on what channel to find *American Idol*.

This is the END of the road for your brain, Freeman. You've spent too many years in retail having to recall employee numbers. Your brain cannot take any more. It's fried times four.

When I became 441064, there was no special ceremony like a graduation or bar mitzvah and I did not receive a 441064 official certificate, engraved necklace, fashionable tee, henna tattoo, or bumper sticker. The number 441064 was presented to me illegibly scrawled across a small piece of orange scratch paper that wasn't even a Post-It. HR Manager Tammy unceremoniously handed 441064 to me and said, "Memorize it and never forget it. Those six numbers are connected to everything you do, including your paycheck."

I stared at my beastly mark like it was part of *The Da Vinci Code*.

How will I remember this? I hate numbers. It took me months to remember my cell number. If my paycheck is riding on this number, I'm in deep shit.

The first few days of trying to remember 441064 were worse than trying to remember my locker combination in high school. Within hours, I lost the slip of paper and mixed up the order of the numbers like a blender on purée. Every time I tried to enter them into the register it beeped loudly while my customers sighed impatiently.

Was it 460144? BEEP! 446014? BEEP! No, that's not it. Are the double 4s at the beginning or the end? 440164? BEEP! 406144? BEEP! 441046? BEEP! BEEP! BEEP!

Why can't my employee number be 12345? Or 420? Or 666? Or 8675309? I can remember those numbers! BEEP! BEEP! BEEP!

The register noise and impatience of Douche standing behind me, ready to ring up half the department, alerted General Judy, who was on me like some freaky ninja-manager.

"FREE-MAN!" she yelled, "YOU NEED TO REMEMBER YOUR EMPLOYEE NUMBER! WHAT'S WRONG WITH YOU? Don't force me to write it down and pin it to your tie."

Fearing humiliation, I took to writing 441064 on my palm with a red pen. As it turns out, this was not such a great idea. The heat from the handbag department coupled with my nerves produced enough sweat to fill up a Marc Jacobs satchel. I ended up smearing red ink all over a pink DKNY leather tote that a customer was about to purchase. "What are you doing?" she snapped, "Your hand is red! My God, you're bleeding on my new bag!"

Thank God Marsha in the Corral was with me at that moment and not Judy. "Oh, it's nothing, hon," she said, quickly opening a drawer and producing a bottle of magic leather cleaner. Seconds later, the red smudge disappeared. Then Marsha opened another drawer and pulled out a 5"×7" card that had a list of all the department's employee numbers—including yours truly, 441064.

"We use this for reference when ringing up holds and whatnot."

"Why didn't Judy just show me that?" I asked, feeling my retail blood start to boil.

"Because she's a nasty bitch and likes to yell at people," Marsha replied. "Now ring up your customer, dear."

From that point on, I never forgot 441064. I also ended up unwillingly memorizing everyone else's numbers, *including* the General's.

Ultimately, I think stores like The Big Fancy should let sales associates create their own employee numbers. Then they could choose easy-to-remember digits that have personal significance, like birthdates, anniversaries, favorite Super Bowls, or dates of loss of virginity. If I had been given creative control of my employee number, I definitely would have made some retailicious improvements on 441064.

For instance, I'd have cut the 1, 0, and 6, making it 444444! How sweet is that?! Nice and easy on my number-challenged brain. Or, 242424 because it's three 24s in a row and *24* is the Fox TV show starring Kiefer Sutherland, whom many say I look like. (Dumbass Customer: "Are you Kiefer Sutherland?" Me: "Why, yes, I am. I'm selling handbags to make extra money between explosions and tortures.")

What if my employee number were a countdown number, like 654321? After entering the 1 on the register, I would do something dramatic, like yell, "BLAST OFF! You are about to get rung up by the Jack Bauer of handbags!"

If I'd had a more attractive group of numbers like 323232, they could be a decorative border for my business cards. 32323232323232323232323232323232. Employee number art!

I can't help but think that my number might have been luckier if it had been 123456, a straight flush, or a big jackpot number like 777777. I also would have loved 1313 as an employee number because it's *The Munsters'* home address on Mockingbird Lane, or 111111, because it looks mysterious like an *X-File.*

But as far as employee numbers go, I guess 441064 isn't the worst set of Big Fancy employee numbers to ever grace the top of a receipt. I could have been given something really fucked up like 392754186. What a bitch *that* employee number would have been to remember.

As The Big Fancy days turned into years, and 441064 saturated my very being, the thought of actually becoming 441064 crossed my mind more than once. I'm 441064 at The Big Fancy; why not in life? Prince did it when he changed his name to that symbol. Why not me? No one has the name 441064!

Eat your heart out, Moon Unit, Apple, Moby, and 50 Cent.

Not only would it confuse the shit out of the IRS when they got my taxes, but can you imagine the look on a cop's face after he pulls me over and reads 441064 on my driver's license? And if annoying telemarketers ask to speak to the man or woman of the house, I could proudly respond, "There is no man or woman here, only 441064."

It would certainly be strange living as 441064, but I suppose I'd get used to it, like 007 did. My friends would say, "Hey 441064, s'up?" They could also shorten it to an affectionate nick-number and say, "You rock, 44 . . . props, 44!"

But there are times, I fear, when being called 440164 would have major downfalls. My tombstone would read, "Here lies 441064"; my full signature would take forever to write: Four four one zero six four; I'd have no last name; and I'd hate it during sex when my boyfriend called out, "Oh, yes, 441064! You are the stud among studs, 441064!"

Maybe being 441064 wouldn't be such a good thing after all.

As END ravaged my brain on a daily basis at The Big Fancy, making it difficult for me to play Sudoku and sing *99 Bottles of Beer on the Wall,* one thing was for sure. The number 441064 left an indelible mark. A hideous, permanent graffiti stain. Like the name of a cattle ranch branded on some poor steer's ass.

441064 is forever.

The Customer Is *Always* Right

According to corporate America, The Big Fancy, and consumers everywhere, "The customer is always right."

Even when they're not so right.

The way I saw it?

If the customers were always right, that was fine by me.

It was my absolute pleasure as a sales associate of The Big Fancy to provide them with the most outstanding customer service I could and let them act however they wanted to.

"Hi. Can you help me?" asked a woman with wiry black hair so out of control and full of static, she must have French-kissed an electrical outlet. The bitch looked completely insane.

"I'm looking for a handbag in a purplish brown color," said Electric Hair.

"Purplish brown?" I replied, unsure of what she meant, although the visual of a black eye did pop into my head.

"Yes, a brown with purple."

"You mean like an eggplant color?"

Like a shiner?

"No. Brown and purple."

"Like a Bordeaux?"

"No, more brown."

Like dog poop?

"Like a cordovan?"

263

"No, more purple."

Like purple dog poop?

I'm really confused now.

"Is the brown chocolaty?" I asked.

"Yes, but with purple in it," replied Electric Hair.

Like your alien blood?

"Is the purple a deep purple?"

"Yes, very deep."

"Chocolaty brown with deep purple in it."

"Yes! Exactly. That's what I'm looking for. Do you have it?"

If we do, I don't know where it is.

"I don't know," I said, hoping she would go back into the mall's wilds.

"I really need to find something," Electric Hair pleaded, "it's for a very important event. Can't you please help me find something?"

Against my better judgment of helping freaky-looking women with dangerous hair, I put Queer-Eye Handbag Guy into action and gave her a Brown Handbag Tour.

"It needs to have purple in it," she said after seeing each one.

So then I gave her a Purple Handbag Tour.

"It needs to have brown in it," she said after seeing each one.

I showed her every handbag that looked like rotting eggplant.

"Not the right shade," she quipped, "Almost, just not quite right."

I showed her every handbag that looked like freshly dumped doggy poo.

"No, there's not enough purple," she groaned, "I need purplish brown."

Then Electric Hair went all high-voltage hell bitch on me:

"I'm frankly surprised you don't have anything in that shade. It's the hottest color of the season! Your buyers need to be more on top of what is going on in the fashion world. This color was all over last month's *WWD*. Why aren't you salespeople better educated? This is such a disappointment. I was planning on buying my purplish brown handbag today. They shouldn't have a man working in Handbags who knows nothing."

I'd had just about enough shock therapy from Electric Hair. She was full of static shit.

Even though The Big Fancy had never sent me to New York's fashion week, I decided to pretend like they did, and tell her what she wanted to hear.

"Oh, I know what you are looking for!" I said overly dramatic, "You want burple. I could not agree with you more. Our buyers are so out of it. Burple is HOT!"

"Burple?"

"Yes, burple! It's all the rage in handbags!"

"It is?" she said gazing at me like I had just given her a key to the power company.

"That's the color you saw in *WWD*. It's what all the designers are calling a mix of brown and purple. I personally think it's fashion accessory genius. Burple bags are going to be huge."

"I know, I know," said Electric Hair getting excited, "That's why I want to get mine now."

"There will be burple shoes, burple clothing, burple makeup, burple everything. Hey did you see last month's *In Style*?"

"No, I missed it."

"Madonna and J-Lo are already wearing burple. There was a whole spread about it."

"Wow," said Electric, completely mesmerized.

"You know it's pretty sad, we should have it in by now, but we don't. My suggestion would be for you to try all the other stores. Just make sure you ask for the color by name: burple. That way salespeople will know exactly what color you're looking for and everyone will be so impressed that you're on the cutting edge of fashion!"

CUSTOMER: "I know what I saw! It was a white handbag with black stripes and purple dots. It was about this tall, there was a handle and a strap, it wasn't too big or too small, and it was right here on the counter. On this very spot."

No clue what she was talking about.

Her self-proclaimed photographic memory seemed to be crashing.

ME: "I'm sorry, ma'am, we've never had anything like that."

CUSTOMER: "It was right here on the counter. I saw it last week!"

ME: "Perhaps you were in another store."

CUSTOMER: "Are you calling me a liar? I know what I saw. Are you new?"

ME: "No, I'm not."

CUSTOMER: "Then how long have you worked here?"

ME: "Longer than last week."

CUSTOMER: "Well, then, I'm sure you must have seen it. Maybe I'm not describing it right. It was stark white with black stripes and big purple dots. Kinda big with a long strap."

ME: "There was no white bag with black stripes and purple dots here last week."

CUSTOMER: "You're lying to me or maybe you just don't know your merchandise very well. I know what I saw and IT WAS RIGHT HERE ON THIS VERY SPOT!!!"

In Big Fancy Retail Hell I found there was only one way to deal with a Black Stripe Purple Dot Hallucinating Psycho Bitch Customer like this.

Tell her she's right.

ME: "OOOOOOOh, *that* bag! I remember it now. It was a white bag with black stripes and purple dots. Really big, long strap. I think it was sitting right here on the counter. On this very spot!"

CUSTOMER: "Yes! That's it. You remember it now! I knew I wasn't imagining things."

But you were. That's what smoking too much angel dust does.

ME: "Yes, I remember it very clearly now."

CUSTOMER: "Well, it's about time. Where is it? I want to look at it."

ME: "I'm so sorry. It got marked down to 50% off yesterday and I sold it about fifteen minutes ago. You are just fifteen minutes too late."

Because I'm such a service-giver to those Always Right Customers, I offered to go above and beyond.

ME: "If you want, I'll call our Long Beach store. I hear they have one left. They can hold it for you. I know it's a long drive through rush-hour traffic, but it would be so worth it for you to get that cool white bag with black stripes and purple dots!"

CUSTOMER: "Yes! Please! I want to take a look at it."

ME: "My pleasure."

The Do's and Don'ts of Shopping

Whether you're a Retail Slave or not, one thing we all have in common as humans is that at some point or another, we are *all* customers. Whether we're looking for shampoo, cheeseburgers, designer shoes, or fishing rods, there will come a time when we need to go in search of stuff.

Having experienced hell as both a salesperson and customer, I've put together a few Do's and Don'ts to make your shopping experience one that doesn't end up feeling like a root canal. You don't want to end up the joke of the day in a store breakroom, or even worse, the subject of someone's angry rant on a blog somewhere.

Know what to DO as a good customer and when to keep your douchebag customer in check with a DON'T!

The Do's and Don'ts of Shopping:

DO smile and say hello after a store greeter has acknowledged you are an actual person and offered up a friendly, "Hello. How are you today?"

DON'T act like you don't speak English, turn your head away, and walk by silently as if greeters are dead people you can't see. When you have a question or need help, you might just become dead people *they* can't see.

DO use shopping sense when you need assistance. Example: You're in the hardware department and you see someone wearing a uniform, nametag, and headset doing stock work. Walk up, say hello, and ask an appropriate question (e.g.: "Where are the hammers?").

DON'T be a dumbass and ask, "Excuse me, do you work here?" followed by asking an equally annoying question in the hardware department: "Do you know where I can find cherry red lipgloss?"

DO be friendly, polite, and patient. You'll reap rewards you didn't know existed. People behind the counter have the golden key to your savings and shopping experience. Kissing their ass will get them to use it for you.

DON'T be a Bitchista. Otherwise, no discounts or mentions of upcoming sales for you! Your douchey rude ass took care of that. Remember: Nice customers *always* walk away with the best service and deals from a store.

DO go shopping in a decent mood and with a sense of respect for humanity. The people working at stores and restaurants do have brains and some may even be smarter than you. Being condescending will only encourage them to use those brains to find a way to give you the worst service possible.

DON'T go shopping when you're in a rush, off your meds, feeling frisky, stricken with swine flu, hours away from giving birth, seeking psychotherapy, or basically feeling like you want to kill someone. You are not making a contribution to society going out in the world like this. Stay home and shop online.

DO shop with your cell phone. Text and chat away as long you're not disturbing the peace by loudly discussing your mother's bowel movements or blocking busy aisles while texting like a teenage girl.

DON'T yammer away on your cell while being waited on! End that call. NOW! And the same goes for texting. Retail Slaves everywhere are fed up with rude cell phone behavior and have been known to actually stop helping customers who are engaged in cell calls.

DO be an amazing parent by paying attention to your children every moment you're in the store. Administer parental discipline when they start to turn into Hell Spawn and throw shoes like they're baseballs and run up and down the escalator.

DON'T be a shitty parent by turning your back and pretending you don't hear the screaming or loud crashes from two aisles over. Watching your little monsters will save you from dirty looks, paying for destroyed merch, lawsuits, being banned from the store, and having to explain to the police why you were shopping for frilly underthings at Victoria's Secret while your kids were destroying *Twilight* books at the Barnes & Noble across the street.

DO save your receipts for returning!!! Consumers are constantly complaining about returns. The only problem with a return is when you DON'T HAVE A RECEIPT! Save your receipts, people! Or expect to fight like Rocky and then be told NO when you try to demand a refund for your pasta-stained dress.

DON'T throw a freaky merchandise-throwing tantrum and expect a store to magically recognize you and the merchandise even though you've lost all your receipts. You might get your refund after your diva-like meltdown, but be warned. Someone in line behind you may have captured the moment on her iPhone. Yes, your shopping shit-storm could end up on YouTube.

DO be a Conscientious Shopper. Put merchandise back where it belongs so the next customer can find it, be careful about shopping with food, and ask for assistance if you want to see what's inside an item.

DON'T be a Piggy Shopper, with a taco in one hand and a slushy in the other, dumping stuff where it doesn't belong, throwing clothes on the floor, tearing open packages, and basically ruining merchandise like you are a descendant of King Kong.

DO exhibit good fitting room etiquette, which includes returning clothes to the attendant hanging or folded properly. These actions help the merchandise reach the floor quicker.

DON'T be a Piggy Shopper and dump clothes in a pile like they're dirty laundry, hang them inside out, leave behind dirty diapers and bloody tampons, or treat the fitting room like it's your own personal food court, motel, or toilet.

DO read merchandise signs and tags. Ask the sales associate to explain discounts and markdowns that are confusing to you. Shopping illiteracy is at an all-time high and is the cause of MAJOR Retail Hell for slaves and customers alike.

DON'T be an annoying Discount Rat and ask for discounts when there are clearly none offered. Unless the store is closing down for good, the ENTIRE store is never on sale, so don't bother asking.

DO have your form of payment ready when it comes time to pay. It will make the line move faster and you'll get on your way faster!

DON'T wait till the salesperson is staring at you to retrieve your credit card, which is buried at the bottom of your handbag like an Indiana Jones lost treasure.

DO rush into a store right before closing, grab what you need, and be at the register when the closing announcement is made.

DON'T continue shopping after that announcement, demand a makeover, and expect personalized attention for as long as you desire. You are interfering with sales associates' lives because they are now forced to change their plans due to your indecision and rudeness. As a result, you'll receive rushed, bad service. And guess what? You're an inconsiderate ass who deserves it!

Retail Hell Readers' Discussion Guide

1. At the beginning of Act 1, a greasy hobbit-like customer demands to return a beat-up Ferragamo handbag with her dirty bra inside.

If you work in retail, what's the worst return you've ever experienced? Have you ever tried to return something to a store you know you had no business trying to return?

2. As I train to become a sales associate at The Big Fancy, I am forced to climb eight flights of stairs every day, attend migraine-inducing pep rallies, and follow the insane direction of a store manager who acts like a psychotic Snow White on acid.

What kind of annoying procedures have you had to endure at your job? How do you handle a high-strung boss who should be taking meds? What rules at your workplace do you think are ridiculous?

3. When I was hired by The Big Fancy to sell handbags, I didn't know the difference from a mock-croc hobo or a lambskin clutch and I quickly learned to never use the p-word!

What kind of handbag do you carry? If money was no object, what bag would you buy? What a woman keeps in her handbag says a lot about her personality—what's inside your handbag?

4. In Act 2, readers meet the boisterous and foul-mouthed Lorraine Goldberg, who quickly becomes my own personal Shoposaurus on steroids with an insatiable appetite to buy everything in sight and stock up as if the world is about to end in ten minutes.

If you work in retail, do you have an over-the-top customer like Lorraine? Are you a Shoposaurus? Do you buy stuff you don't need and consider yourself a future candidate for the TV show *Hoarders*?

5. It doesn't matter whether you work in a shoe store, a fast food restaurant, or at the library, the ways people can cause Retail Hell are universal. A few of the customers I tell hellacious tales about are Piggy Shoppers, Discount Rats, Picky Bitches, and Nasty-Ass Thieves.

What customer archetypes have you had to deal with? How did you handle them? Would you ever compare yourself to one of them?

6. Act 3 opens on one of Big Fancy's sales events with the familiar scene of two women feuding over the last fugly sale bag. We all love to get shit on sale, but let's face it: Sales are not only brutal to work, they can also be brutal to shop.

What do you hate most about working or shopping a big sale? Have you ever fought another customer for the last one? Do you have a haggling story, either as a sales associate or customer?

7. Unruly children (aka Hell Spawn) are one of the worst nightmares sales associates face. Although the story of a child humping my leg like a poodle in heat was the scariest experience I've ever had, I've witnessed all kinds of demon behavior from little monsters.

What's the craziest thing you've ever seen a Hell Spawn do? Is it okay for a sales associate to use a disciplinary tone when stopping a child from doing something dangerous or destructive? Have your kids ever done anything in a store that embarrassed you? How did you react?

8. When Retail Hell rears its ugly head, both Retail Slaves and customers can suffer the drama.

When things go to hell in your store, how do you get through it? If you're a customer experiencing Retail Hell, are you patient or do you freak out? What was your worst experience waiting on someone? What was your worst experience as a customer? Most important, do you believe in Retail Heaven?

Acknowledgments

Retail Hell was ten years in the making and it wouldn't have been possible had I not encountered so many amazing, supportive people along the way.

To my cousin and fellow writer Beach Weston—from word one you gave me your passion, encouragement, creative talent, and laughter. Love you Cuz, we did it!

I am most fortunate to have the best sister in the world, Billee Burchett—you are a pillar of strength and wisdom, I love you dearly. And to her wife, Michelle Quevedo—you instill me with confidence and courage. Love you. Thank you both for your unwavering support. You got me to the finish line!

Daiva Venckus—your love, advice, and guidance throughout this process has been invaluable.

Harold Stoll—I raise my glass in a toast. Thank you for believing in me. You are an inspiration.

To my retailicious agent, Holly Root at Waxman Literary Agency—what can I say? I've won the agent lotto. Thank you for being my champion and guiding me through the wilderness.

There would be no *Retail Hell* book if Adams Media editor Chelsea King hadn't taken it under her wing and led it on a journey of transformation—I'm deeply grateful for your dedication and hard work.

Wendy Simard—you are a Rockstar story editor and you've taught me so much. You raised my game. Thank you.

Heartfelt thanks to everyone at Adams Media for their tireless efforts—you are my publishing dream team and I feel like the luckiest author in the world. In particular, I'd like to thank Karen Cooper, Beth Gissinger, Frank Rivera, Colleen Cunningham, Leslie Norris-Hendrickson, and copy editor Jen Hornsby.

Thank you publicists Meryl L. Moss, Deb Zipf, and Jane Summer.

Brandy Rivers—my manager extraordinaire.

Vanessa Schafer—you are my muse, always there to inspire and make me laugh.

Jeff Swan—your optimism and friendship has kept me going.

Dr. Janna Segal—I'm forever grateful for your inspiring wit and humor.

Teresa Bozek—my cousin by blood, sister by heart. Thanks for being there.

To my moms away from mom: Colleen Peeler, Nancy Foster, and Betty Gomez, three amazing, strong, funny women—I'm thankful for your love and support.

To my peeps, retail and non, I love you guys: Krystine Chaparo, Christiana Glasner, Barb Roche, Michael Jameson, Bronwyn McKune, Andi Palmer. Andrea Morgan, Gail White, Ken Arlitz, Kelby Peeler, Terri Mills, Bruce Cassaro, Mark Brey, Jerry and Theresa Briggs, Leyla Mutlu, Kerry Daley, Julie Darling, Calindy Mann, Gina Mae Temelcoff, Richard Gasbarro, Johnny Law, Sharon Manning, Frances Roach, Stacy Lam, Beth Gates, Kari Del Mastro, Lisa Abreu, Elisabeth Walter-Marchetti, Kathyrn Foster, Benjamin Kissell, Sherina Florence, Melinda Filardo, Debbie Blute, Mandy Plax, The Ezran family, The Nakano family: Jean, Wayne, and Erin, and The Kibby Family: Walt, Danusha, and Walty.

Thank you to my family: Freeman and Lucy Burchett, John Burchett, Dave and Lee Marquardson, Bill Bozek, Missy Goss, Lana Cariaso, and Pam Vallandingham-Saralaqui.

And to the people whose talent has inspired and taught me: Stephen King, Steven Spielberg, Trey Parker, Matt Stone, David Sedaris, Augusten Burroughs, Anne Rice, Amy Tan, Armistead Maupin, Michael Thomas Ford, Michael Tonello, Thomas Lennon, Robert Ben Garant, Kerri Kenney-Silver, Marc Cherry, Bill Lawrence, Sarah Jessica Parker, Michael Patrick King, Ellen DeGeneres, Oprah, Tyler Perry, Louise Hay, Marianne Williamson, Carolyn Myss, Eckhart Tolle, Kathy Griffin, Chelsea Handler, Lady Ga Ga, Madonna, Green Day, Sarah Brightman, Loreena Mckennitt, and my boy Spongebob.